FEEDBACK

JOYCE ESERSKY GOLDSTEIN

How to Cook for Increased Awareness, Relaxation, Pleasure, & Better Communication with Yourself & Those Who Eat the Food

FEEDBACK

How to Enjoy the Process as well as the Product   How to Use the Kitchen as a Source of Nourishment; Emotional, Physical, & Sensual

Foreword by Dr. Leonard Pearson

Richard Marek Publishers, New York

Acknowledgments:

Lines from "The Fun in Fun" by William Barry Furlong are reprinted by permission of *Psychology Today* magazine
Copyright ⊕ 1976 Ziff Davis Publishing Company

Lines from *The Only Dance There Is* by Baba Ram Dass are reprinted with the kind permission of the Hanuman Foundation
Copyright ⊕ 1970, 1971, 1973 by Transpersonal Institute

Lines from "Hers" by Lois Gould © 1977 by the New York Times Company. Reprinted by permission.

Library of Congress Cataloging in Publication Data

Goldstein, Joyce Esersky.
    Feedback.

Includes index
    1. Cookery—Psychological aspects. I. Title.
TX652.G64   641.5′01′9   77-29263

SBN: 399-90002-0

Printed in the United States of America
First printing

In memory of Josef Albers, Paul Jacobs, and Essie Goldstein (who knew that seeing, feeling, and tasting were all part of the recipe)

ACKNOWLEDGMENTS

I have been told by friends who are writers that this is the page that nobody really reads—that is, nobody except for those invaluable persons who helped to make the book possible and kept the author sane during the lengthy writing process. So I would like to say THANK YOU! To Danny Kopelson, for love, support, and infinite patience; to my children, Evan, Karen, and Rachel, and to students and friends who tasted all the food and offered "feedback"; to friends who shared family recipes and traditions; to Joe Camhi and Zoe Snyder of the Gestalt Institute of San Francisco; to Helen Palmer, Carol Field, Kathy Slobin, Carolyn and Jim Robertson, Frederick Mitchell, Russell Everett, Chet Lieb, and Janine Kraemer, who read the manuscript in various stages of its development, asked the right questions, and offered good criticism and even better advice; to Millea Kenin, for typing skills and an amazing ability to decipher cooking hieroglyphics; to Anne Borchardt, for working so hard on my behalf; and to Joyce ("Joycie") Engelson, whose editing skills, insights, high energy, and endless support helped transform my ideas into a reality.

Note on Serving Portions

Most of the recipes in *Feedback* are supposed to feed six people with moderate appetites. However, it is wise to remember that portions are almost impossible to estimate precisely (unless you are serving food in a restaurant that has a "portion control"). Lasagna for eight might barely satisfy four teenage boys. And if you serve a number of different courses you will be able to squeeze extra servings out of each individual recipe. Occasionally I have structured a recipe to feed ten to twelve because there is so much preparation involved and there are so many different ingredients it seems silly to go to all that effort just for two. (Of course, if you feel like paella for two, who am I to tell you no?)

Foreword

It is rare that a reader has an opportunity to personally *observe* the concepts and techniques to be presented in a new book before it is written. I was fortunate to be invited to Joyce Esersky Goldstein's home months before this book was finished, to *experience* the novel ideas she is espousing in her classes. I vividly recall that luncheon—served late in the day because of our schedules, yet easily served—the many dishes to choose from, among them a curry I had never considered as typical "luncheon" food, but wonderfully fitting the mood, after all, of that cool afternoon in Berkeley; the unhurried tempo; the feeling I received of being welcomed, cared for, from the way the dishes were arranged by Joyce, a total stranger. We spent several hours leisurely eating and talking. Her teenage son joined us briefly, preparing his own food in a slightly different way in the adjacent kitchen area. I had the opportunity to see how conveniently, how efficiently, the kitchen was arranged, and what a warm feeling that room had, a place where it was easy to lean against the counter top and carry on a conversation, sipping a cup of coffee or tea. It was impressive to see how relaxed the cook was, her system allowing her to be a participant in the eating process instead of focusing on the need to prepare, watch for proper temperatures, etcetera.

Based on that experience, as well as on reading *Feedback,* I feel that Joyce has added a unique dimension to all of the other tools that exist to help people learn more about themselves, to function in a common area without the stresses so frequently a part of that daily activity. As a psychologist, I mean to recommend this book for those who are overweight, underweight, hate to cook, love to cook, who want to use cooking as a way of manifesting their care and tenderness for another person, as well as those who want to treat themselves and use the time of food preparation and eating as an additional form of meditation, energy use, stress reduction, and toward the enjoyment of a more fulfilling life.

Finding parallels to my own experiences, I feel that Joyce has presented new psychological insights into the way people can misuse food, or ignore bodily signals, and how being out of touch with the personal meaning of food and cooking can lead to problems not only of over- and under-eating but also of strained personal and family relationships.

Actually, of course, Joyce Esersky Goldstein deals with a great deal more than cooking in *Feedback.* She concerns herself with feeding, expressing care through food, and meals and food as a system of communication. Nevertheless, I was surprised myself at how hard it is to stop reading her work, once you allow yourself to be drawn to the journey she shares with you. (It's difficult to think of her as other than "Joyce" because her style is one of sharing, self-revealing, and self-disclosure—so all of her readers will feel we know her personally.)

What holds the interest in the manner of a suspense novel are the descriptions of the ways in which Joyce learned about herself through cooking, the changes that took place in her own career as a cook, as owner of a gourmet cooking school well-known in San Francisco, as the person who began the use of food preparation as meditation, who discovered her own inner feelings through food, and the ability to express affection to others that way, as well her key discovery: caring for oneself by selecting the recipes according to one's own mood. It is fascinating indeed to a psychologist like myself to see here the unfolding of ways in which cooking can be a facet of exploring oneself *and being good to oneself.*

Ram Dass has recently described the guru who becomes violently ill because he can sense the negative emotional mood of the cook! By reading *Feedback* and listening to it with one's "inner voices," it should become impossible to prepare a meal with anger. Such negative attitudes have taken their toll of those preparing food for others—most often the women in our society—and this book presents a way of liberating the entire process so that one is free: to respond to food and cooking in terms of one's own feelings as well as of the occasion, whether it be for oneself alone—an honored guest, as Joyce makes clear—or family, a friend, a loved one.

In many ways, Joyce Esersky Goldstein has reclaimed food, cooking, and eating, too, from the devalued sex-role status it has too often been associated with. Her book makes it possible for men and women both to perceive in a fresh way that most basic, primitive aspect of all of our lives, food and the sharing of it with others.

What Joyce has done in fact is to present the entire process of eating, from selection of food to preparation to meditation or self-energizing in the course of cooking, in an unusual context: one that is psychologically sophisticated and sensitive. Reflecting her own development, skills, and knowledge of food, cooking, gestalt therapy and interpersonal relations, this book can serve a variety of purposes, adding an unusual window on self-awareness for those of us who have a daily relationship to food, eating, cooking, serving; namely, all of us!

LEONARD PEARSON, PhD
Professor of Psychology
Sonoma State College, California

Past President, American Psychological Association,
Division on Psychotherapy

Contents

PART FOUR: WHAT AM I COOKING?

FEEDBACK

Part One

Why Am I Cooking?

Chapter 1

COMING OUT OF THE KITCHEN CLOSET

For eleven years I have been teaching cooking, privately and at my California Street Cooking School in San Francisco. Not a week has gone by during those years that someone hasn't asked, "Well, when are *you* going to write a cookbook?" I've always copped out, made up any convenient answer. I was in no rush and I wanted to write a book when I felt that I had something to say—and had the time to do it right, not sandwiched in between eight classes a week.

When I finally started to write, I realized that I didn't want to put together just another collection of recipes to be filed on the shelf along with last year's fashionable favorites, Peasant Food, Cuisine Minceur, or Multicultural Gourmet Machine Cooking. A therapist friend suggested that I go straight: come out of the Kitchen Closet, where I have been doing "undercover growth work" with my students for years. So now I want to say it loud and clear for all to hear: I am not so much interested in WHAT we cook, be it moussaka, coq au vin, Szechuan shrimp, or corned beef hash. What is really important to me is WHY we cook, FOR WHOM we cook, and HOW we feel when we are cooking. You can have the best equipment, the most perfect recipes, masterful technique . . . and still be missing the point. Cooking does not take place in a vacuum. It's not just an intellectual game of skill with obstacles to overcome and formulas to follow. If you know all the tricks of the trade, you may be merely tricky.

One of the most important ingredients in cooking never appears at the top of the recipe: PEOPLE! Cooking is too complex and idiosyncratic to reduce to just technique or robotlike reproduction of recipes. It involves human beings making things for human beings, those who cook and those who eat the food. *Cooking is a physical activity with emotional fallout.*

There is much to be learned about life through the metaphor of the kitchen. Situations arise there that have parallels in our day-to-day existence, our work, our relationships. In cooking we express feelings, take risks, release tension and body energy, strive for praise and recognition, do things for others as well as for ourselves. We learn to share space and to master it. We deal with success and failure, competition and self-esteem. *The kitchen is a source of nourishment, both physical and emotional.*

So if you are looking for an elegant dinner-party-menu book to help you wow your acquaintances with your prowess, this book is not for you.

If you are looking for a book that tells you how to boil an egg, that 3 tsp. are the equivalent of one Tbsp., that slant-sided pans are best for omelets, then this book won't give you any data that you can't find in any basic cookbook you probably already have.

If you want lectures on health and nutrition, dieting, food as religion or morality, food as romance, I don't think I'm going to be of any special help.

If you need outrageous recipes, or novelty, or chic, or drama, or fashion, stop reading.

Anybody left out there? O.K. This book is going to tell you how to have a good time in the kitchen, how to enjoy *your own company* (and indirectly the company of others) via food. We all have to eat to live, so we might as well learn to enjoy making the food. Just because cooking is a necessity it need not be a chore. Why not learn to make the job work for you? Why not learn to enjoy the *process* of cooking as well as the *product?*

This book will try to do two things:

1. Get you excited about the process of cooking (what I call the HOW) and *show you how attention, concentration,* and

creative involvement in the cooking process can expand your awareness of yourself. You can explore your thoughts, feelings, and sensations while chopping, shredding, kneading, measuring, stirring, tasting, even cleaning up. You can get in touch with your present mood and contact your physical and mental energies: *how you experience yourself* NOW. If you "center" yourself—come into a state of inner balance—while engaged in these physical tasks, you may transcend their sometimes mundane natures and learn more than just cooking. You may also learn something about yourself. Your meals and your consciousness will both flourish. *Consciousness* is more than simply knowledge. It is the expanding totality of awareness, an openness to the "inner" and "outer" environments.

2. Show you *how cooking can be used effectively as a means of communication with yourself and others.* When you are cooking *consciously,* you are in contact with your own experience and can share that experience with those FOR WHOM you are cooking. WHAT you cook, WHY you cook, and HOW you cook make a statement about yourself. That statement can be vague, soft, incoherent, thoughtless, or it can be clear, firm, coherent, thoughtful, and a pleasure to others.

If you have avoided cooking because it seemed time-consuming and difficult to master, if you are one of the walking wounded in the kitchen for whom cooking has never been fun, despite the number of cookbooks you have read, classes you have attended, equipment you have purchased in hopes of easing the burden, perhaps this book will make a kitchen convert out of you. Cooking is a part of life; wouldn't it be satisfying to reflect some of that life in *your* cooking?

Of course *Feedback* will have practical information about kitchen logistics and technique, recipes well tested by myself and hundreds of students, recipes collected from friends and cookbooks; however, the major emphasis of this book will be on the *act of cooking, the physical, mental,* and *emotional aspects of the cooking process* and *its effects on yourself and others.*

Chapter 2

"INNER COOKING":

Cooking and Emotion

After a long day of office work or changing diapers and housekeeping, it's no wonder people need to play tennis, jog, pick up the guitar, get a massage, or go dancing. They need to unwind. If the tension that has been building up all day is not released in some physical way and is kept bottled up, it may cause emotional and perhaps even physical harm (in the form of ulcers, heart attacks, and other stress-related diseases). For most people, doing is better than stewing. But in this book you'll see that stewing can be doing.

While sports, dancing, even taking long walks are easily recognized outlets for letting off steam, tension may be dissipated in ways that are not so readily identified. For years, whenever I was angry or feeling uptight, I would clean the house. Things were no dirtier than usual, but I had to get that pent-up emotion out of my system without causing mental or physical harm to myself or to someone who happened by chance to be in my vicinity. After I scrubbed the floor, my anger and anxieties flowed out with the water on the mop. I felt relaxed and not the least bit tired.

Others may find relaxation in driving a car, fixing a motorcycle, doing needlepoint, building a fence, or weeding the garden. Cooking is another wonderful *escape valve*. If one of your children or roommates comes bouncing into the house when you are feeling "crowded," tie on an apron, perhaps turn on the radio, and get cooking! Transform that negative energy into positive action!

Cooking promotes relaxation and is a good outlet for channeling stress. It can calm frazzled nerves and provide an opportunity to clear the mind of inner chatter. While no substitute for professional help in stress-related disorders, it certainly may be considered "therapeutic" and an adjunct to treatment. Not only is cooking an excellent means of transforming negative emotions, it enables you to give expression to positive feelings, too. What better way to show affection and single someone out for attention than to cook a special meal for him or her!

Were you ever surprised to find out that a famous athlete or politician was a dedicated cook? That your stockbroker or lawyer was a master at bread baking and lasagna? Certainly nothing about their work or outward life-style gave you any clue to this offbeat hobby. Many may actually prefer cooking to their "real" work. There are quite a number of chefs and restaurant owners who were once teachers, accountants, lawyers. Yet no one is really surprised to learn that painters like Richard Olney, Ed Giobbi, and Robert Motherwell, or filmmakers like Francis Coppola and John Frankenheimer, or writers like Lillian Hellman, Anthony Powell, and Lawrence Durrell, love cooking.

What they have discovered is something that artists almost unconsciously "know": A person who is academically educated and intellectually oriented needs to get in touch with feelings and imagination if he is to be "in balance."

Because we "think" with our eyes, our hands, and our bodies as well as with our minds, we may express ideas and feelings physically as well as mentally. Cooking can satisfy this need for balance in the human spirit. It can provide a complement to one's other activities; it involves both body and mind. There is more than just the obvious physical gratification of eating a good meal. The inventing, preparing, and sharing of that meal are emotionally, intellectually, and physically satisfying.

When you create something in the kitchen, you are expressing yourself through the medium of food. You can be Picasso, Pavlova, the Mad Scientist, the Interpreter, the Wild One, the Poet, the Fool. There are special moments of elation or revelation that the cook shares with no one. Like the tactile enjoyment that comes while chopping, kneading, blending, and tasting. Or the moments of discovery when you try a recipe for the first time or master a difficult sauce or technique. There is the kick that comes from getting more proficient at doing something, like cleaning three pounds of shrimp in a half hour instead of your usual two. Or slicing mushrooms elegantly and uniformly, if that has been your goal. Most people won't notice anything different about the mushrooms or the shrimp, but they will enjoy eating them because your enthusiasm in their preparation has been contagious.

The development of a food idea also can be exhilarating: the blending of tastes and textures to reflect your mood, your feelings, your thought processes. You grow, you learn as you create; your personal discoveries are precious to you. Not everyone will know that you have invented something "new," but you still will be sailing off the energy of the adventure and your guests will taste that. And even if no one but you tastes the dish, cooking it will have been a very positive experience.

Living in California in the late 1970's, one cannot remain unaware of the incredible "Personal Growth and Self-Awareness" movement that pervades our environment. We have encounter groups, Gestalt, Transcendental Meditation, est, Arica, polarity or radical therapy, and on and on. People gravitate from one "growth" cult to another in search of self and joyful fulfillment. They might be surprised to learn that a medium as old-fashioned and down-home as cooking can be a means to increased awareness and personal growth, providing a release of body and mind energy, enabling you to get in touch with your feelings.

At first I thought the theory of cooking as a means of expanding one's consciousness might pertain only to me and a few more cooking freaks. But after teaching hundreds of students, working with them for extended periods of time, I found there were just too many people responding to cooking as a "growth" experience for this notion to be only a personal aberration. They were learning recipes and techniques, but they were also going through (what is called in the jargon of the consciousness trade) "changes." Cooking had helped them liberate their physical, mental, and creative energies. After working out in the kitchen cooking for themselves and friends, they were more relaxed and self-assured, more sensually attuned, increasingly aware of themselves, and certainly more aware of others.

I don't think that this can be dismissed as just another nutty California craze. Cooking as a means of expressing emotion and reducing tension is not simply a regional or contemporary fad. In many different places and times people have experienced cooking in this personal way. They just haven't labeled it "growth" or "centering" or a "means to expanded con-sciousness." But they have felt the inner peace and reaped the emotional benefits just the same. If you have always wondered why your friend emerges from the kitchen looking radiant and relaxed, while you stagger out feeling harried and exhausted, perhaps you haven't been asking the right questions when you cook. Possibly you have been too wrapped up in the WHATS of cooking: recipes, technical expertise, the latest equipment and trends in menu planning. Maybe it's time for you to ask WHY, FOR WHOM, and HOW you are cooking so that you, too, may be able to make cooking work for you, not against you.

Chapter 3
EXPANDING YOUR KITCHEN CONSCIOUSNESS

Meditative and High Energy Cooking

Have you ever had a day when the alarm didn't go off and the kids were mad at you because they were late and missed the bus? Or the plumber couldn't fix the leaky pipe that day or even that week? Or your boss rejected the design scheme you'd been working on for three months? Or you had a fight with your best friend? Then you find yourself going into the kitchen and starting to chop onions. You smash the garlic to smithereens. You peel the carrots, dice the celery, and slice the mushrooms so thin you can read through them. Before you know it you are humming to yourself. You are moving more rhythmically, faster or slower, but with ease. You are no longer tense, angry. As a matter of fact you feel pretty damn good, even a little high. What has happened? Well, you've let off some steam in smashing the garlic. You've steadied your pace with the rhythm of the onion chopping. You have slowed yourself down while watching the peels of the carrots slip off the knife in thin curls and concentrating on how it feels to slice the mushrooms so slowly, evenly, repetitiously. You are relaxed because you have taken the time to pay attention to what you were doing while you were doing it, and how you felt—the specific physical sensations of each task. What you have experienced might be called *Kitchen Meditation*. While assembling the meal you are super-"tuned in" to the process. By focusing on simple cooking chores, you become "centered." You have used your time in the kitchen to unwind and make some *emotional space* for yourself.

Perhaps you've been sitting at your desk all day. Your legs and rear are numb and you're feeling somewhat hungry. You have lots of physical energy that you'd like to express. However, your mind is a little tired and you don't want to follow a recipe with lots of complicated instructions. You would like to get moving. Feel loose. Work out. You turn on the stereo and get some music that will supplement your natural rhythm. Then you open the refrigerator, see what is there, and start to cook a meal that will keep you and your pans in constant motion. Nothing so mentally taxing that it will dissipate or suppress your physical energy. You are in a good mood, with lots of positive energy to release, so you tie on your apron and sail into action. You sauté a steak and prepare the pepper sauce while steaming the broccoli and reheating the leftover rice. You move with agility; your body language is in harmony with your cooking vocabulary.

Here the *physical* activities of the cook are more important than the details of preparation. You need to get the energy *out* rather than focus *in* on yourself. You are going on natural body fuel, feeling your physical power and selecting the methods that tap and release that power.

Sometimes you don't have to be feeling speedy or adventurous to get energized for cooking. You could be tired or indifferent. Just what you need are people coming for dinner! You invited them a few days ago when you were in an expansive mood. Today has been exhausting, not one of your best. Well, here goes nothing. Just can't face doing that old, tired chicken-with-mushroom-soup recipe. What's new to try? Maybe use some of that leftover fruit salad from the night before. Hey, that tastes pretty good. What does it need? Maybe a little cinnamon, some lemon rind . . . Wow! Why not some noodles instead of rice . . . some zucchini with nuts. You're really flying around the kitchen. Who said you were tired? You are excited, energetic, could go on for hours—even knock out a soufflé.

Here the inventing of the meal acts as the energy catalyst. Instead of running on physical fuel, you are going on *mental* steam. The *creative* aspects of the cooking process produce lots of *high energy* and turn your mood around, leaving you with power to burn. Quite a difference from the person who cooks for two days for an Important Dinner Party and is too pooped to enjoy the food or the guests.

I have just described three different responses to the question "HOW AM I COOKING?"—the results of *being in communication with yourself*. These examples represent the modes of cooking that I call Meditative cooking and Physical and Mental High Energy cooking. Once you understand how these work you will be able to summon the kind of cooking energy that reflects your needs, and you'll be able to make cooking work *for* you and *with* you. (It's possible that you have been cooking in harmony with these energies but have been aware of them only unconsciously or by chance. After reading this book I hope that you will be able *consciously* to arrive at the mode of cooking energy you need. Instead of having Meditative and High Energy Cooking happen to you occasionally, accidentally, and with hindsight, why not learn to get in touch with your moods so you can make them happen and enjoy them!)

Meditative cooking is introspective and personal. The cook is usually alone—if not in body, in mind. Like painting, gardening, sewing, the experience is reflective and tactile. The cook's attention is completely focused on chopping, mincing, slicing, the physical sensations of cooking, especially those which have repetition, rhythm, and routine or ritual. *Action and awareness become one.* Time is slowed down, or "lost." While simultaneously paying attention to subjective sensations and the objective activity, the cook emerges from the experience calm and centered, relaxed and alert.

High Energy cooking involves a release of energy outward, toward the object (the food) rather than inward, toward the subject (the cook). It is both *physically and mentally* active, tapping the body's creative and intellectual resources. Physical movements are rapid; time "speeds up." A sense of urgency develops. You are involved in a process that cannot be interrupted. You are near your goal. In High Energy cooking you don't have time to focus on yourself. Relaxation comes not during the process of cooking but *after* the process is completed (like finishing two sets of tennis or running the mile).

Whereas Meditative cooking is private and introspective, High Energy cooking is more sociable. Because much of the cooking is last-minute, family or friends who are to eat the food may be in the kitchen watching or helping. Much of High Energy cooking is virtuoso public performance. Stir frying, deep frying, assembling a soufflé or hollandaise, because of their rapid pace, imply that the eaters are not too far away so that they can get the goodies when they are ready, moments later.

In Meditative cooking the cook's primary feedback is from the process. Meditative cooking is something you do for yourself, although others may benefit later. What is most important is being and doing, the awareness of self merged with an awareness of the activity, the emotional centering of mind and body on the physical sensations of preparing the food.

In High Energy cooking the cook gets some feedback from the process, but the primary feedback is from the eaters and from him/herself. How they and the cook felt while things were coming together, how they both liked the new creation. Less energy is spent in elaborate preparation and more on body action in the actual cooking. In the creative aspects of High Energy cooking lots of mental energy is expended. And there is more sharing of the kitchen space.

Given these two alternatives, before any particular meal you can see HOW you are feeling, get in tune with WHY and FOR WHOM you are cooking, and then select the way of being in the kitchen that will mesh with your motives and feelings of the moment.

It is important to work in harmony with your state of being. If you are *present-centered*, you know HOW you feel when you are about to cook, so that you will *make the most of your time* in the kitchen. Do you want to be alone? Do you need lots of time and no pressure of a deadline? Do you want to have almost everything ready before you serve the meal? Sounds like Meditative cooking is what you need. On the other hand if you feel like thinking on your feet, being wild or experimental, want to try coordinating your timing with the precision of a choreographer and daredevil combined, if you want to have people in the kitchen when you're cooking, High Energy cooking may be your method of the moment.

Actually, in the course of preparing a meal you can go, if you like, from Meditative energy in the early "prep" stages to Mental High Energy while modifying the original recipe and then into Physical High Energy for the last stages of the cooking process. You don't have to choose one over the other if you don't want to. Your mood may change or evolve during the entire cooking experience. Some dishes are almost entirely Meditative, like making strawberry jam or a soup that simmers slowly after a complex prep. Some are mostly High Energy, like sautéed veal scallops or steak au poivre. And some dishes combine the two, like assembling spring rolls and deep frying them at the last minute, or stuffing grape leaves and preparing the avgolemono sauce just before serving. The boundaries between the energies are not always clear. Once you become aware of these different modes, emotional, mental, and physical, select the one that reflects your needs of the moment. You'll learn to sense the transitions and changes of energy in the kitchen and in yourself as you become immersed in the cooking process.

A word or two on the use of music in cooking. Some people enjoy cooking in silence, hearing the vegetables crunch under the knife, the sounds of water flowing, foods crackling in the pan. If that is your way, enjoy the natural silence and the subtle sounds coming from your movements in the kitchen.

However, there are days when a blast from Jean Luc-Ponty or Stevie Wonder might just set your pace and reflect your mood in the kitchen. The music may supplement your tempo; you'll respond to the rhythm and gear your body movements to the sound coming from the stereo. There is a time for Mozart and Vivaldi and a time for Debussy or Keith Jarrett. Know your mood and work rhythm and you can choreograph your cooking.

Cooking is a means of communication with yourself. It can

produce two kinds of energy. One mellows you, the other leaves you sailing. Both produce a "high," an increase of felt energy. It is far more difficult to describe how a process works than it is to experience it directly. There are no magic formulas to achieve these states. When I say that the physical acts of chopping, kneading, smelling, and tasting set your Meditative energies to flowing, I can't play "Dr. Feelgood" and prescribe one half hour of chopping, three minutes of dicing, five minutes of tasting, and expect it to produce the desired effect. How do you get energetic from cooking? How long do you have to cook? How fast do you have to be moving to be doing High Energy cooking? I cannot tell you. All I can suggest is that you try it with these ideas in mind and find your own comfortable rhythms. What may speed *me* up may calm *you* down. What may speed *you* up one day may calm *you* down the next. It is never exactly the same. You have to train yourself to hear your own messages and to answer your own needs—just as you can tune in to the messages that your body sends you when you are tired or hungry. Once you have experienced the kitchen "meditation" or the energy "high," you will understand immediately what I am driving at. (And there is a good deal more in later chapters about the specifics of these energy styles.) All of the emotional, physical, and mental activities in cooking can help you to get in touch with yourself, after which you are better able to get in touch with others.

Chapter 4

COOKING AND PAINTING AS COMMUNICATION:

The Meal as the Medium for the Message

People are always asking me how and why I got interested in cooking. Did I take lessons? Was my mother a fabulous cook who spent endless hours in the kitchen teaching me all she knew? When I lived in Europe, had I attended the Cordon Bleu cooking school?

The answer to all of these questions is no, no, and no. I stumbled into cooking quite by chance and was heavily addicted before I had time to analyze why. In fact, I was an unlikely candidate for the role of cooking teacher. As a child I hated to eat! Skinny, finicky, I found mealtime a source of great agony. I couldn't swallow, and food accumulated in my mouth, earning me the nickname "The Pouch." I would delay drinking that eternal mealtime glass of milk hoping against hope that my mother would leave the room so I could pour it down the sink. I didn't give a damn about the starving children in Europe, or India, or even Brooklyn for that matter.

A competent analyst could figure it out: Eating was

unpleasant for me because my parents would fight at the dinner table. Food was used as one more means for a parent to wield power over a child: They knew what was good for me to eat, whether I liked it or not. Between the arguments and the forced feedings I had little appetite.

My first opportunity for "reprisal eating" occurred when I went away to college. I existed for a year on pizzas, burgers, brownies, and black coffee. So much for good nutrition and the starving children of Europe. During my sophomore year I gained twenty starchy pounds on dormitory food. No traumas at meals, but not much protein either. I dieted stringently to become fashionably thin, even with my heritage of Middle European hips. I guess the whole food experience would have been lost to me for a long, long time, maybe forever, if I had not had the opportunity to go away to graduate school and have my own apartment.

You may still wonder why I got so involved in cooking. After all, there are thousands of people who have their own apartments and never venture into the kitchen except to boil water for instant coffee. So what was it that I found so interesting, so all-engaging about preparing a meal? (It was a time when women were not looked at as simpleminded home-ec drones just because they liked to cook. There was no stigma attached to the act of cooking when I began my career in the kitchen.)

I had never been allowed to cook at home. Perhaps if I had been involved in the preparation of the meal I might have gotten interested in eating a whole lot sooner. But my mother thought that cooking made a mess, and she believed that cleanliness was next to Godliness: Children were not by nature neat, so we should not be allowed into the pristine lab that was the source of our nutrition.

You can well imagine that it was a wild and heady moment when I stepped into my kitchen and made my eggs the way *I* liked them. It was absolutely mind boggling how delicious lamb stew could taste if the peas were not cooked till they were gray and the potatoes soggy and grease-laden, and to discover that homemade soup didn't taste anything like those canned wonders I'd eaten for years! I was drunk with power. I was in control of what I put into my mouth, when, how much, and how it would taste. I had embarked upon a giant adventure that still excites me every time I roll up my sleeves, tie on an apron, and step into the world of the kitchen.

I was enrolled as a graduate student in painting at Yale University. One of my teachers was Josef Albers. Whenever he came into my studio cubby, called a "booth," Mr. Albers would talk about painting as "cooking." He might say, "Ach, girl, I see we are into a little Persian cooking today" if my color range or choice of shapes reminded him of Persian miniatures. Or, "Some Russian cooking today?" when I was at the height of my fascination with Russian icons. Anyway, in my New Haven kitchen I discovered that cooking was painting, that adding some herbs and parsley was like adding color from my palette, that chopping the nuts coarsely was like adding certain rough textures to my painting medium, and that planning a harmonious meal, one that looked and tasted delicious with just the right number of contrasts and counterpoints, was like composing a canvas. I was home at last. The kitchen was a studio and the studio was a kitchen.

Furthermore, cooking had the added sensual delights of taste and smell. It provided a framework of style and tradition and the implied artistic challenge which said, "O.K., kid, accept or reject the past at will. Learn techniques. Invent your own. Play, choose, innovate, grow."

I'm sure that if I had been a nutrition or home-economics major, my approach to cooking would have been very different. My meals were not formularized solutions of one serving of starch, one leafy vegetable, one piece of meat or fish. I did not ask how many units there were of vitamin D, how many proteins, carbohydrates, and minerals. This doesn't mean I was unaware of their existence and importance, but they were not the starting points of my cooking process. I asked How can I combine the smoothness of the pureed eggplant with the crunchiness of the chopped nuts? How can this be made to look creamier, and that feel crisper? Why can't I make it seem more Indian than Arabic in inspiration if I like?

For example, here is a simple Italianate recipe for eggplant puree:

EGGPLANT PUREE

Pierce two eggplants with fork. Place in hot oven (450° or broil) until soft, approximately 30 minutes. Cut in half, drain excess liquids, and scoop out meat. Mash with fork or purée in blender or processor, but don't overblend. Leave a few pieces here and there to provide interest and variety for the tongue.

Season eggplant puree with the following: Two finely minced cloves garlic sautéed (not browned)* in butter. Add two Tbsp. or more parmesan cheese. Add 2–3 Tbsp. olive oil, and salt and black pepper to taste. (Serves 6.)

The Arabs name it baba ghanouj and take it in a different direction. To the eggplant puree they add 2 cloves raw garlic, finely minced; 3–4 Tbsp. sesame tahini,** and the juice of 2 lemons, and garnish it with pan-toasted pine nuts and parsley. It is served with pita or Arab bread.

Here's the recipe they use in India: Fry 2 minced onions in 4 Tbsp. butter, add eggplant puree and 2 tsp. turmeric, and cook slowly for 15 minutes. Add 1 Tbsp. garam masala*** and cook some more. Season with salt to taste, and garnish with pan-toasted almonds, yoghurt.

By adding a few tomatoes the Moroccans have a salad. They

*A good heavy cleaver is ideal for smashing and chopping garlic. The blow of the cleaver usually removes the peel, and additional pounding will pulverize the pulp as well. It will also make you feel powerful and provide you with a good release of energy. Incidentally, this method of chopping garlic produces garlic that is less bitter than that pushed through a press. The oils remain imbedded in all the tiny fragments instead of being separated from the pulp. At least this is my belief from taste experience. Some people prefer to mince garlic by grinding it in a mortar and pestle with some salt. Overbrowning garlic gives it a bitter taste.

**Ground sesame seeds with oil. Can be found in health food stores and shops that specialize in Middle Eastern foods.

***Garam Masala

3	Tbsp. black pepper	3	Tbsp. coriander
2	Tbsp. cumin	1	Tbsp. cloves
1	Tbsp. cinnamon	1	Tbsp. cardamom seed

Grind coarsely in blender and store in airtight jar.

peel and mash the baked eggplant pulp, put it in a salad bowl rubbed with garlic, and add 3 peeled and slightly mashed tomatoes, one small grated onion, 2 Tbsp. chopped parsley, ¾ C. olive oil, 3 Tbsp. wine vinegar or lemon juice, and ½ tsp. each cumin and paprika. Allow to marinate at least one hour before serving. Salt or sugar may be needed to round out the flavor. (Serves 6–8.)

My decisions as a cook were determined in part by WHAT I had in my pantry and by my budget. Some decisions were purely aesthetic: What would look best on the table with the other foods I had prepared? What dish would provide an accent or contrast with another ? But above all my choices were affected by an awareness of WHO WOULD EAT the food. If I was cooking for myself I would pay attention to what my palate craved: Did I want something spicy or tart? If I was cooking for a friend who liked spicy food I might make the Indian version. If a Mediterranean food freak was coming for supper then I knew that some good olive oil, garlic, oregano, and chopped tomato would really talk to him/her in a personal way. The recipe was selected because of the message I wanted to send: I was thinking of you when I prepared this eggplant.

While I was quick to notice that cooking was a natural extension of painting and my creative energies, I was a little slower to realize that it tapped my social energies as well. Cooking was a good way to let myself be known and to get to know others, a means of communication and contact.

When I was at graduate school many of my classmates were from different countries and ethnic backgrounds. Some were on such tight budgets they barely ate enough to keep their minds from wandering as they painted. We would sit, as students do, and talk for hours over endless cups of watery coffee in the Waldorf Cafeteria across the street from the art school. Interspersed with heated discussions would be food confessionals, reminiscences of meals gone by, reveries about foods no longer eaten but still yearned for. As I was one of the few people at school to have a working kitchen, however minuscule, I was elected to cook some of these "dreamed-of" meals.

If John was coming for supper I ran to the library and read up on Greek food so I could give him a personal present of a meal from his homeland. I might prepare moussaka or pastitsio to make him feel "at home" while away from home. Perhaps some oranges with orange flower water for dessert. Or special cookies like kourabiedes.

MOUSSAKA À LA GRECQUE

Peel 2 medium eggplants and slice about ½" thick; sauté in butter and set aside.

Sauté 2 medium onions, minced, and 4 cloves garlic, minced, in 4 Tbsp. butter till soft and transparent. Add 1 lb. ground lamb to the onions and garlic and cook 10 minutes more.

Then add:

2	Tbsp. tomato paste or 1 C. tomato puree	1½	tsp. cinnamon
			Salt and pepper
¼	C. or more parsley	½	tsp. oregano or
¼	C. red wine		marjoram (optional)

Cook till the liquids have been absorbed, stirring often.

Separately, combine ½ C. grated parmesan cheese and ½ C. bread crumbs.

Cheese Custard Sauce

4	Tbsp. butter	4–6	eggs, well beaten with a fork
3	Tbsp. flour		
2	C. milk	½	tsp. nutmeg
1	C. ricotta cheese		

Melt butter and add flour to make a roux. Add milk and stir till smooth and thick. Stir in the ricotta cheese, eggs, and nutmeg to taste.

Grease a 9"x15" baking dish and sprinkle the bottom lightly with the bread crumb mixture. Alternate layers of eggplant and meat, sprinkling each layer with crumbs and cheese. Pour the cheese sauce over all and bake in 375° oven for 1 hour. Cool

15–20 minutes. Cut into squares and serve. (This can be assembled up to two days ahead and baked later; or after baking, can be kept three or four days before reheating.) The flavors have a chance to mellow this way. Reheat at 350° for 25–30 minutes. (Serves 6–8.)

For the pastitsio variation cook ½ lb. ziti or macaroni in 4 quarts of salted water till "al dente." Drain. Add layer of noodles between the meat and the custard layers.

ORANGES WITH ORANGE PEEL AND ORANGE FLOWER WATER

Remove peel from 3 large oranges with a potato peeler and cut peel into tiny julienne strips, removing all white pith. Separate these oranges plus 3 more into sections.*

Syrup

1½	C. sugar	2–4	Tbsp. honey
½	C. water	3	Tbsp. orange flower
1	2" piece of cinnamon stick		water

Make syrup of sugar, water, cinnamon stick, and honey and cook till thick (about 230°). Add peel and orange flower water. Pour over oranges. Chill well for 4–6 hours for maximum flavor.

A French variation omits the cinnamon and orange flower water and adds ¼ C. Grand Marnier. (Serves 6.)

KOURABIEDES—Greek Butter Cookies

1	lb. sweet butter**	2	Tbsp. brandy
1–2	egg yolks	4½–5	C. flour
3	Tbsp. powdered sugar		Whole cloves
⅛	tsp. baking soda		Powdered sugar
	Juice of ½ orange		

*See p. 143 n. for more on julienne.

**The salt in butter acts as a preservative but it produces lots of water and residue when the butter is melted. Sweet butter costs more but has less debris; therefore you may not be wasting money by using it.

Cream butter till very light and fluffy. Gradually add egg yolk and powdered sugar. Beat. Dilute baking soda in orange juice and add to batter. Add the brandy. Beat again. Add flour gradually until a soft dough is formed. Knead a little, then roll into little balls or crescents. Place 1 clove in each ball. Place on ungreased pan and bake about 20 minutes, or until light brown. Remove from pan. Let cool a little.

Gently roll each cookie in a bowl filled with powdered sugar. Pat the sugar on generously. The cookies are extremely fragile to handle at this point, so be careful. They're best eaten a day later (if you can wait). (Makes about 50 cookies.)

If Steven or Melvin dropped by at five o'clock on the pretext of borrowing some drawing paper and it happened to be close to supper time, their food needs and emotional desires for the contact of home could be satisfied at the same time. They missed their mothers' cooking. So if I knew in advance that they were coming to visit I would prepare:

JEWISH BRISKET OF BEEF POT ROAST

3½–4 lb. piece of fresh brisket, not too well trimmed of fat	(Del Monte is traditional in our family)
3 medium onions, chopped coarse	About 12 carrots, trimmed and cut into 3" pieces
3 Tbsp. chicken fat or margarine	Sautéed mushrooms (optional)
1½ C. canned tomato sauce	Salt and pepper

Brown the brisket in its own fat in a hot pan. If it is too lean use 2 Tbsp. margarine or chicken fat. Set it aside. Season with salt and pepper.

In a kettle that has a lid, sauté the onions in the chicken fat till soft but not brown. Put meat atop onions. Cover kettle and simmer 1 hour. Add the tomato sauce. About 20 minutes later, add carrots. Simmer 1 hour more. You may add mushrooms the last 15 minutes if desired. Adjust seasoning—you may want more salt and pepper. This is good with pan gravy and mashed potatoes but even better with latkes. (Serves 6–8.)

LATKES—Potato Pancakes

3	large baking potatoes	4	Tbsp. flour
1	onion		Salt and pepper
1–2	eggs		Crisco or corn oil

These must be fried at the last minute if they are to retain their crispness.

If you like to suffer, grate potatoes and onion into a bowl and add eggs. If you are not a kitchen masochist you may use the blender (not the processor—it leaves chunks): Cube potatoes and onion. Puree the onion in the blender with one egg. Add half the potato cubes gradually and blend till grated. Remove most of the potato-onion batter from the blender. Reserve a little, which will act as the liquid for the remaining potato cubes. If the potatoes are difficult to puree, then add one more egg. You should be able to puree all of the potatoes this way. Add 4 Tbsp. flour, salt, and pepper, and fry in very hot Crisco or shortening or corn oil. The pan must be very hot so the batter will not stick and the potatoes will cook quickly. When pancakes brown at the edge, turn and brown on the other side. *Be careful* because the hot fat may splatter when you turn the latkes over. Drain on paper towels and serve with sour cream, applesauce, or pan gravy. You may make the batter ahead of time; cover and refrigerate it. Stir just before frying. As the potatoes sit they may give off more water. Drain the excess. You may have to add more flour to hold the batter together. (Serves 6.)

June and I would discuss life and art and other esoteric topics over cups of Constant Comment tea and an occasional nosh like:

SOUR CREAM PECAN COFFEE CAKE

1 C. chopped pecans	2 eggs
2 tsp. sugar	1 C. sour cream
1 tsp. cinnamon	½ tsp. vanilla
1 C. sweet butter, room temperature	2 C. flour sifted with 1 tsp. baking powder, ¼ tsp. salt
2 C. sugar	

Preheat oven to 350°. Grease and flour a tube or bundt pan. In a bowl mix the nuts, 2 tsp. sugar, and cinnamon. Cream butter and 2 C. sugar till light and fluffy. Beat in the eggs one at a time. Fold in cream and vanilla on lowest speed of mixer. Fold in flour mixture. Place about ⅓ of the batter in cake pan. Sprinkle with ¾ of the nut mixture. Spread the rest of batter over the nuts. Sprinkle with remaining nuts. Bake 1 hour. Cool on rack. This freezes well. You may reheat it to serve warm. (Serves 10 austere eaters or 6–8 sweet addicts.)

While I learned a great deal about food from practical experimentation and reading and comparing recipes, I also learned from talking about the meals we had eaten, critiques not too different in tone from those with Josef Albers in the studio. "Too bland." "Needs more spices." "The texture is off." "Should have been crisper." "Not subtle enough." "Too heavy-handed." "Back to the drawing board." And I learned a great deal about my friends, seeing them relaxed over the dinner table, able to open up and give of themselves intellectually and emotionally. Here was cooking as communication at its fullest expression. I had given something tangible in the form of a meal, but indirectly given something of myself. They got my message and were able to return it to me in the form of friendship and good feeling. We all profited; we learned something and we ate well too.

I don't want to imply that you should entrap or seduce people with food. It has, of course, happened. I am not as insecure as I once was, so I no longer need to use good food as a means of making and keeping friends. But I do find that the meal is a natural context for people to get together and spend time in a relaxed and pleasant manner. There is an aura of well-being that pervades the room after a good meal is shared by friends. (It is not the same when we go to the movies or talk on the phone.) There is a letting down of defenses, an opening up that occurs because of the sharing of a sensual experience that may or may not include sexuality. Eating is a sensual activity that people can share without having to be lovers. It promotes physical intimacy, and physical intimacy seems naturally to progress to emotional intimacy.

Naturally this doesn't happen at every meal. I'm sure that you can recall excruciating dinners with nice people, groping for conversation. That failing, you end up discussing the food, because the "opening up" never came. This is a common occurrence when people are eating together out of forced friendliness or a sense of obligation, motivated by social or business advancement. Even well-meaning folks who want to send a loving message but are ill at ease with their feelings can produce a tasty but uncomfortable dinner. The host and hostess do what they can to make everyone feel comfortable, but their anxiety can be somewhat contagious. Although their feelings are right, the format is wrong.

If people's intentions are good, the quality of the food they serve you is relatively unimportant. When friends invite you for supper because they haven't seen you for a while and want to spend time with you, and they serve you hot dogs or leftovers, you shouldn't be critical of the meal. They did not ask you over to wine and dine you, but to wine and dine *with* you. Even a "mediocre" meal can convey good feelings and energy. In fact sometimes silence—sipping a glass of wine and sharing a close space at the dinner table—is more intimate than spending the night with someone. (You wake up in the morning wondering who that person is, hoping not to have to make conversation at breakfast. Intimacy over food will not happen unless you are with people you really like. It may be easier to sleep with strangers than to eat with them.)

Over the years I have discovered that cooking can be an incredible growth experience, a means to self-knowledge. Through cooking I have become aware of how I think, how I work, how I feel about others and myself. The kitchen is a microcosm of all my activities and a safe place to try out new ways of doing and being. You may have to call my name a few times to get me back. Either I will be calmly working in a Meditative space-time dimension that is all my own or I will be dancing, humming, and chopping all at the same time, enjoying my own High Energy.

In the kitchen I have discovered how to enjoy my own company. And now that I am comfortable with myself I am better able to enjoy the company of others. Of course it's fun to cook by myself, the "artist" in the "studio," creating a work that will be enjoyed later, but it is also wonderful to cook with family and friends sharing that space. I get high with their questions, their suggestions, their presence. They help create the good energy and love that is stirred into each dish. If that is not communication I don't know what is.

Hospitality, the breaking of bread, is a sacrament. Cooking satisfies our need for community and communion with others. So I have become a Cooking Evangelist! I have crossed from the valley of hating to eat and a fear of trying new things, and have come out to the other side where eating is an adventure and cooking is as creative and exhilarating as painting, filmmaking, or writing a poem. I want others to join in the journey and discover the pleasures of the kitchen.

Chapter 5

MULTIPLE FEEDBACK:

Teaching and Learning

I became a cooking teacher quite by chance—almost the way I became a cook. One day my friend Darlene asked me to teach her how to cook. She and her husband were tired of taking their friends and clients to restaurants, yet she felt unprepared to cook for all the people they needed to entertain. She was terrified that she might be judged and found wanting. Not that that would have been the case. Even if she had opened a can of baked beans and served dinner on paper plates, people would have enjoyed her company and that of her husband, a charismatic art dealer.

However, because I loved her and thought it would be fun, I invited her to come and live in my kitchen for a while, to learn what she could by eye and practice the written recipes at home, when she had the time. She became a capable cook fairly quickly, and invited some friends over for dinner who said, "Darlene, when did you learn how to cook?" And the next thing I knew there were eight women sitting in my kitchen, friends of Darlene's. After that it was word of mouth, French cooking led to Continental, led to International; led to French Two, led to Middle Eastern, and on and on.

I saw that people came to cooking classes for a wide variety of reasons. Some were there because they were fearful, intimidated by cooking, either from what they had heard or read or because they'd suffered a few bad experiences in the kitchen. They were the cooking disabled, the walking wounded. Others came to class to get the basics. They found books an incomplete means of learning and wanted to see for themselves: the Harry Truman approach. Others came to perfect their techniques, to learn why things work and how to prevent disaster. Some came for new recipes or a renewed impetus to cook, an energy boost, an inspiration. Still others came because they wanted to spend time with other people, and a place to go for the evening; other people, a good meal, and maybe they'd learn something too. In fact, there were people who had tried encounter and singles groups and found them traumatic but felt very safe in a cooking class, talking over dinner and testing out their social wiles in a neutral "undercover" environment. "I'm not here to meet people. I'm really here to learn how to cook (and if I meet someone, well, that's O.K. too)."

I suspect that is why people join groups—whether the focus be gardening, woodworking, running, or cooking. These activities provide an opportunity to work alone and then the occasion to share the experience in a group format. People learn more about themselves and they get to learn about others. Cooking classes are increasingly popular because of this basic need for communality and communication. People want to learn how to cook and to share the food and sensual pleasure and energy high that comes from putting the meal together. For many it is the best night of the week: a chance to share their feelings about the food and themselves because the kitchen has become a nonthreatening environment.

As a cooking teacher I found I could play many roles. I could be a technician, a historian and social commentator, a magician, a coach, or a philosopher. Any or all of the above. A good teacher teaches more than just technique. He/she teaches the reasons behind the recipes. If you only learn to reproduce recipes, like memorizing a piece of music for the piano without understanding its organic structure, you will forever be dependent upon the teacher every time you want to master a new recipe, a new technique. You will become a cooking-class addict. (Of course, not every student wants to become independent. Some want to keep coming back again and again because they need the constant support and feedback the class situation provides.)

Sometimes the cooking teacher plays historian. He/she tells you the background of the dish you are preparing, its technical, cultural, and social tradition. Does it represent aristocratic or peasant cooking? For what ceremony or person was it created? How was it presented?

By creating a safe space for the student, the cooking teacher acts as a sort of magician or faith healer. Once you see the trial run in class the recipe loses its aura of mystery and danger. You learn that the risks are not so risky and you see how to pull the rabbit out of the pot after you have added too much wine to the sauce.

The teacher communicates inspiration and enthusiasm as well as expertise, so the student wants to run home and cook that dish. He/she is like the "coach" who gives the team the old pep talk: "C'mon, you can do it. Your omelet will be just fine. You can't fail. Everyone will love it. Have a good time cooking."

Just as the meal is the vehicle for the exchange of energy from the cook to the eater, the cooking lesson is the vehicle for conveying the energy and philosophy of the teacher to the student. He/she conveys an approach to food and to life and their interrelationship. The teacher reveals to the student the powers of the cook, the WHY of cooking, and can make you aware of your motives and your role as the medium between the food and those who partake of it.

While I was teaching people how to prepare the food, indirectly I was also showing them how to communicate with themselves and others, to be aware of multiple feedback. They could see how I felt while I was cooking. They would taste the dish, consider how they felt about it, and then feed back their reaction. Later they would go home and cook it for friends, get their friends' reactions, and return to class to tell me how their interpretation of the dish tasted and how others responded to their food and their energy. I got feedback on their feedback!

I was amazed to discover how many people were afraid of doing things for others. They feared that they might not get anything in return, or that they might not measure up. Cooking for *personal pleasure* is one way of getting past this impasse. It's not so difficult to go from cooking for *yourself* to cooking for *others* (or even cooking *with* others). Once you learn to master your own space in the kitchen you will be better able and willing to share with others.

Students who had never ever enjoyed cooking, and were so tense and anxious that they went into shock if someone set foot in their kitchens while they were preparing the meal, began to invite people over so they could cook *together*! The kitchen became a place of enjoyment. If something went "wrong," they put their heads together, laughed, sipped some wine, and salvaged the dish in some ingenious way. It tasted even more delicious having shared this "secret failure" with friends.

Susan has been divorced for about a year. She is just starting to feel good about being alone, making tentative overtures to old friends to see if they still like her even though she isn't part of a couple. She's also been meeting new people and is wondering what would be the best way to get to know them better and have them get to know her. When she was married, she and her husband, Greg, entertained quite a bit: formal dinners, lots of wine, and elaborate foods. Those dinners always made her nervous, although Greg liked them. That style of entertaining never felt comfortable to her. She was exhausted for days after each meal. Susan decided to take cooking lessons so she could explore what her style might be. How does Susan alone differ from Susan and Greg? Although her budget ain't what it used to be and her new friends are not the pâté-and-caviar types, she has discovered that she loves cooking! She realizes that cooking *with* her old and new friends, rather than for them, may be one way to break the ice and to establish her new identity. So she invites everyone for brunch or early supper on Sunday, and each can cook a favorite dish. She and her husband never did that. Next month when the weather is better she might organize a pot-luck picnic and ask everyone to meet her in the park.

I now learn of students sent to cooking classes after the end of a love affair or a death in their family. Someone who cared about them and was concerned about their recovery realized that they needed to get involved in something that took them out of the house and away from their grief. Cooking seemed to be an activity that enabled them to unwind and deal with their feelings. It also brought them out of isolation and into contact with others. Eventually they were able to use the cooking process as a means of emerging from a difficult time of life. They learned a skill, opened up to classmates, and eventually were able to invite others into their space to enjoy the food.

For the first time in fifteen years Charlie is on his own. When he started dating after the death of his wife, he was shy, out of practice, ill at ease. Taking dates to restaurants all the time was getting him down. It was expensive, and not very personal or private. One night two old friends invited him to a cooking class. Charlie never cooked when he was married. Now he discovers that he really has a knack for this cooking business, loves it in fact. He and his friends decide to cook together once a week. They plan the meals, market, and get together to "create" and then feed some other friends. They laugh over their failures, take pride in their triumphs, have a grand time. The old friendships are cemented and the new friends are delighted to be part of the fun. Charlie's dates are thrilled. How much better than going to restaurants every week. How nice to be cooked for. How personal.

A few psychiatrists have actually referred patients to me for cooking lessons. And I get feedback from them on the results of the "cooking therapy" as a supplement to therapy in the more traditional sense.

Unbeknownst to me, I had a student who was having trouble in achieving orgasm. Her doctor, my neighbor and friend, tried a variety of methods, referred his client to radical therapy, massage classes, group sessions, but no go (or come). At one meeting with the doctor the patient mentioned that she did not like to cook or to make things for other people. So, of course, he advised her to take cooking lessons in order to explore the problem. In one class we discussed the incredible sensual taste and textures of honey mousse, its fragrance, how sexy it felt on the tongue. That week the patient-cooking student went home and prepared honey mousse for her boyfriend and bingo! She thawed her libido with the frozen dessert. The psychiatrist never said a word, but years later he showed me an article in a scientific journal which described this particular case history. I'm sure that the dessert itself has no aphrodisiacal properties, but it did something for the emotions of that one particular person. It's all in the mind, you know.

HONEY MOUSSE

6 egg yolks	1 C. heavy cream, or a bit
¾ C. honey—I like Wild	more*
Mountain	Shaved chocolate

Beat egg yolks with honey till very pale and thick. Whip cream till stiff and fold into honey mixture. Ladle into individual serving dishes or a bowl. Top with shaved chocolate. Cover with a double thickness of tin foil and place in the freezer for at least 4 hours.

Remove from the freezer and place in refrigerator for 1 hour before serving for small molds; a few hours for one large bowl. Keeps frozen for 2 months. (Serves 6–8.)

This story is related not to titillate you or send you rummaging for all the "hot" recipes in the book, but to make you aware of the power of direct physical activity, the sensual liberation of working with foods and the incredible satisfaction that comes from sending a message and having it received.

So many people know of the sensuality of eating, but how many are aware of the sensuality of cooking? How tactile, feeling whipped cream, putting your hands in flour or sugar, fondling avocado flesh. What aromas when you peel a peach, chop fresh herbs, heat butter and garlic in a pan. Tasting the

*Most ingredients respond better when they are at room temperature, with the exception of heavy cream that is to be whipped. It should be *very* cold. (Heavy cream=whipping cream. When just cream is listed, it means cook's choice, heavy or light or half and half.)

food, savoring its flavor, texture, and aroma, and imagining how the person who will eat it may respond are sensual, often erotic, experiences. That's why I love my work. Sometimes it is play, although at times it can be physically exhausting. Marketing and putting away massive quantities of groceries, doing prep and cooking for two classes of ten and my family of five can be a real workout. But seeing my students learn how to cook and enjoy the process as well as the product, discovering how to make the kitchen a safe space to explore their feelings and expand their sensual awareness, are sources of great satisfaction to me.

Not all of us may be teachers. Nor may we all take lessons from a teacher who is perfect for our needs. Yet we still can participate in that energy exchange called feedback. It is not just confined to the classroom or to the pages of this book. Because *Feedback* is not only about *my* experience. It is also *yours*. When you are present-centered, paying attention to *how you are now*, you constantly activate and interpret the feedback in *your own kitchen*. You become increasingly aware of the effects of cooking on your own emotions, sensations, thoughts. You discover how your cooking communicates with those who eat your food and share your space and energy.

I may not be able to make you love fish if you hate it. I may not turn you into a sweetbread or broccoli fanatic. But I will guarantee that if you enter your kitchen with an open mind, present-centered, alert to feedback from the cooking process and from yourself, you will become a cooking afficionado, a cooking lover. I have seen it happen. I can recognize the signs. The maitre d' at your old favorite restaurant asks, "Hey, where've you been?" Your friends say, "When can we get together and try that new lemon chicken recipe you've been talking about?" The regulars at your market smile as they see you getting excited by the beautiful produce or whirling around the market to pick up some last-minute items for dinner. You are not the same person who used to go shopping with a grim expression on your face and that compulsive list in hand. Once you open up the lines of communication with yourself, you will be able to communicate with others. You will be sending messages all over the place and receiving them too. Multiple Feedback!

CHAPTER 6

THE POWERS OF THE COOK:

Negative and Positive Powers

Recently there has been an avalanche of books about *"power,"* how to get it, how to use it, woman power, man power, people power. Believe it or not the cook also deals with *power,* every time he or she steps into the kitchen.

As soon as we stop asking first WHAT am I cooking? or HOW am I cooking? and start wondering WHY am I cooking? we enter the realm of the *powers of the cook.* Some powers are easy to recognize, others not so obvious, too subliminal, or just not owned up to. Some are positive, used to benefit the cook and others in a healthful and loving way. Others are negative and may come disguised in well-meaning apparel, but in fact do more harm than good.

Negative power. Well, what do I mean? Let me give you some examples: "You eat this or you don't leave the table." "I say you'll eat it because it's good for you." "No spinach, no dessert." "If you don't clean your plate there'll be no TV for you." "You must finish all of your milk or you won't grow up to be big and strong." "If you are good I'll give you an extra piece of pie." Do any of these sound familiar? Enough to make you lose your appetite? I think this is called "power tripping." Food—which can be nurturance, comfort, love—is used as punishment or reward.

It's too easy to hide this manipulativeness under the guise of concern about health and nutrition. "I want him to eat a well-balanced meal." Of course, cooks can affect health and physical well-being by the foods they prepare. But they can affect it for ill as well as for good. What about those who force too much food (because if food is love you had better eat a lot to show me you love me)? "What, you only ate two helpings, didn't you like it?" No, it's not Mrs. Portnoy or a bad joke. How many mommies have given the child an extra candy bar after the visit to the doctor's office, or the lollypop for the A on the report card? Boy, are they lucky! Now look what they've got. Only twenty extra pounds. Thank you!

Is it any wonder that we are a nation plagued with compulsive dieters, binge eaters, junk food addicts, secret stuffers, and the obese?

O.K. That kind of punishment is unconscious on the part of the cook. "She meant well" is a refrain that resounds in my ears. Does the cook "mean well" by knowing a guest is on a diet, pushing dessert or extra helpings, making him feel guilty for not eating all these "special treats" prepared "just for you."

Speaking of guilt, have you heard this one? "Look how I've slaved all day to make this wonderful dinner and you say you're not hungry. You don't appreciate how hard I've worked to get this dinner together for you. I'm not even hungry after cooking all day, but you should eat and appreciate it. I'll keep you company and watch you eat." Eating can be a chore for those who feel victimized by food and by the cook.

Some cooks are so nervous and insecure in the kitchen that they cause anxiety in others. Will they make it? Will dinner come out? Will the dishes come to the table at the same time? What will be burned or dropped tonight? *How many compliments will I have to give before she'll relax and eat something? Will she be so uptight that I get indigestion?*

Other cooks are insecure in a different way. They serve six elaborate courses when three would suffice. But it means more compliments, insurance that their effort will be appreciated—"Oh, you liked it. No, it wasn't too hard. Only took a few days to make. Nothing, really."

Competitive cooks, the sportspeople of the kitchen, are *out to win.* "My dinner was so good they'll never beat it. That'll impress my husband's boss. So what if it makes his wife feel like a dodo? I'll get noticed." These game players use their power to impress while simultaneously making others feel inadequate.

When I was doing television news reporting on food issues, I covered two stories which really impressed me with the power of food to keep people down. Both involved the California prison system. I was following up a story on the San Quentin food strike where hundreds of prisoners refused to eat because of the way the food was served. The prison authorities claimed that the prisoners were getting good food and well-balanced meals. But would you want to eat your pork chops and cream gravy and bread topped with a scoop of ice cream? All the foods were piled on top of each other on the plate, the gravy on the ice cream, the meat covered with both. Not too appealing. What did it tell the convicts? The message was We've got you. You're hungry so you'll eat this. Too bad if you don't like the way you're getting it.

At a fund-raising dinner for the United Prisoners' Union, instead of the usual catered hors d'oeuvres, a special food was served: "Isolation Loaf." The recipe was smuggled out of the prison kitchen, and it was prepared exactly as written. Mostly bread, beans, and spices, with a little meat thrown in. Perhaps it was nutritionally sound (I'm sure some dietician worked this out with care) but it tasted horrible! And it is served to the prisoners in solitary every day. Constant humiliation, a daily reminder of who they are and where they are. I think it was the first fundraiser I ever attended where nobody touched the food. One whiff was all it took for people to make a donation. I can imagine resentment rather than reform under such a system of "nourishment."

Of course, food as punishment can be a lot more subtle. What about those who are deprived of nourishment to teach them a lesson—the send-'em-to-bed-without-supper syndrome? Or people who punish themselves by eating badly, junk foods, poor nutrition? What they are saying, in effect, is "I don't deserve any better than this, because I am not willing to put in the time for myself. For others, maybe. But for me, no."

Fortunately, most cooks use their powers to comfort and nurture in a loving way. They can single someone out for special attention even though it's not a birthday or some such event—just a way of saying "I care about you."For example, your dear friend has had a terrible week. Things have not been going well at work, she's strained her back playing tennis and has had a tension headache for days. What do you cook? A centering meal that says Relax, enjoy this. Things will be better. This is just for you. And then serve a favorite dish that lets your friend know that she is loved.

The cook has the power to seduce as well as show love with food. The way to a man's heart, or a woman's, is through the stomach—that is not just an idle cliché. Those candlelight dinners for two can promote more than culinary satisfaction. Eating is, of course, incredibly sensual. And sensuality can be heightened by the way the cook presents the food and how well he/she knows the preferences and predilections of the person being cooked for.

Despite the vast aphrodisiac mystique, very few foods have the physical property to sexually arouse.* But the cook has the power to promote sensual awareness, to set the scene and prepare someone emotionally for the food.

First the setting. Do you serve it at the table by candlelight? Or on the floor? In the bedroom? (I suppose if you've gotten that far you know something about sensuality, but it doesn't hurt to embellish a good thing.)

Eating out of doors can also be very voluptuous. You are not only appreciating the food, its aromas and textures, but those of the physical environment. You smell the trees and grass, you hear the birds and insects. You notice the colors of the sky, feel the heat of the sun on your skin. You are more sensually aware, so the food is one more element of this heightened awareness.

Do you use elegant crystal, china, and silverware, or do you eat with your fingers? Food that you bring to your mouth (or to someone else's) can be very sensual because you not only feel it

---

*Asparagus, oysters, and shellfish have chemical properties which may stimulate the urinary tract; juniper berries (gin) irritate the prostate. Alcohol and grass are prime relaxers, so people who use them may be more open to physical and emotional sensations.

in your mouth, you feel it on your fingers. A double physical awareness. Actually I believe that cocktail parties (deadly if you are not in the mood) can be incredibly erotic if you are turned on to someone there. All those people standing around eating with their fingers, feeding each other little tastes of this and that, drinking. It can be quite stimulating, perhaps more arousing than sitting around a formal table. So much body language!

Foods that are highly perfumed and aromatic—like raspberries, peaches, orange flower and rose water—have this double whammy effect; you are eating a taste and also eating a smell.

Another way to heighten sensual awareness is to serve food that stimulates multiple sensations on the tongue, like hot and cold, sweet and sour, creamy and crunchy. The contrasts make one aware of the flavor and the texture of the food. You are tasting and feeling at the same time. You can serve foods that are erotic in appearance (like bananas, figs, oysters, asparagus) or in texture. Many people are turned on by steak tartare because it is reminiscent of flesh. So are melons, peaches and mangoes, avocadoes, smoked salmon, not to mention rare steak or roast beef. Obviously, sensual arousal is partly physical and partly mental. If you tell someone a sexy anecdote about a dish and then serve the food, he/she will be turned on by the idea that it was supposed to be erotic. Sex by association. So if a recipe worked for Casanova, or a famous mistress of some king or poet, it is bound to arouse your friend if you tell him/her the original context.

Here are a few sensual time bombs, if you know what your friend likes to eat. First the *fleshy textures*:

STEAK TARTARE

1 lb. chopped sirloin steak	Salt, pepper, Tabasco,
1 Tbsp. Dijon mustard	Worcestershire sauce to
2 egg yolks	taste
Large onion, grated, or	
¼–½ C. finely minced	
onion	

Combine well. Serve with toast, rye rounds, and capers, and additional chopped onion on the side. You may garnish with tomatoes, capers, green onions. Serve at *room temperature*. Do not mix the capers in with the meat if you prepare this ahead of time: they will discolor the meat.

It is essential that the meat be freshly ground. Many recipes suggest grinding it twice, but I find that it gives the meat a pasty consistency.

NARSAI DAVID'S GRAVLAX

2 lb. piece of salmon filet with skin	¼ tsp. ground black pepper
1 tsp. dill weed and dill seed (dried) or 2 Tbsp. fresh dill	¼ tsp. allspice
	¼ C. wine vinegar, brandy, or aquavit (Narsai prefers aquavit because the salmon stays much pinker in color)
3 Tbsp. coarse salt	
3 Tbsp. sugar	

Sprinkle salmon with dill. Place skin side down on Pyrex or china plate.* Mix salt, sugar, spices, and pat lightly into fish. Sprinkle with vinegar. Cover with plastic wrap and weight down. Refrigerate 2 days, basting juices over fish occasionally. Remove weight after first day. Drain before serving. Slice thin. Accompany with a mustard-and-dill-flavored mayonnaise, or sprinkle with lemon juice. You may eat this with your fingers!

*Meats and fish that must marinate in wine- or vinegar-based marinades should be put in ceramic, Pyrex, or stainless steel dishes to prevent discoloration and weirdness of flavor.

RUBEN MEDINA'S CEVICHE

2 lbs. scallops, cut in
   bite-size pieces
   Juice of 2 limes or more
⅓ C. olive oil
1 Bermuda onion,
   thin sliced
1 4-oz. can peeled green
   chilis, cut in half and
   sliced
1 ripe tomato, peeled and
   chopped

½ tsp. sugar
2 fresh jalapeño peppers
   or more, chopped
   (optional)
   Salt to taste
   White pepper to taste, if
   jalapeños omitted
   Cilantro (Chinese
   parsley or fresh
   coriander) (optional)

Combine all in a bowl. Mix well and marinate in refrigerator at least four hours, but overnight is better.

Remember caviar and clams! (See caviar cake roll, p. 287), caviar omelet, p. 282, etc.; and stuffed broiled clams, p. 141.

Anyone who saw Alan Bates eating figs in *Women in Love* will understand the erotic power of this dessert:*

BAKED FIGS

12 purple figs
½–¾ C. brown sugar
½ C. water

Cloves and cinnamon,
or Chinese Five
Spices**

Sauce

1 C. sour cream
2–3 Tbsp. sugar

4 Tbsp. Grand Marnier

*Instead of dissecting it politely with knife and fork, he held the fig in his fingers, peeled it open, and scooped up its fleshy interior with his tongue.
**A Chinese spice combination which consists of cinnamon, star anise, fennel seed, cloves, and Chinese pepper corns.

Prick figs with fork in a few places. Place in buttered baking dish. Sprinkle with sugar and add water. Bake in 350° oven for 25 minutes, basting often. Dust with cinnamon and cloves or Chinese Five Spices. Mix sour cream, sugar, and liqueur and spoon over figs just before serving warm or at room temperature. (Serves 4–6.)

Don't forget the fleshy papaya, the melon and the peach!

STUFFED PEACHES

Pour boiling water over 6 ripe peaches and slip off the skins. Halve the fruit and remove the pits. Fill the cavities (you may enlarge the cavities a little and mash the extra pulp with the rest of the stuffing) with:

8–10 crumbled Amaretti or macaroons	8 Tbsp. sweet butter
4 Tbsp. sugar	1 tsp. ground ginger (optional)

Bake in buttered baking dish in 375° oven for about 25 minutes. (You may baste with Marsala or white wine.) Serve warm with cold vanilla custard sauce (see p. 257) or cold zabaglione sauce (see p. 255). (Serves 6.)

Not only do you have the fleshy texture of the peach, but the aromatics of the almond macaroons and the sensual contrast of warm vs. cold.

Strawberries or peaches with raspberry sauce (p. 356) are sensually satisfying, and for a textural and *aromatic* debauch, try:

ALMOND MERINGUE STRAWBERRIES

½ C. (about 5) egg whites	3 boxes of ripe strawberries, cleaned and hulled
1 C. sugar	
Pinch of salt	
2 tsp. almond extract	2–4 Tbsp. amaretto (almond liqueur)
1 C. heavy cream	

Beat egg whites with salt till stiff. Gradually beat in sugar and keep beating till shiny. Add almond extract. In a separate bowl, beat cream till thick. Combine with the egg whites. Pour almond liqueur over berries, an hour ahead if possible. Top with meringue-cream mixture.

Note: The meringue-cream is a last-minute topping and will not hold up longer than 20 minutes.

For another sauce for strawberries, don't forget the epicurean zabaglione (p. 254) served at body temperature, with one spoon for two people.

As far as *eating a smell*, remember orange flower water, rose water, and crystallized rose petals, violets, and mint leaves.

ARABIC BANANAS AND DATES

2 bananas, sliced ½" thick
½ C. pitted dates, cut into ¼" bits with scissors
1 C. heavy cream

3 Tbsp. brown sugar
1–2 tsp. orange flower water (optional)

Cover bananas and dates with cream and sugar. Refrigerate 2–6 hours. You may add orange flower water if you like it.

For a tropical variation top with chopped nuts and coconut that have been sautéed in butter for a few minutes. (Serves 2–3.)

See Iranian Baklava, (p. 353) and oranges in orange flower water (p. 40). Be sure to eat this with your fingers and feed some to a friend.

EKMEK KADAIF—Turkish "Palace Bread"

4–5 Tbsp. sweet butter
¼ C. dark brown sugar
½ C. dark honey
3 C. firm bread, 1" cubes,

crusts removed. (Sweet or sour French bread is excellent)
½ C. heavy cream
1–2 tsp. rose water

Melt butter. Add sugar and honey and stir over low heat till dissolved and bubbly. Stir in bread cubes and coat well with syrup. Pour into flat buttered serving dish, such as a pie plate. Cool about 2–4 hours at room temperature. From time to time stir the bread cubes in the syrup. Whip cream and add rose water. Serve with bread.

Just a few *finger foods* follow—but don't forget:

CROSTINI

½ lb. chicken livers
4 Tbsp. minced onion
2 Tbsp. butter and
1 Tbsp. oil*
Salt and pepper

Lemon juice
Sage
Marsala wine to taste
Bread rounds, fried or toasted

Sauté the livers with the onion in butter and oil about 10 minutes, till the livers are soft. Mash or puree coarsely in the blender. Season with salt, pepper, lemon juice, sage, and Marsala. Spread on warm toasted bread, lightly buttered, or bread rounds that have been fried in butter and oil till golden. Serve immediately.

Crostini, a Florentine specialty, are served warm. You may assemble all the ingredients in the pan ahead of time, but heat and puree the livers just before serving.

*Adding 1 Tbsp. of oil to butter while sautéeing will reduce the risk of burning the butter and prevent most scorching and smoking.

GUACAMOLE

2–3 ripe avocados
½ medium onion
3-6 cloves garlic
    Juice of 1 lime
    Salt
    Half of one small (4 oz.)

can diced green chilis
(about 2 whole peppers)
Worcestershire,
Tabasco sauces
(optional)

Mash the avocados with a fork. Puree the onions, garlic, lime juice, and chili peppers in the blender. Add to the avocado. Season to taste. Serve with corn chips.

Resist the temptation to throw the avocados into the blender, too. The texture of guacamole is more interesting if the avocados are mashed.

DEVILED EGGS

6 hard-boiled eggs, shelled and cut in half

Mash yolks with:

4 Tbsp. mayonnaise
2 Tbsp. chili sauce
    Salt and pepper

Dash of Tabasco or
Worcestershire sauce
1 tsp. Dijon mustard

Stuff mixture into yolk cavities in whites. Sprinkle with cayenne or paprika.

Other things that mix well with the egg yolks to stuff back in the egg whites:

    caviar
    pâté
    chopped smoked salmon
    chutney

64

MARINATED MUSHROOMS

Add ½ lb. mushrooms to the following mixture and place in a crock:

⅔	C. red wine vinegar	½	tsp. salt
½	C. olive oil	2	Tbsp. water
1	clove garlic, mashed		Pepper and Tabasco to
1	small onion, in rings		taste
1	Tbsp. sugar		

Marinate 2–3 hours. Stir occasionally.

The secret to the deliciousness of marinated mushrooms is their texture. They are only marinated for a few hours—enough time to absorb the flavor of the marinade but not long enough to get soggy. Spear with toothpicks or forks. If you have any left, toss them in salad and use the marinade combined with your regular vinaigrette dressing.

Because the cook has the power to seduce, he or she should be careful not to abuse it. It's hard to have too much sympathy for the person who feigns surprise or gets indignant when someone makes a pass after a very sensual meal. What message *was* being sent? Don't underestimate the power of food to convey feelings, even those you didn't know you were expressing.

Food has powerful emotional connotations. When people are deprived of food, it takes on fantastic, obsessive proportions in the mind. When one is hungry, taste and style are unimportant; mere nutrition is needed for survival. But once this is no longer the issue, food can trigger all sorts of memories, feelings, waves of nostalgia. Food messages can be almost subliminal. Did you ever walk into someone else's kitchen and smell something cooking that took you back to another place, another time? Biting into an apple or a ripe tomato can remind you of a childhood picnic or lunch eaten with a friend, seated on a park bench in the city. Marcel Proust had his "Madeleine," and you can have a Milky Way to set off remembrances of meals gone by.

One of the powers of the chef is to evoke a memory in others who eat the food. Sometimes the memory is a wonderful one—a special event, a favorite dish, a meal that reminds you of someone you love.

Unfortunately, not all of our memories will be pleasant ones. It took me almost 35 years before I could be in the same room with the smell of lamb stew. I don't remember the specific childhood event that brought about my intense bad feelings. I suspect that my reasons for rejection of the dish were aesthetic as well as emotional. One day I said, "Joyce, this is ridiculous. You are a cooking teacher. You ought to be able to make it edible, even good. Give it a try." But how does one get over negative food conditioning to be able to approach the dish with an open mind? I had to detach myself from the past and from the emotions, and deal with it as an artistic challenge. Here are some carrots, some onions, some pieces of lamb. How can I put them together in a way that will allow them to express their individual character and taste good in combination? As an abstract cooking question it is then easy to tackle the subject of lamb stew without being blinded and held back by Uh-oh, lamb stew, bad memories. I can't eat it and I can't cook it. Instead one thinks, Aha, crunchy orange carrots, how can I keep their texture? Soft, juicy meat, yet resilient. How can I cook it to just the right degree of tenderness and not dry it out until it loses all its flavor and chewiness? Round white onions, smooth and firm. They must be made tender but not mushy in this mélange. What goes in first? The lamb. Then the broth. After a while the carrots. The onions are too tricky to dump into the pot as is. They must be cooked separately and added later so that they can impart some flavor to the meat and the pan juices. The little peas are also a last minute addition, because I need some green and parsley is not enough. Do I want the stew to taste of Greece? Then I add some cinnamon and marjoram. Is it Italian in inspiration? Then oregano and lemon juice. Is it French? Then how about some thyme? And is it Joyce? Then add some garlic, perhaps a sprinkling of mint. Thus I am able to turn on my creative juices and "invent" lamb stew for the "first time" and enjoy it. Years of bad memories and brainwashing are down the tube.

LAMB STEW

2–2½ lb. lamb, cut in 1½–2" cubes
Seasoned flour
1 onion, chopped
2–3 cloves garlic, minced
1 tsp. thyme or fines herbes
Butter and oil
¾ C. water, wine, or beef stock
6–8 carrots, scraped, cut into 2" lengths crosswise
4 turnips, peeled and chunked (optional)

12–14 white onions, parboiled 5–7 minutes* and peeled (optional)
1 package frozen peas, thawed
1 C. sour cream or yoghurt (optional)
Sautéed mushroom caps (optional)
2 C. cooked tomatoes (optional)
Cinnamon and pine nuts (optional)
Chopped parsley

Dredge meat in flour that has been seasoned with salt, pepper, paprika, nutmeg, garlic powder, etc. and cinnamon if desired.** Sauté in butter and oil. Place in heavy kettle or dutch oven. Add onion, garlic, herbs, and cook 3 minutes. Add liquid, cover the kettle, simmer 1½ hours, adding carrots last 30 minutes, turnips last 20 minutes, white onions last 10 minutes. Add peas last 5 minutes. Sprinkle with chopped parsley and pan toasted pine nuts if desired.

Optional: You may stir in 1 C. sour cream or yoghurt when stew is ready, and some sautéed mushroom caps. Cooked tomatoes could be added during the last half hour. (Serves 6.)

If I wanted to take the stew in a Middle Eastern direction, I might treat it as couscous.

---

*It is easier to peel small white onions if you parboil them for a few minutes. You can peel peaches and tomatoes easily too by dipping them in boiling water for a few seconds.
**Cinnamon could go here or at end after tasting the stew and deciding that it "needs something"

COUSCOUS

2–2½ lbs. lean lamb in 1½"
    cubes
2 onions, cut in chunks
1½ tsp. salt
2 tsp. black pepper (or ½
    tsp. cayenne, ½ tsp.
    black)
1 tsp. ginger
½ tsp. saffron
1 tsp. paprika

6–8 Tbsp. oil or butter
3 C. cold water
3–4 carrots, 2" lengths
3–4 zucchini, 2" lengths
2–3 turnips, peeled and
    chunked
15½ oz. can chick-peas,
    drained
½ C. raisins

In heavy kettle sauté the lamb, onions, and spices in butter for 5 minutes. Add water and bring to a boil. Then simmer 1 hour. Add carrots, zucchini, turnips, and cook 15 minutes. Add chick-peas and raisins, and cook 10 minutes.

Couscous

1 lb. couscous
4 Tbsp. butter
¼ tsp. cinnamon

Salt
2 C. water

Cook couscous in lightly salted water according to package directions. Separate grains by rubbing between hands and add butter and cinnamon and place in top part of steamer.

Mound couscous on a platter. Surround with meat and put vegetables and raisins in center. Pass extra sauce and hot sauce. (See harissa, p. 283.)

Incidentally, this couscous is excellent if made with *just vegetables* and no meat, in which case, sauté the onions and spices, add vegetables and just 1½ C. water and cook as directed. You may of course increase the amounts of vegetables and serve this with rice or wheat pilaff as well as couscous. (Serves 6.)

Another time I might make the stew with beef and red wine

and call it beef Bourguignonne, or chicken pieces and call it coq au vin. They are all stews!

You as the cook have the special power to please yourself, to satisfy your own food cravings. You can derive pleasure from perfecting your craft, inventing a new dish, making a personal discovery in the kitchen. You have the power to reveal yourself through the foods you choose to prepare. With every dish you are saying something about yourself.

Not only do you, the cook, have the power to please yourself, you have the power to please others. If someone you love asks you to make something special, you cook with the joy of knowing that your work will be truly appreciated for itself and for your efforts. It is only when you are doing things that you don't want to do that honoring a request makes you feel resentful and used. Of course you must respect your own feelings and be honest with the person who asked you to cook that dinner for six "important business associates." If you feel anxious about it and you cannot transfer your cooking energy to the person who asked you to cook and away from the unknown (and therefore threatening) guests, then you had better decline the request.

The cook also has the power to awe and enthrall others. You can create a meal that is magic, adventure. You can take people to foreign countries without having to spend the air fare; you can whisk your guests off on incredible voyages of sensual delight. You can expand their horizons by introducing new foods and giving them insights into other cultures by the way the food is prepared and served. *But there is the danger of going too far.* You should not go so far out that the guest is overwhelmed and intimidated. You can train yourself to pay attention so you'll know what format suits each guest for the optimum effect: who likes drama and fantasy and who needs the comforts of home. It's better to delight than dismay.

And the cook truly can be a teacher to friends and family who want to learn how to cook. Louis is divorced. Every weekend he picks up his two boys at his ex-wife's house and the three of them make a trip to the supermarket. After months of eating out at hamburger stands or, the other extreme, at fancy restaurants ("the Disneyland Daddy syndrome"), they've discovered that it's fun to cook supper together. Teaching his children is a wonderful way for Louis and his boys to get to know each other better. Their hours in the kitchen, chopping, stirring, tasting, sharing, are nourishing for them emotionally as well as physically. It affirms their closeness, their family bond.

Carolyn is in the process of getting a divorce. One day she is up, feeling good about her decision. The next day she is in the pits of despair. On the nights that her husband has dinner with the kids she is depressed and either drinks her supper, forgets to eat, or punishes herself with a boiled egg and some vanilla ice cream. On the nights that she has the kids she is so busy trying to make them feel better that dinner is tense, absentminded in preparation, often a joyless affair. After four or five months of this she realizes that the meals are actually a ritual that is keeping them a family, a bond between them, and that she will try to enjoy it, to make it a joyful time for all of them. No matter how horrible things may be, it is the one fixed event of the day with her children when they still feel like family again. Carolyn now finds being alone in the kitchen from time to time very relaxing. She enjoys the preparation of the food and her own company in a way she had not known before. And on the days that the kids want to help she is unruffled and happy with their company. The meal is a *centering* force in their fragmented life.

The cook is the keeper of the family flame. He or she has the power to maintain and continue family traditions, to keep the family in touch with its ethnic and cultural roots. By using recipes handed down from great-grandmothers, aunts, and cousins, by teaching these recipes to the children so that they in turn can pass them on, and by making traditional family meals and holidays memorable and happy occasions, he/she renews family ties, affirms the identity and meaning of the family.

The cook also has the power to bring people together, to set the scene, to control the social environment just by who and how many are invited for dinner, not to mention intuition about which people will like each other. I used to know a man who perversely invited people to dinner he knew would get into a fight. It provided an interesting evening for him, listening to all the arguments and seeing his "friends" in this way. Of course, you can well imagine that not too many people accepted his next invitation. Yet you certainly know what a wonderful feeling it is to bring a group of people together and see how much they enjoy each other's company.

The cook has the power to make newcomers welcome in the community, to make strangers feel "at home." Sharing a meal is sharing your life. Hospitality is an honor to give as well as receive.

The cook also has power as a conciliator. What if two friends have been at odds, unable to come to an agreement, even though they still care for each other. The cook can invite them to dinner and hope that the warm environment may soften them up a bit, enabling them to meet each other halfway, to reaffirm their friendship even though they may still choose to disagree. What if in fact the cook has had an argument with someone and feels like making up or at least making peace. Why not serve a dinner with some of the friend's favorite foods and say, Look, we may not have settled this one, but our friendship is too important to let slide over a disagreement. Let's sip some wine, eat dinner, and let bygones be long gone.

The cook also has the power to "cement a deal," as one of my young executive students so aptly described it. What if things have come to an impasse in negotiations and somehow progress isn't happening as fast as one would like. Why not invite the person to dinner and see if you can get closer, so that a contract can be signed or an agreement can be reached. Crass? Crude? Not really, not if you like the person well enough to eat with him or her; not if you think him or her worth your time and effort. If the deal falls through anyway, the good karma you put out will surely come back another time. At least you can try.

A good meal can get you the attention you think you deserve and bring you closer to someone you would like to know better. If you own up to your motives you will be able to cook with confidence instead of guilt.

And here you thought cooking was learning how to slice onions, how to make omelets and a perfect béarnaise sauce! Bet you didn't know that when you stepped into the kitchen and tied on your apron you became "Wonder Cook," with the power to affect minds and souls as well as bodies. Why do you cook? I hope it's because you enjoy it. If you nourish yourself, you nourish others, and if you nourish others you nourish yourself.

•

Chapter 7

BARBARA'S DREAM:

"Why Am I Cooking?"

Two weeks before Christmas Barbara had a dream. She was in
her kitchen, crouched atop her electric stove, cowering. Below
her the kitchen floor was a sea of alligators, hundreds of them,
mouths open and snapping.

I met Barbara at a dream workshop, a group where we told
each other our dreams and worked with their imagery in order to
better understand ourselves. The timing of her dream episode
and my classes in Holiday Cooking couldn't have been better. I
had just spent a few sessions discussing the trauma of holiday
meals on both the cook and the guests, and here was Barbara
with her nightmare, made to order. After considerable work she
came up with these insights.

The alligators were, of course, those who were to eat the
Christmas dinner. The electric stove (of which she was so proud)
was up to date, completely automatic. All she had to do was turn
the switch on or off, high to low. Barbara's behavior around the
holidays was also automatic, dependable. They just clicked her
switch and she cooked. Only there she was, fearful and trapped
atop the stove, and she didn't know how to get free.

What was really happening in Barbara's life was that she and her husband, who usually celebrated Christmas with his brother and sister-in-law and their kids every year, were going through a difficult time and frankly didn't feel like participating in the family dinner. This year they wanted to stay home and have dinner alone. Only they didn't know how to say No, thank you, this Christmas we need some time for ourselves. Instead, Barbara and her husband worried about how the other members of the family would take it. They felt trapped and unable to do what they really wanted to do for themselves. "What shall I cook, Joyce?" asked Barbara.

"WHAT shall you cook, Barbara? I wonder *if* you should cook. WHY are you doing this?"

But Barbara, just like thousands of other people around the holidays, never stopped to think, "WHY am I cooking? Do I want to do this?" She was locked into a pattern, a tradition that held no meaning for her this time around. At best the food she could produce would be as tired and reluctant as she was. Automatic, detached, mechanical, competent, but definitely not bursting with holiday cheer.

How many dinners have you attended where the food was well prepared, the table properly set with the best glassware, china, and silver, the cook too tired or tense to enjoy the meal? The guests dutifully ate everything, thanked the cook for a nice dinner, and left feeling full in the tummy and empty in spirit. Another performance signifying nothing.

Far too many people march robotlike into the kitchen without ever stopping to think WHY. They just go. The format of entertaining, the cook's set role, is never questioned. It's a habit. It's expected of them whether they feel like cooking or not. There they are, like Barbara, with their on and off switches, their automatic and dependable response.

I suspect that more people would enjoy cooking if they stopped to ask themselves WHY and even FOR WHOM they were cooking before they wondered about WHAT and HOW they were going to cook. Their approach might change, time and energy would be saved, real feelings would be expressed; no one would feel put upon or obligated.

For example, if you asked yourself WHY am I cooking, your

response might be, "I'm hungry but I'm tired, and I don't feel like making anything. So I won't cook." Then you don't have to bother to ask FOR WHOM, HOW, and WHAT. Energy is saved and real feelings respected. If you ask, "For whom am I cooking?" and the answer is, "For people who make me uptight or whom I don't know well enough," then you stop at point two. No need to go on to HOW or WHAT. Just say, "Wait a minute, there's something uncomfortable for me in this situation. I don't feel like cooking today. Maybe when I know them better I will. But tonight we'll eat out." Again, feelings and efforts are spared. If you decide that the WHY and FOR WHOM are all favorable, then you can get into the HOW and WHAT of cooking with enthusiasm.

If you have accepted the responsibility of cooking for your household regularly, you still have some options. First you can decide FOR WHOM you are cooking—a specific member of your family, or for your own pleasure. Then you can get in touch with HOW you are feeling, whether you need the time for yourself and will use cooking as a Meditation, or whether you want to cook quickly and simply and tap your High Energy. If you do not feel like cooking at all, you still have some choices. After all, this is no ironclad contract you have with your family. You can take a night off from time to time. If your budget is limited and you can't afford to eat out en masse there is really nothing wrong in suggesting that everyone make his or her own favorite sandwich. Or perhaps other members of the family might like the opportunity of cooking that evening. You have only yourself to answer to if after asking yourself WHY, you realize you don't want to cook and then you do it anyway, feeling miserable later. Having taken the responsibility to cook for others, you owe it to yourself to take some responsibility for yourself and your feelings.

Cooking is communication. And most of us are so busy thinking about reaching others that we don't take enough time to communicate with ourselves, to get in touch with our own feelings. In part this is due to the traditional role of the cook as the keeper of the flame, the one who looks after others. But the cook must learn to look after him/herself, or those who eat the food will suffer; not that they won't be fed, but they may ingest some bad feelings along with the food. And that could cause a case of emotional indigestion that just might not be worth the effort for the cook and and the eaters.

Cooking involves motives as well as methods, reasons as well as recipes, feelings as well as food. The meal is not only a source of physical nourishment, it is emotional nourishment too. None of us wants to be on survival rations.

PART TWO

For Whom Am I Cooking?

Chapter 8

THE MEAL AS A MIRROR:

You Cook Who You Are

After we know WHY we are cooking, we must stop to consider FOR WHOM we are cooking. Sometimes we are cooking for ourselves alone, even if we are not alone when we eat the food. What if you have read a new recipe that sounds intriguing and you are eager to try it, to see if it is as you have imagined. You are then cooking for yourself, to explore and discover. Implicit in this experiment is the knowledge (or hope) that others who eat the food will be delighted with your spirit of adventure and share your desire to try new things. You're all in it together, a "food conspiracy" of sorts. If the recipe turns out to be just so-so, you will not feel judged and defensive. Let's face it, we've all bombed occasionally. And what you were in the mood to cook may not have been what your family or friends were in the mood to eat. You can't connect every time.

Occasionally we find ourselves in situations where we are cooking for people we don't know too well. An old acquaintance of your husband's has moved to town and been invited for supper, to reconnect. Or a new woman has been hired by your office and you'd like to get to know her better. You both eat lunch out every day so meeting at a restaurant just doesn't fit the bill. So you invite her to your home for dinner. As you don't know her well, FOR WHOM will you cook? *Yourself*, of course. You cook something that you like, a dish that may reflect your style. After all, you are both trying to get to know each other better. And the meal will give her some clues about who you are.

In his book *The Only Dance There Is*, Baba Ram Dass says:

> The only thing you have to offer another human being, ever, is your own state of being. You can cop out only just so long, saying I've got all this fine coat—Joseph's coat of many colors—I know all this and I can do all this. But everything you do, whether you're cooking food or doing therapy or being a student or being a lover, you are only doing your own being, you're only manifesting how evolved a consciousness you are.

We cannot help but reflect our living in our cooking. My life is ny work—not the other way round. My personal "style" and sense of self pervades every level of my existence: cooking, writing, painting, teaching, being a woman, a mother, a lover. My environment and the people around me are also factors that affect my being and certainly color my cooking: WHY I cook, FOR WHOM I cook, HOW I cook and WHAT I cook.

Cooking reveals a great deal about the cook's "being." As well as sending messages about your mood and how you feel about those you are cooking for, the meal reflects your economic situation and aspirations, your upbringing, and your personality. People usually approach cooking the way they approach life. For instance, you cook what you can afford (or you make sacrifices to cook what you can't afford so people will be impressed . . . or so you will be impressed). Poverty cooking is very different from prosperity cooking. That doesn't mean that bean soup doesn't taste as good as crab or tomato bisque, but they represent two different economic levels and two different points of view.

TOMATO BISQUE

6	Tbsp. butter	1	6 oz. can tomato paste
1	Tbsp. olive oil	3–4	Tbsp. flour
1	onion, chopped	2	C. chicken broth
¾	tsp. garlic, minced	1–1½	C. light cream
6	large tomatoes, very		Salt and pepper
	ripe, or 1 2-lb. can of	4	Tbsp. dry sherry
	Italian plum tomatoes		Chopped chives

Melt 4 Tbsp. butter with oil. Add onion and garlic and simmer till golden. Add tomatoes, sliced. Cook over low heat for about 8 minutes. Stir in tomato paste and flour, and gradually add chicken stock. Bring to a boil, stirring constantly. Puree in blender and strain out seeds. Add cream. Season to taste. (If the tomatoes have poor flavor, use less cream and/or more tomato paste.)

Reheat, but don't let boil. Add sherry and 2 Tbsp. butter. Garnish with chopped chives. May be made up to 5 days ahead. Freezes well. (Serves 6.)

Variation: Simmer with grated rind of one orange, or with a cinnamon stick. Or serve with homemade croutons.*

*When I say croutons, I do not refer to those tired, packaged pellets that resemble dog food. I am talking about homemade ones. I have discovered that if I make a batch of these early in the day for soup that evening, they will mysteriously disappear before the soup hits the table. Now I usually make three times what I need because they are loved for themselves alone. They don't need soup to taste delicious, and if by some miracle you have any left over, you can add them to salad. What is the special recipe for these fabulous croutons? Well, they are simply 1" cubes of French bread, either sweet or sour, with the crusts trimmed off, fried (not toasted and buttered, FRIED!!) in butter and oil till brown. You may add some finely minced garlic to the pan at the last minute or sprinkle lightly with garlic powder or herbed salt if you want a spicier flavor. Not too much.

COLD CREAM OF CRAB SOUP

¾ lb. crab meat, shredded
with your fingers
3 Tbsp. grated onion
2 tsp. lemon juice
1 tsp. salt
¼ tsp. white pepper
½ tsp. paprika

1 tsp. curry powder
4 C. *hot* chicken stock
1½ C. heavy cream
1 small cucumber, diced
2 Tbsp. minced parsley
2 Tbsp. minced chives

Mix ½ lb. crab, onion, lemon juice, and seasonings and 2 C. stock in blender for a minute. Add to remaining stock and simmer 2 minutes. Cool well. Lightly whip the cream and fold into the soup just before serving. Garnish with cucumber, parsley, chives, more crab meat. (Serves 8.)

SHOURABA IL ADDIS—Syrian Lentil Soup

3 Tbsp. butter
1 onion, chopped
2 stalks celery with
leaves, chopped
2 carrots, chopped
¾ lb. lentils (about 1½ C.)

4 pt. water or stock
Salt and pepper
1–2 Tbsp. lemon juice
1 tsp. cumin
1–2 bunches spinach or
Swiss chard (optional)

Melt butter and sauté onion, celery, and carrots. Add lentils and liquid. Simmer, covered, for an hour. Add salt, pepper, lemon juice, and cumin, and cook a little longer. Use blender to puree the soup, if desired.

You may shred the well-washed spinach or chard and add to the soup and simmer 10 minutes. Rice may also be added to this soup. Good served with fried garlic croutons (p. 79n.). (Serves 6–8.)

If you make bean soups way ahead of time you will find that as they sit they thicken up quite a bit. You may have to add more water to stock to achieve the consistency that you first had when the soup was finished cooking.

NORTHERN ITALIAN WHITE BEAN SOUP

2 C. dried white beans,
like Cannelini or Great
Northern (1 lb.)
Water
2 onions, diced
4 or more cloves garlic,
minced
4 Tbsp. olive oil (enough
to film the pan)

1 ham bone
2 C. chicken broth
1 C. ham, diced
Regular or cracked
pepper
Salt to taste (undersalt
because of the ham)

Cover beans with water and bring to boil. Then turn off the heat and let them sit covered in water for 1 hour. (Overnight soaking of beans is not necessary if you follow this method of softening.) Drain.

Cover now with 2 quarts of water. This is a good ratio for 1 lb. of beans. Simmer for 1 to 1½ hours or till beans are tender.

Place onions and garlic in a soup pot with olive oil and cook on medium flame. Add beans, drained, and ham bone, then chicken broth. You can also puree some of the beans at this point. Add ham and simmer about 10 minutes. Adjust seasoning according to saltiness of ham.

Variations: Add sautéed sausage, or ham hock, or hot dogs. You might add coriander, celery salt, caraway. Italians would add more olive oil and pepper. Mexicans would add Tabasco sauce and vinegar. To stretch soup, add pasta or rice.

Your upbringing is expressed in the choice of food served, either a reflection of that heritage or in reaction to it. If your childhood has been happy, then ethnic "roots" foods will always have a centering effect. Those foods remind you of home, family, the good times, security, and love. If, however, your childhood experiences have been unpleasant, many ethnic foods will serve as unhappy, possibly traumatic reminders of bad times. One more serving of matzo balls or manicotti could push you over the edge. Well, that's a bit extreme, but you get what I mean.

When people brought up in poor circumstances finally achieve a measure of financial success, they tend to spend a lot of money

82

on good food and fine wine because they never had it. The prime ribs, filets, pâtés and Lafitte-Rothschilds are symbolic of having "made it," of moving up in the world. (Some who were raised in abundance and richness may be much more austere when left to cook on their own—sort of an embarrassment about how much they have had while others have had so little, a reverse "making it," or "unmaking it.")

Cooking is a language. With some practice you can increase your vocabulary so you can communicate more effectively. There are days for poetry and days for simple prose. To be good, foods need not be esoteric, elaborate, or expensive. Don't underestimate the power of a simple statement over a costly cliché.

RIB ROAST (when you can afford it)

Leave roast out at room temperature all day and/or overnight. Insert slivers of garlic all over roast. Brush well with Kitchen Bouquet. Place in pan.
Bake at 350°,
12 minutes per pound for very rare meat
15 minutes per pound for medium rare
18 minutes per pound for medium
Any longer and you shouldn't spend the money on rib roast!

HELEN CORBITT'S GINGERED ROAST BEEF

8	lb. lean eye of rib roast, well trimmed	1	C. soy sauce
1	Tbsp. salt	1	C. sliced onion
2	Tbsp. grated* ginger root	1	C. sherry or bouillon

Rub meat with salt, ginger, and soy. Place in roasting pan on

*Fresh ginger root is different in flavor and intensity from dried ginger powder. So they are not interchangeable. Ginger root can be peeled and stored in a jar of sherry for quite a long time. Some books say that you can freeze it but I find that it gets stringy and very difficult to grate.

top of the sliced onion. Baste with sherry or broth. Allow 10 minutes per pound at 350° for rare. Let stand 10 minutes before slicing.

You may marinate a whole filet of beef (about 3½–4 lbs. trimmed) in half the above mixture, adding a bit of olive oil. Bake in a 400° oven for about 30–40 minutes (130° on meat thermometer).

KALBI KUI—Korean Barbecue Ribs

3	lbs. English short ribs (the bones from the prime rib you didn't buy)	2	cloves garlic
		1	red pepper or 1 tsp. red pepper flakes
4	Tbsp. sugar	3	Tbsp. sesame seeds, pan toasted and ground in blender
3	Tbsp. sesame oil		
8	Tbsp. soy sauce	½	tsp. ginger
2	green onions	2	Tbsp. flour

Make deep cuts in ribs every three inches. Rub ribs with sugar and oil. Let sit 30 minutes. Mix other ingredients and add to ribs. Let sit 30 minutes. Broil till done, about 5 minutes per side, 20 minutes in all.

AN UNCONVENTIONAL BEEF WELLINGTON

Beef Wellington is an elaborate and terribly rich dish that has achieved great popularity in this country among the aspiring gourmet-food addicts. To me the meat, wrapped in its thick pastry crust, always tastes as if it has been sitting on a steam table. Many students asked if they could learn how to make it in class, but I didn't want to teach it until I could solve the problem of the steamed taste. Finally, after some experimenting, I have come up with a satisfactory solution. The fillo dough* is more porous, thin, and crispy, so the meat tastes roasted and juicy, not steamed.

*Paper-thin sheets of dough, sold at Middle Eastern specialty shops. See pp. 193–94 for details.

3 lb. filet of beef, trimmed of all its fat and sinews (the meat should be weighed after trimming, although you will have paid for everything that the butcher throws away!)

½ lb. fillo pastry in the largest sheets you can find (if the sheets are cut small you may need a pound of fillo to envelop the filet entirely)

½ lb. melted butter

1 C. liver pâté, homemade, or canned puree de foie gras (don't buy the most expensive canned pâté, because it melts while cooking).

Watercress

Madeira gravy (see pp. 83–84)

Preheat oven to 400°. Rub the filet with a little pepper and sear it in a hot pan in a bit of butter till brown on all sides. This keeps the juices in. Prepare about 10 layers of fillo pastry with melted butter brushed between each layer. Spread with half of the softened puree de foie gras or pâté. Place filet on pastry and cover with the rest of the pâté. Roll up filo sheets to cover meat. Then top with more layers of pastry and butter each layer. Be sure that the filet is well sealed in the pastry and that there are at least 10 extra layers of fillo on the top. Place in a greased baking pan and bake about 45–50 minutes. When crust is browned and crisp, remove filet to serving platter and garnish with watercress. Serve with Madeira gravy. You may assemble the filet in pastry, chill in the refrigerator, and bake later, after bringing it to room temperature.

Timetable for other sizes of filet strips: 2½ lbs.: 40 min; 2 lbs.: 35 min.; 3½ lbs. 50–65 min. For *rare* beef, the only way to eat filet.

MADEIRA GRAVY

4 Tbsp. butter
1½ Tbsp. flour
¾ C. beef broth
2 tsp. Kitchen Bouquet

¼ C. or more Madeira
Mushrooms or truffles (optional)

Melt 3 Tbsp. butter, add flour. Stir and cook 5 minutes. Add beef broth, Kitchen Bouquet (for color), and Madeira. Swirl in 1 Tbsp. butter when done. You may add mushrooms or truffles, minced. Without the Madeira this is a simple "Brown Sauce."

For a variation add 2 Tbsp. tomato paste. Good over meats and some poultry.

For those who can't afford filet but like the idea:

MEAT LOAF IN FILLO—The Poor Person's Beef Wellington

1 large onion, chopped fine	1 tsp. bouquet garni (mixed green herbs)
1 clove garlic, minced	Nutmeg
3–4 Tbsp. butter	1 egg
1 lb. ground chuck	4 Tbsp. bread crumbs
2–3 Tbsp. minced parsley	½ lb. butter, melted and cooled
½ tsp. or more cinnamon	
Salt and pepper	½ lb. fillo

Sauté onion and garlic in butter till soft. Add meat and seasonings and sauté till done. Add 1 egg, bread crumbs. Cool. Butter 6–8 sheets fillo. Place half the meat in a strip along one end, tuck in ends, and roll up like strudel, buttering as you go. Do one more roll. Bake at 350° for 40 minutes. Serve with sour cream.

MEAT LOAF

2 lb. ground chuck or 1½ lb. chuck and ½ lb. ground veal or pork sausage	Salt and pepper
	1 Tbsp. bouquet garni for beef or Italian seasoning (green mixed dried herbs)
3 slices bread, soaked in milk or water, squeezed and crumbled	½ tsp. seasoned salt
	½ tsp. garlic powder
2 eggs	2 hard-boiled eggs for center (optional)
1 large onion, finely minced (or 4–6 tsp. dry minced onion)	1 C. chili sauce or 1 small 8-oz. can tomato sauce

Mix meat, bread, eggs, and seasonings well. Form into a loaf, around the hard-boiled eggs if used. Put in greased baking pan. Cover with chili sauce or tomato sauce and bake 1 hour and 15–25 minutes.

KUFTEH TABRIZI—Persian Meatballs Stuffed With Hard-Boiled Eggs

2 lbs. lean beef, finely ground	Salt, pepper
3 slices white bread, crusts removed	Chopped parsley
1 onion, finely chopped	1 egg
½ cup yellow split peas boiled in 3 C. water till soft (40 min.)	4 hard-boiled eggs
1 tsp. cinnamon	8 soaked, pitted prunes
½ tsp. nutmeg	Butter and/or oil
	1 8-oz. can tomato sauce
	water

Combine meat with bread, onion, drained peas, spices, and egg. Divide the meat mixture into 4 parts and pat and press each one well around 1 egg and 2 prunes. Form into jumbo meatballs and fry in hot butter and/or oil till browned. Add the tomato sauce diluted with a little water and simmer for 45 minutes. Serve hot or cold with yoghurt or additional tomato sauce. You also may bake these in a 350° oven for 45 minutes, basting with the tomato sauce.

CHILI CON CARNE

Meat

¼ C. olive oil
2 med. onions, coarsely chopped
4 cloves garlic, minced
1 lb. chuck steak, diced in ½" cubes, or 1 lb. ground chuck
1 lb. beef chorizo (hot Spanish sausage), crumbled
½ tsp. basil

2 tsp. oregano
½ tsp. ground cumin
1 tsp. salt
½ tsp. pepper
2–3 Tbsp. chili powder (not chili pepper!)
1 can tomato paste
1 C. water or beer
1 2-lb. can Italian plum tomatoes with liquid

Beans

1 C. dried pinto or kidney beans
1 onion, peeled and chopped

2 cloves garlic, minced
1 tsp. oregano
   Salt to taste

Soak beans in water to cover overnight. Drain and put in a kettle. Cover with water one inch over beans. Add onions, garlic, and oregano and simmer 1 hour. Add salt and cook till tender but not mushy. Drain. Or use a 2-lb. can of kidney beans, drained and rinsed, with or without the seasonings.

Heat oil in large skillet. Add onions and fry till golden. Add garlic, meat, and spices and mix well. Add remaining ingredients and cook, partly covered, stirring often, for 1 hour. Stir in beans when done.

People's personalities are expressed in their cooking. Timid persons tend to be more traditional and controlled. They may be less likely to invent new dishes or to take chances in the kitchen. They follow the written recipe; it is safe, tested and predictable. This doesn't mean that people won't change and grow, that tomorrow's recipe follower might not become the next far-out inventive chef. As your life goes through changes, so do your eating and cooking habits. If you become more outgoing or self-confident, so does your approach to cooking.

Cooking isn't always just a reflection and extension of one's individual style. Occasionally, it can reveal and help develop another aspect of one's personality. Those who lead loose and casually disorganized lives may actually find pure enjoyment in the mechanical aspects of cooking. What a refreshing contrast to their general chaotic or haphazard approach to the world. People are full of surprises: Bob, who constantly locks his keys in the car; Sue, who loses her mail on the way home from the mailbox; Jennifer, whose desk looks like a tornado has blown over it—all may be most impeccable and precise when cooking. In cooking they embrace the discipline that they would resist if it came in another form.

Some people are exacting, orderly in their work, and for them precision and measuring in cooking may feel safe and familiar, a continuation of what they experience in daily life. Others may say, "The hell with this. I need to break out and the kitchen is the place to do it." For them cooking is an escape, an opportunity to express themselves in ways they might never dare in day-to-day existence.

I am a cooking pusher, but I won't push trendy recipes or formula menus which promise (but rarely deliver) social success. I do push the *process of cooking*. I will feel that this book has been successful if it sends you into the kitchen comfortable to Cook Who You Are.

As in painting, there are different styles in cooking: classic and baroque, austere and opulent, traditional and innovative. Anybody can fill in the numbers on a predesigned painting, but it takes an individual to create his own! If you feel at ease preparing simple homely fare like baked apple or rice pudding, instead of crème brulée or tarte tatin, fine! Chicken pot pie can be as satisfying as chicken en croûte. Prepare the menu that reflects you, not what fashion and tradition dictate.

STUFFED BAKED APPLES

6 Rome Beauty apples,   at the base (I use a
  cored but not punctured   melon-ball scooper)

Filling

Combine with hands into a thick paste:

½ C. chopped walnuts or   mixed, or just raisins,
  pecans or ground   chopped
  almonds or macaroons ¼ tsp. ground cardamom
¼ C. brown sugar   or powdered ginger
1 tsp. cinnamon 6 Tbsp. sweet butter
1 tsp. orange peel ¼ C. honey and juice of 2
½ C. raisins and dates   oranges for basting

Fill apple centers with nuts-fruit-butter mixture. Place apples in buttered baking dish. Bake in 350° oven about 45–60 minutes, basting with honey and orange juice. You may serve with cream, sour cream or sweetened yoghurt.

You may bake without filling and baste with butter, brown sugar, and orange juice. (Serves 6.)

or

TARTE TATIN

½ C. butter and ½ C. sugar 6 Golden Delicious
  melted together till   apples, peeled, cored,
  caramelized and   and sliced
  browned

Preheat oven to 425°. Pour butter-and-sugar caramel into the bottom of a 10" pie plate or two 8" square baking pans. Arrange apple slices in the pie plate (no more than 2 layers of fruit slices).

Dough

1⅓	C. flour	½	tsp. grated lemon peel
¼	C. sugar	¼	lb. butter
2	egg yolks		

Combine dough ingredients with your fingers. Form into a smooth dough. Roll, between pieces of waxed paper for easier handling, into a large circle or 2 squares and cover the pie pan(s) and pat down dough on top of apples. Bake for about 45 minutes. If crust gets too brown, cover lightly with foil. Remove pie from oven and let stand 10 minutes. Preheat broiler. Invert pie onto heatproof platter. Sprinkle the top with ⅓ C. sugar and caramelize under the broiler. Repeat this process one more time. Serve tarte warm, with whipped cream.

RICE PUDDING

2	C. milk	½	C. yellow raisins, plumped in warm water
½	C. heavy cream		
½	C. sugar	½	tsp. cinnamon
2	tsp. grated orange rind (optional)	1	tsp. vanilla
		¼	C. Cointreau (optional)
2	Tbsp. butter (optional)	3–4	eggs or 2 whole eggs plus 2 yolks
1	C. cooked rice		

Heat milk and cream. Add sugar, orange rind and butter. Add rice. Simmer about 5 or 10 minutes. Add raisins and a bit of cinnamon. Simmer 3 minutes more. Add vanilla and Cointreau, if desired. Add hot liquids gradually to lightly beaten eggs. Pour into a buttered baking dish and bake in 325° oven for about an hour. You may sprinkle the top with cinnamon before baking. Chill and serve with heavy cream.

If you like creamy rice pudding rather than one you can slice, bake in pan of hot water and increase milk by ½ C. This can be made days ahead of time.

For bread pudding, omit rice and pour custard mixture over 6 slices of stale French bread, toasted, buttered, and sprinkled with cinnamon.

ORANGE CRÈME BRULÉE

3   C. heavy cream
6   egg yolks
6   Tbsp. sugar
    Grated rind of 1 orange

¼   C. Cointreau or Grand
    Marnier
¾   C. or more brown sugar

Scald the cream. Beat the egg yolks with the sugar until thick and light. *Slowly* pour the hot cream into this mixture, *stirring constantly.* Cook over very low flame till it coats a spoon (about 6–8 minutes). Remove from fire. Add rind and liqueur. Pour into an ovenproof serving dish (shallow and rectangular is best—Pyrex is good), put the dish in a pan of hot water, and bake in a 325° oven for 20–30 minutes. Chill well. When cold, and on the day of serving, place a thin layer of brown sugar over the custard and put it under a hot broiler to melt the sugar. You may repeat this step another time to get a thicker layer of caramel. Chill again till serving time. You may serve with berries, too.

CHICKEN POT PIE

Combine:

3   C. cooked chicken, diced
1   C. or more of sautéed
    mushrooms
1   C. frozen peas, thawed
1   pkg. frozen baby carrots,
    thawed
4   Tbsp. butter or
    margarine

4   Tbsp. flour
1½ C. milk, light cream,
    chicken broth in any
    proportion
    Salt, pepper, nutmeg
    Pinch of cayenne

Pour into a buttered baking dish and cover with a piecrust or some frozen puff pastry patty shells that have been rolled out to form one layer. Brush with egg or milk and bake in a 400° oven till golden, about 40 minutes.

The chicken mixture can be put into individual pies or pieces of dough and rolled up into turnovers. They will take about 10 minutes less to cook. Or it may be served over rice—called chicken à la king. (Serves 6.)

Cooked Chicken

Simmer chicken in water or canned broth to cover. Add one or two carrots, a few stalks of celery with leaves, a sprig of parsley, 4–6 peppercorns, some salt, and a whole onion. Cook 25 minutes for chicken parts, or one hour for a whole medium chicken. Discard vegetables, strain stock, and cool the chicken. Enrich the broth with powdered chicken-soup base if you plan to serve it separately. For chicken vegetable soup, sauté sliced onion, celery, and carrots, add broth, and simmer 20 minutes. Add shredded chicken, noodles, and cook 5 minutes more. Adjust seasoning.

CHICKEN BREASTS EN CROÛTE

3 large chicken breasts, skinned, boned and split in half

¼ C. sautéed mushrooms

½ C. or 1 small can of puree de foie gras or homemade pâté

Pastry

6 oz. cream cheese

1½ sticks butter

1½ C. flour

Cut a pocket in each chicken breast and stuff with pâté. Sauté in butter for three minutes on each side till golden. Cool.

Combine cheese, butter, and flour, and roll out pastry into 6 ovals. Place chilled chicken breasts on each piece, top with sliced mushrooms, and seal the pastry envelope by wetting the edges of the dough and pressing down with the tines of a fork. You may decorate with pastry cutouts. Brush with egg. Prick with fork. Bake in 425° oven on ungreased baking sheet for 30–35 minutes. Serve with Madeira sauce (see pp. 84–85).

Chapter 9

"KITCHEN KARMA":

You Get Back What You Put Out

In his book *The Only Dance There Is,* Baba Ram Dass talks about cooking as communication.

> My teacher is so delicate; he is a very beautiful Brahman. He said to me, "Don't eat any food that isn't cooked with love or with mantra . . . because it will poison you. The vibrations of a person cooking food enter into the food when it is cooked over fire." Fire transmutes, converts, brings that energy. . . . Well, now, I can go into a restaurant along the road and eat something that is cooked by an angry chef and I won't experience it because I am so gross yet. My teacher would get violently ill; but even if the food were brought to him by a loving person and he didn't know anything about who cooked it, he would still get ill, because those vibrations are as real, as you get nauseous from the color green or blue or purple or whatever your thing is. . . .

While we may not be as highly evolved as the guru in this story, we can teach ourselves to become aware of the powers of the cook to affect people with food and feelings.

93

The cooking process is a producer of energy, and the meal is the vehicle for the exchange of energy with others. If you get high on the process, you generally convey that feeling and others can share in your high and can feed that energy and good feeling back to you. That is the optimum complete exchange. If you cook for your own pleasure you are bound to convey pleasure to others. If you are nervous, any negative energy you experience is also felt by others. When dinner is only "payback," an obligation with ulterior motives or an imagined social debt to be dealt with, the meal may be as contrived and constipated as the reasons for its being. After cooking a few of these dinners and feeling wiped out later, you may have wondered why. Perhaps now you realize that unless you put out the energy and cook because you *want* to, not *have* to, the meal will be as formularized and tired as you are. This is the doctrine of Kitchen Karma: You get back what you put out.

Whether you are preparing an elaborate feast for friends or a hard-boiled egg sandwich to be eaten alone in the kitchen, you are still sending a message. If you are depressed, or feeling sorry for yourself, you will eat badly, perhaps suffer indigestion or restlessness or lack of energy. You know people who say (not in these exact words, but their message is clear): "I'm bored and alone. My boss doesn't appreciate me. No one loves me. I don't even love me. I think I'll skip supper and eat a quart of ice cream and a bag of potato chips in bed and watch TV." But if you had a bad day yet felt good about yourself ("I am worth the time and effort") the act of cooking dinner for yourself could be a comforting vote of confidence.* What was to be a plain boiled egg may emerge as an omelet or French toast, and the lonely dinner can be transformed into a pleasurable time where you can enjoy your own company. That omelet may taste better than a six-course dinner eaten with others just to pass the time.

Betsy comes from a family in which her mother did all the cooking and was very good at it. Her husband's mother was no

---

*Of course there are nights when we feel lazy and sinfully self-indulgent, cheerfully willing to eat a supper that consists of a Baby Ruth, a dozen Oreos, and some Rocky Road ice cream. But if you have a weight problem or do this too often, the hedonism may be self-defeating.

slouch in the kitchen either. Betsy is a competent and careful cook. She has taken a few classes in Gourmet Cooking, has read lots of books recommended by friends and experts, and has an elaborate supply of equipment. But Betsy still doesn't enjoy cooking. She feels insecure every time she steps into the kitchen. Her husband may say that the chocolate mousse was better at the French restaurant where he had lunch, or his mother's "duck à l'orange" was crisper. She recalls her mother's seven-layer cake and knows that her own is only worth three and a half layers in points.

Elaborate baking and cooking always make Betsy feel like an automaton, and she gets tense at the first mismeasurement. None of these "gourmet" foods are her favorites. Betsy prefers simple dishes, stews, hearty soups, peasant foods that have few rules, things that "just happen." So why doesn't she wise up? Why doesn't she say, "Look, those other foods aren't me. I'm not my mother, I'm not George's mother. I am me and I want to cook what I like in a style that is comfortable to me."

Betsy has been locked into cooking patterns that are alien to her nature and her palate. If she stopped to ask WHY she was cooking, she'd answer, To nourish my family, to please them and to please myself too. I am cooking for me as well as for them. HOW am I cooking? In a style that pleases me. I want to be relaxed in the kitchen—not tense and miserable.

Unfortunately, many cooks are Betsys; they cook for others at the expense of their own happiness. It's not too surprising that no one *really* enjoys those meals, because the cook is doing something that isn't *in harmony with his/her being.* If you are cooking in a manner that pleases you, your sense of peace and joy enters the food, and others who eat it later partake of this feeling. You can tell when this happens at your house. It's the moment at the table when everyone stops chattering and there is a most wonderful silence. You know that your message has been received.

SPECIAL FOOD FOR SPECIAL FOLKS

Although our food tells others about WHO we are and HOW we are feeling, we can also choose to send a specific message to someone with the food. Obviously, the optimum message is, "I like you and I made this especially for you." Even if there are six people at the dinner table, the person for whom you made the pie will know it was for him.

When you set out to cook for a friend, how do you go about projecting his or her tastebuds and head onto yours? Despite the booming interest in out-of-body experiences and the occult, we are not all mind readers and psychics yet.

So it helps to pay attention. Use your powers of observation. How does he or she approach food—heartily or with restraint? Did he enjoy the food of his origins? Will a family meal be a centering or a jarring experience? Does she like adventure, travel, trying new things, or is she timid, traditional, conservative? Is he set in his ways ("I'm just a meat and potatoes person")? Does she prefer to be fussed over or to be treated like one of the family? The person for whom you just prepared a six-course gourmet French dinner may be intimidated, awed rather than pleased. Know your guest. Cook for him, not AT him.

However, knowledge is *more* than facts. What about intuition? What are your "gut feelings" about your guest? Both facts plus feelings will give you the knowledge of how to cook for someone so when he tastes the first mouthful of the food you have prepared he will know "This was made just for me. It has my name on it."

In some sense we do become interpreters, mystics, mediums. We try to put ourselves inside the head or mouth of another person to "psych out" what he or she would really like to eat. What if your friend likes cheese? Do you ask what cheese is supposed to taste like? Is there an abstract cheese module imprinted on your tongue? You may know what you want it to taste like, but you may not know how to get it to taste like that. And here is where decisions get complicated. You are not cooking for *your* taste of cheese but for your friend's taste of cheese.

Should the cheese stand alone? Should it solo or become part of the chorus? Know your friend and you will know the answer to the question.

The cheese stands alone:

MACARONI AND CHEESE

12 oz. macaroni	¼ tsp. cayenne
6 Tbsp. butter	¼ tsp. nutmeg
4 Tbsp. flour	2 C. grated sharp cheddar
2 C. milk	cheese
¼ C. cream, optional	Bread crumbs for
Salt and pepper	topping (optional)

Cook macaroni "al dente" (see p. 275 for definition). Drain and add 2 Tbsp. butter.

Melt 4 Tbsp. butter, add flour. Stir in milk and optional cream and cook until thickened. Add salt, pepper, cayenne, and nutmeg. Mix in with the drained macaroni. Stir in most of the cheese, setting some aside for topping. Pour macaroni into buttered baking dish. Top with remaining cheese (and bread crumbs, if desired) and bake in 400° oven for 25–30 minutes.

This recipe calls for cheddar cheese alone, but we have used various combinations of cheddar, Swiss, Monterey-Jack, mozzarella, and parmesan, so use your favorites.

But cheese can sing subtly with tomatoes:

MACARONI ALLA SORRENTINA

1 lb. macaroni	1 lb. peeled diced
6 Tbsp. butter	tomatoes, or 2 C.
1 C. dry white wine	canned plum tomatoes
2 Tbsp. minced onion	6 Tbsp. grated parmesan
1 tsp. garlic	1 C. diced mozzarella

Melt 3 Tbsp. butter and sauté onion and garlic till tender. Add white wine and cook 2 minutes. Add tomatoes and lower heat. Simmer ½ hour till a thick sauce is formed. Puree the sauce. (Or eliminate the above, and use 2 C. canned marinara sauce.)

Cook macaroni al dente and drain. Mix with 3 Tbsp. butter and the sauce. Pour into buttered baking dish and top with cheeses. You may do this in two layers. Brown in 400° oven till bubbly.

Cooking personally for someone is quite different from going to the recipe file and pulling out Standard Company Dinner Menu Number 42. Instead of routinely reproducing a recipe, think about who is going to eat the food. If you can take the time to shop and cook, surely you can take the time to think about your guest. After all, isn't it a lot more satisfying to cook for someone you love *with him or her in mind* as you are cooking? It's not just a case of making mousse for dessert if your friend likes chocolate. You have to be aware of that person's "being," tuned in to his/her personal style. Does she like her chocolate, like Gail, in megadoses, or does he, like Danny, want a hint of chocolatiness? Is the answer to this cooking question one of more chocolate or of setting up a counterpoint of vanilla to heighten the taste of the chocolate you already have?

For the "chocoholic" there is Chocolate Decadence (p. 306) and:

CHOCOLATE PIE

1	C. butter	2	tsp. vanilla
1½	C. sugar, superfine	4	eggs
4	squares unsweetened chocolate, melted and cooled*	1	9" baked and cooled pie shell
			Whipped cream

Beat the butter with the sugar until it is very well blended, smooth, fluffy, and pale yellow. Blend in the chocolate and the vanilla. Beat in the eggs, one at a time, taking 5 minutes to incorporate each and using the electric mixer at medium speed. Turn the mixture into the pie shell and chill several hours, preferably overnight. Decorate with whipped cream before serving.

Equally rich, but a little less chocolatey:

*Don't stir melted chocolate with a wet spoon. It will get grainy. If you do this by accident (and we all have grabbed for a spoon and found out, too late, that it was wet), stir in 2 Tbsp. solid vegetable shortening to revive the smooth texture.

CHOCOLATE-BUTTERSCOTCH PIE

3 C. light brown sugar
½ C. butter
3 eggs
1 tsp. vanilla
½ C. light cream
1 square unsweetened chocolate, melted

1 9" unbaked, chilled pie shell with stand-up edge
1 C. sweetened heavy cream, whipped
Chocolate shavings

Preheat oven to 350°. Beat the sugar and butter together until creamy. Beat in the eggs, one at a time. Add vanilla. Beat in the light cream, add the chocolate, and beat to mix completely. Pour into the pie shell and bake 30 minutes. Reduce the oven heat to 300° and continue to cook about 50 minutes longer, or until set. Cool before decorating with whipped cream and chocolate shavings. The pie puffs up during cooking, then falls as it cools, so don't panic. (Serves 8.)

A middle-of-the-road chocolate mousse—not too dense, not too light:

CHOCOLATE MOUSSE

12 oz. semisweet chocolate bits
1 C. light cream (half and half)
4 eggs, separated, at room temperature

Salt
1 C. heavy cream, whipped
2 Tbsp. cognac or Kahlúa

Place chocolate bits in the blender. Heat the light cream to almost boiling. Pour over bits. Cover and blend till completely smooth. Add the egg yolks. Blend 2 seconds. Immediately pour into a large bowl. (Don't forget and leave this mixture in the blender: It will solidify and you won't be able to get it out).
Beat the egg whites with a pinch of salt till stiff. (You may add 2 Tbsp. sugar to keep them stiffer.) Lightly whip the cream. Pile

part of the cream and egg whites (about ⅓ of each) on the cooled chocolate mixture. Then stir well. Carefully fold the remaining whites and cream into the mixture and fold in the cognac or Kahlúa. Pour into one large serving bowl or individual cups and chill well. Can be made a day or so before. May be frozen.

CHOCOLATE CAKE ROLL

6	eggs, separated	strained to break up
½	C. plus 2 Tbsp. sugar	lumps
½	tsp. almond extract	Powdered sugar, with
1	tsp. vanilla	optional additional
6	Tbsp. cocoa, sifted or	sifted cocoa

Filling

1	Tbsp. unflavored gelatin	3	Tbsp. sugar
¼	C. water	1–2	Tbsp. rum and/or 2 tsp.
1½	C. heavy cream		vanilla extract

Preheat oven to 350°. Butter a 10"×15" jelly-roll pan. Line with waxed paper or bakers' parchment and butter the paper.

Beat egg yolks for about 10 minutes, till they are thick and creamy. Gradually beat in sugar. Stir in almond extract, vanilla, and cocoa. Carefully fold in stiffly beaten egg whites.

Carefully spread the batter in jelly-roll pan. Bake 15–20 minutes. Cover with dish towel wrung out in cold water and chill in refrigerator till cool, about 7–10 minutes.

Make the filling: Dissolve gelatin in water over low heat and let cool for 5 minutes. Whip cream with sugar and rum. Beat in gelatin mixture.

Turn cake out of pan onto towel and carefully peel off paper. Spread with filling and roll up, using the damp towel as a pusher. Roll onto a jelly-roll board or flat platter. Sprinkle rolled cake with powdered sugar, or sugar and sifted cocoa. Refrigerate.

For a total chocolate "experience," you may frost this with chocolate butter cream, or add cocoa or melted chocolate to the filling. Or you may spread the cake with softened ice cream (chocolate?) and freeze it. Serve with hot fudge if desired.

Chapter 10

THE DINNER-PARTY SYNDROME:

Cooking for Pleasure or Points

Once upon a time, I tried to "entertain," too. Casually, like it says in the magazines. A few friends, a simple buffet dinner, clean napkins, and snappy conversation. For two weeks beforehand I would lie awake nights counting tidbits-in-blankets and worrying about the (Raspberry) Bombe. Days I spent selecting dangerous ingredients I knew perfectly well would explode when mixed. . . . The menu was revised and edited more times than the lead paragraph of a seven-hundred-page historical sex novel. . . .

When I "entertained," I celebrated quietly in the kitchen, splattered with piquant sauce to match the wallpaper. I would hover there anxiously, somewhere between the crusted casseroles and other burnt offerings. . . . I could always hear the guests laughing in the other room. I would thank heaven they were amused, which meant they hadn't noticed how long I'd been out of the room fumbling. . . .

When I "entertained," I would drink too much wine and laugh high terrified laughter. I would choke on my own coffee and spill on my own sofa, murmuring reassuringly, "Oh, it's nothing at all." . . .

When I "entertained," I did not have a lovely time, thank you.

Lois Gould

* * *

The basic format of many cookbooks has been the inevitable Dinner Party, the culinary snow job for friends and would-be friends. If people would put out half the energy cooking for and with their families, not to mention cooking for themselves, there would be fewer therapists at work. Somehow it has evolved that outsiders are to be impressed, wined, and dined, while the family often gets the leftovers—and the leftover energy. There's something wrong here, a combination of misplaced energy and values gone awry. I don't mean to imply that you should cook only for your family. It is wonderful to break bread with people whom you like and respect, but why knock yourself out just to impress virtual strangers and "company"? Good friends would like to pitch in on occasion, help you chop and slice. What is so hallowed about dinner that no one can set foot in the kitchen because it makes you nervous? If cooking makes you so nervous and uptight, better question your motives. Is it in fact the cooking or is it the stress of social pressure and big presentation that the phrase Dinner Party connotes?

I don't mean that special events never occur, that dinner can't occasionally be theater. But why should *every* meal with "company" be an elaborate production number organized with Cape Kennedy countdown precision and hosted by a semiprostrate chef too tired or wired to enjoy the food?

My basic advice is to cook only for people you like! This ought to include: 1) yourself, 2) family, 3) then friends, and 4) acquaintances you'd like to know better. If this isn't the case, your energy should be used to find out WHY, not spent reading thousands of cookbooks and planning elaborate meals for strangers. If this sounds like crazy moralizing ("who is she to tell me whom I should cook for"), it is! I've become a bit fanatic on the subject after seeing hundreds of students plotting endless "successful Dinner Parties" only to hear later of divorces, of children who stopped coming home for dinner or who preferred to hang out at a friend's house and cook dinner with another family. In fact many kids have become vegetarians or food faddists or "junk" eaters just to get back at parents on the big social-food trip. There's too much tension when Mom is preparing for the big night, a ten-course dinner for some office buddy of Dad's. There are the trips to the florist and six different markets to find the perfect ingredients. She then serves TV dinners or leftovers to the family, which gives some kids the message that maybe they aren't important enough to rate the prestige meal; and what a drag it is to be around the house when Mom is so nervous and frazzled.

Entertaining has become serious business! People call weeks ahead for menu-planning advice, anxiously discussing each scheme and recipe as if it could make or break them socially. They get so involved in the food game they lose perspective. Cooking becomes their entire existence. They miss out on the enjoyment of a simple dish, selecting only those that are esoteric and complex. They sweat and slave over creations that others eat enthusiastically, but it is with dismay that they watch their hours of work consumed in seconds. What may be the major event in their day may be only dinner for others!

Of course they are missing the point. Cooking can be enjoyable, relaxing, and a good way to *release* tension rather than manufacture it. It also can turn you on, get you high, space you out; but it ought not send you to the beautician, the bottle, or bed with a migraine. Let's put cooking back in the kitchen where it belongs.

Years ago kitchens were the center of the home, places where you could linger for hours, sitting around the table over a pot of tea talking about the day's events, smelling the incredible aromas seeping out from under pot lids, shelling peas, stringing beans, sorting fresh fruits and vegetables to be canned or dried or prepared for dinner that day or the next. Now the average kitchen has been reduced to an efficient corridor that looks as if it is awaiting the photographer from *House Beautiful*. Gleaming chrome and formica, gadgets and machines, abound. The counter just barely has room for the blender, mixer, ice crusher, and electric coffeepot. Not only are there no comfortable nooks and crannies, there's hardly any room for a table.

Somewhere along the line, values got distorted. The efficiency experts, the food technologists, the women's magazines, helped to make this change, maybe to keep the economy moving with an influx of new products. While saving time (for what?) and saving effort in cleanup, and saving space for more important things like a TV or rumpus room, they took the soul out of the kitchen. And the concept of the Dinner Party helped drive the final nail into the kitchen coffin. Display living rooms, elegant china and silver, elaborate multicourse meals, presentation without (seeming) effort. If all the applause was in the dining room, the living room, the wet bar, the bedroom, who needed to be in the kitchen? Besides, there was nothing to do there anymore. The vegetables were in packages, the meat was precut and freezer wrapped. Just in and out. Thaw it, heat it, put it in the microwave, the dishwasher, and get the hell out. And don't make a mess that has to be cleaned up.

I love my kitchen. It's a long way from my first one, that dreary cubicle on York Street in New Haven. I now have a used six-burner restaurant stove that is to me what a Steinway Grand is to Arthur Rubinstein. I have some well-worn pots and pans and practical kitchen gadgets that I use constantly. They have been part of my personal cooking equipage for years. I can count on them to work with me, not against me. Everything I need is within easy reach, on shelves or hanging nearby. I'm a firm believer in open-shelf storage because I find the constant opening and closing of cabinet doors an inconvenience. I don't want to break my rhythm when I'm cooking.

I must confess that I have succumbed to a few pieces of madness and impracticality, things that I rarely use but that look wonderful. (Ah! the old art-school training that placed value on appearance vs. reality! I bought one wire colander only because it reminded me of an early perspective drawing by Paolo Uccello!) I have justified this accumulation of equipment, books, gadgets, and exotic spices by saying, "It is necessary for my work." But I know that behind this facade of utilitarianism there smiles a hedonistic lover of beauty.

By beauty I don't mean a perfectly designed, award-winning magazine kitchen festooned like an art gallery with color-coordinated pots and pans. Nor do I mean elaborately contrived aspic- and parsley-covered still-life platters that pass for food. I am not opposed to artistic presentation, but I am turned off by cuteness and overkill. (As a matter of fact the more elaborate the platter, the more suspicious I am about the food. Some of the most horrible meals I have ever tasted have come in under such false pretenses—all show and no go.)

Of course, I have pretty platters for serving. The yellow Majolica bowls keep the pasta and my memories of Italy warm. The brown Japanese stoneware plates are austerely beautiful and set off the products of Mother Nature with style. I love flowers on the table, a colored tablecloth or a pretty candleholder, just as I can get excited by a pile of green and red peppers at the famers' market, the food stalls in Chinatown, the jumble of cans and bottles in the delicatessen window. In cooking there's so much natural beauty that it is almost unnecessary to bring in "good design."

To my way of thinking, the kitchen ought to be one of the best rooms in the house. It should look as if people live and work there and love it. There are plants, books, sunlight. There's a great old stove, pots that look as if someone uses them, doesn't just polish them for display. There's a table big enough for the whole family and maybe a friend or two. There's an old couch or comfortable chair where one can read or just sit around. There may be a desk so letters can be written while things are simmering, where kids can do homework and be there to help out with dinner prep. They can learn how to cook directly rather than having to take expensive lessons later on, regretting that they never learned how to prepare their favorite dishes.

Some of my happiest times are when I am cooking with my children, working together in that mellow space, chopping kneading, tasting, evaluating, creating a meal. Sure they may make a mess (so do I!), but they have also learned how to clean up and they can cook like inspired demons. We know that the kitchen need not be a pristine lab. We may be performing experiments, but they are not of a clinical nature. We are surrounded by sensual delights, textures, colors, smells. We deal with beauty as well as nutrition.

Slowly there is a change occurring in the American home. The family kitchen is coming back, and maybe so will the concept of the family, natural or extended. Maybe Mom will get to talk with her daughter as she sits in the kitchen reading or helping out, instead of seeing her briefly at the dinner table or on the way to the TV room. Maybe her son will want to prepare the peas the way *he* likes them so he can practice for when his friends come for dinner on Saturday. Dad will know where everyone is when he gets home, so he might not seek refuge behind the paper and the martini in the living room. And Mom, if she's working outside the home, won't have to do dinner herself, tired and resentful, but will be able to get everyone cooking or set up a system of turns, as they do in communal households today. The kitchen will be a place large enough for group effort, group learning.

When friends come for supper they could keep you company while you cook or help to prepare the meal, instead of everything having to be ready days ahead because the company is in the living room and the cook doesn't want to spend any time in the kitchen and be away from the guests. What might be lost in dramatic presentation might be gained in good feelings and time really spent together instead of only at the formal Dinner Party event.

Here are a few recipes that a few people can work on together. The Moroccan Meat Balls can be formed very well by small nimble children's fingers (but be prepared for meat-ball missiles flying through the kitchen).

KEFTA TAJINE—Moroccan Meatballs

Meatballs

1½	lb. ground beef or lamb		Salt, pepper, cayenne
4	Tbsp. chopped parsley	2	tsp. paprika*
1	tsp. ground cumin		Oil for frying
1	large onion, grated		

Sauce

2	onions, chopped	½–1	tsp. black pepper
2	cloves garlic, minced	¼	tsp. cayenne (optional)*
¼	C. chopped parsley		2-lb. can of plum
1	tsp. cumin		tomatoes, chopped
½	tsp. cinnamon	8–12	eggs

Mix the meatball ingredients, into 1″ balls, and brown in oil. Remove from the pan and set aside. Add the onions, garlic, tomatoes, parsley, and spices to the pan oil and cook uncovered for 20–30 minutes, till quite thick. Return the meatballs to the sauce. Simmer about 10 minutes, then break the eggs into the pan, cover it and steam the eggs till set. Or poach or fry the eggs separately and serve over the meatball mixture. This is good over couscous or rice, even on toasted English muffins. (Serves 6.)

Another meatball dinner, this time served with chicken—an unusual, delicious combination invented by a Jamaican cook.

---

*Although this may seem obvious, please *taste* the food *before* serving. The recipe may not always be accurate; you may have forgotten something. I am astounded by the number of cooks who prepare a dish and never taste until they sit down at the table and discover that it wasn't paprika they sprinkled into the sauce but cayenne pepper!

DORCAS WILLIAMS' CHICKEN FRICASSEE WITH MEATBALLS

3–4 lb. fryer, cut into
  serving pieces
  Butter and oil
  Salt, pepper, seasoned
  salt

Paprika (optional)
3–4 large onions, chopped

Meatball Mixture

1 lb. ground chuck
2–3 slices white bread,
  moistened

2 eggs
4 Tbsp. grated onion
  Salt and pepper

Brown chicken in butter and oil evenly on all sides for about 20 minutes. Sprinkle with salt, pepper, seasoned salt, and paprika if desired. Place onions on top of chicken, cover pan, and simmer 45 minutes. Mix meatball ingredients and form tiny meatballs. Add to chicken and steam 15 minutes more. (If onions and chicken haven't produced much liquid, you may add some chicken stock to pan.)

Serve with rice or noodles. You may add sautéed mushrooms the last 5 minutes. (Serves 6.)

Since Gazpacho is my son Evan's favorite soup, I know I can count on his assistance when it comes to mincing all the separate vegetables.

Actually, in the summer we make a big batch of this soup and eat a bowl a day till it is all gone!

GAZPACHO

6 large tomatoes, peeled, seeded, and chopped coarsely
Boiling water
2 cucumbers, peeled, seeded, and diced
6 Tbsp. red wine vinegar
1 onion, chopped
3 cloves garlic, minced
6 Tbsp. lemon juice
⅓ C. olive oil

2 C. tomato juice
1 green pepper, finely diced
3 Tbsp. red onion or green onion, finely minced as (optional) garnish
Worcestershire sauce
Salt and pepper to taste
Fried bread squares or garlic croutons

Peel the tomatoes by dipping them into boiling water for a minute. The skins will slip off easily. Chop the cucumbers in the blender with the vinegar. Puree the onion and garlic and two of the tomatoes with the lemon juice in the blender. Coarsely chop the remaining four tomatoes in the blender by flicking the switch on and off rapidly. Pour all into a chilled bowl and add the oil, tomato juice, the green pepper, and red onion if desired, and season to taste. You may want more lemon or vinegar. Serve with croutons. (Serves 8.)

Even when I am at my Meditative best I find that stuffing hundreds of wontons or empanadas to feed a large crew of people can be too much for me. I get wiped out instead of spaced out. So I am happy that my daughters Rachel and Karen enjoy making interesting shapes with the dough. Not only am I grateful for their help, but we really have fun talking and working together.

WONTON SOUP

Filling

1	lb. ground pork	½	tsp. salt
⅓	C. fresh shrimp, shelled and deveined, chopped	1	Tbsp. sherry
½	C. water chestnuts, chopped	2	tsp. cornstarch
		1	lb. wonton skins*
1	tsp. grated fresh ginger		Boiling salted water
½	C. green onion, chopped	6	C. chicken broth
1	egg	3	C. water
2–4	Tbsp. soy sauce		Shredded spinach
4	tsp. peanut or sesame oil		Chopped green onion (optional)
4–6	dried Chinese or Japanese mushrooms, soaked and chopped (optional)		Leftover roast pork (optional)

Combine all the ingredients for the filling and put a teaspoon or two of filling on each wonton skin. Fold to form a triangle. Pinch to seal. Drop into a large kettle of boiling salted water.

When the water returns to a boil and the wontons float to the top add 1 C. cold water to slow down the cooking. When the water resumes boiling, remove the wontons with a slotted spoon and add them to a pot which has the hot chicken soup diluted with 3 C. water. Garnish with shredded spinach, chopped green onions, optional roast pork. Cook one minute longer and serve immediately.

You may freeze the uncooked wontons for a month or two. Place on cookie sheets till firm, then transfer to containers or plastic bags.

*Purchased at supermarket or Oriental specialty store.

EMPANADAS

Filling:

½	C. minced onions	2	tsp. red chili pepper flakes
1	Tbsp. olive oil		
½	C. water	½	tsp. each cumin, paprika, salt, pepper
2	cloves garlic, minced		
½	lb. ground chuck	8–10	olives, diced
4–5	Tbsp. raisins, soaked in hot water	2–3	hard-boiled eggs, cut into small chunks

In a large pan mix the onions, oil, water, and garlic over high heat till water evaporates. Add meat and stir constantly till browned. Stir in raisins and seasonings, olives, and eggs. Chill the filling.

Use 2–3 packages Hungry Jack flaky biscuits, found in the refrigerator section of your market. Separate the biscuits, pull each one in half or thirds, and pat each piece of biscuit down into a flat circle. Stuff each piece with about a tablespoon of the chilled filling and fold into a semicircle; pinch or roll the edges to seal. (If the filling is hot, the dough will get too soft and won't seal properly). Bake in 400°–450° oven for about 10-15 minutes, till golden. You may brush each with melted butter while hot. Can be assembled on ungreased baking sheets and refrigerated. (Makes about 40–50 empanadas.)

This filling served hot over rice is like a Cuban dish called picadillo. It is also delicious as a crepe or omelet filling. Add canned beans and you have an exotic chili.

For another variation:

CURRY BEEF TURNOVERS

1 clove garlic, finely minced	Salt and pepper
1 large onion, chopped	2 tsp. cornstarch
1 lb. ground beef	Peanut oil
1½–2 Tbsp. curry powder	2–3 packages of flaky biscuits

Heat oil in pan and sauté garlic and onion till soft and golden. Set aside. Heat more oil and sauté beef in pan till it is crumbly and cooked through. Add onion and garlic, spices and cornstarch. Cook two minutes more to blend flavors. Chill the filling. Fill and bake the turnovers as in the empanada recipe above.

The biscuit-dough turnovers can be prebaked and reheated or assembled and chilled on baking sheets, then baked later. Unfortunately, the biscuit dough does not freeze. If you want to prepare these ahead of time for the freezer, you must make a piecrust mix, roll out a sheet of dough, and cut with a round cookie cutter. Then fill and freeze unbaked. The hard-boiled eggs in the empanadas do not freeze well, so if you plan to make empanadas for the freezer, eliminate the eggs.

Chapter 11

PEOPLE'S LIBERATION IN THE KITCHEN:

Changing Sex Roles in the Kitchen

This is probably as good a time as any to bring up the issue of women's liberation, the search for recognition, identity, and self-worth. I don't mean to imply that it's the sole reason sharing supper with friends evolved into the five-course Cecil B. De Mille extravaganza, but it's lurking there in the background. Women married to successful men, home all day when not PTAing or marketing or playing bridge or doing God knows what else to fill their days (after all, with thirty-two appliances even housecleaning can't take eight hours)—these women sought recognition too. And the Dinner Party got them some of the identity that they craved. It was not enough to have the husband say, "Good dinner, dear." But it helped to have people say, "Charlie, that wife of yours really turns out a mean beef stew," or to have other wives talk about your meal and ask for recipes. It was ego-gratifying to hear, "He's a lawyer and she is a fabulous cook!" Not much, you may say. But to some women it was the only recognition they got.

To keep this myth of the life of the glamorous housewife

afloat, women's magazines have been pushing the competitive Dinner Party syndrome, the flashy presentation, the elegant hostess gowns and designer aprons, the ingenious table settings, the homemade tablecloth and napkin sets, the novel flower arrangements, the cute herb gardens on the windowsills. For many a woman, entertaining has become a full-time occupation. With all the stress on social recognition and competition, the enjoyment of the *process*, cooking, got lost in the *production*, Dinner Party.

It's not too surprising that in protest against all these years of domestic propaganda and the Myth of the Merry Housewife, the women's movement urged women to get out of the domestic scene and into the working world. It became embarrassing to confess that you still liked to cook. There were more important things for women to be doing.

But women's liberation in the kitchen is a dual issue. A woman ought to feel free to say "To hell with it" if cooking gives her no satisfaction. If she wants to cook only occasionally she ought not feel guilty for skipping some nights. But she should not have to defend herself from being called a cop-out from the movement if she really loves cooking and marketing. Liberation is also in the mind. Instant pizza, ready-mixed batters, frozen dinners, and microwaves won't make you a genuine card-carrying feminist.

Ironically, a lot of sexism does exist in the world of cooking and it is often women who are getting a bad deal. How many women run the kitchen in prestigious restaurants today? It's acceptable for them to sit and stuff wontons and ravioli, but how many of them receive the same salary as the man who cooks the pasta? If a woman's place is in the kitchen, why can't she get equal opportunity in the professional kitchen? When does the role undergo this subtle change which makes it a man's career in the outside world, but a woman's duty and responsibility at home?

There has been a reverse prejudice about boys and men in the domestic or home kitchen. How many TV shows or movies haven't we all seen where the father told the son to come along with him into the den to read the sports page and to leave the girls alone in the kitchen to do their job? Many a nervous Daddy seemed to fear Junior was doomed to be considered effeminate if he ventured into the kitchen.

For a while it looked as if barbecue was destined to be the only permissible male home cooking technique in America. A man who baked bread or made soufflés was looked upon as a bit of a weirdo, but one who wore an apron covered with funny sayings while turning steaks and hamburgers over a smoky grill was acceptable to the American image of a MAN. Did he need that long fork or spatula in his hand?

Some of the most sexually attractive men I know are fine cooks. And I have attended dinners where the entire family participated in the preparation of the meal: The father stuffed the artichokes, the son the zucchini, the mother prepared the meat, and the daughter helped with the pasta and the dessert. Everyone cooked his or her favorite dish. It wasn't a competition. And no one asked if artichokes were less masculine than meat or if zucchini were more macho than cannoli.

BRACIOLE DI CARNE

Have your butcher cut a 1½"-thick piece of round steak, about 2–3 pounds, and cut it across the thickness almost in half so you can open it up like a book. Pound it thin. (You may use two separate 1"-thick steaks and roll each one individually).

Combine the following for the stuffing base:

2	eggs	2–3	Tbsp. parmesan cheese
	Salt and pepper	2	slices bread, in tiny
1	Tbsp. parsley		pieces
¾	lb. lean veal and beef, ground, or all beef		

Spread the meat stuffing over the steak. Atop this mixture arrange the following:

| 2–3 | hard-boiled eggs, sliced thick | ¼ | lb. Italian salami slices |
| 4 | oz. provolone cheese in 1" x ¼" strips | ¼ | lb. mortadella slices (optional) |

Roll up steaks and tie. Brown in hot oil in a heavy casserole, and set aside.

Pasta Sauce

2	onions, chopped	4	C. tomato puree
2	tsp. garlic, minced	4	Tbsp. tomato paste
1½–2	C. red wine		Salt and pepper

In the pan in which the beef was browned, sauté the onions and garlic till soft. Add the wine and simmer 5 minutes. Add beef roll, tomato puree, and tomato paste. Cover the pan and cook atop stove or in oven on moderate heat for about 1½ hours. Season with salt and pepper. Slice and serve meat with sauce and boiled rigatoni or large ribbons of pasta.

I make this often because the pasta sauce is so fantastic! You may double the sauce part of the recipe and freeze the extra for another meal. (Serves 6–8.)

CARCIOFI ALLA ROMANA—Artichokes Roman Style

Trim and clean 6 large or 12 small artichokes. You may serve the larger-sized ones as a vegetable and tiny ones as antipasto. Cook the large ones quickly in boiling water for about 10 minutes; if the artichokes are tiny, just boil about 5 minutes. Drain and cool. Remove the centers with a spoon or a melon-ball cutter.

Stuffing

1	C. bread crumbs	1	Tbsp. minced garlic
1	Tbsp. dried or 2 Tbsp. fresh mint leaves	2	tsp. salt
2–3	Tbsp. vinegar	½	tsp. pepper
		4	Tbsp. olive oil

Mix all the ingredients and press into the cleaned-out centers of the artichokes. You may stuff some in between the leaves as well. Place in a deep baking dish and add vermouth, white wine or broth to about 2 inches depth for the large ones, 1 inch depth for the small ones. Cover the dish and simmer atop stove on low flame until the artichokes are tender. The large artichokes will take 30–40 minutes; the tiny ones will take about 15–20 minutes. Sprinkle with olive oil and lemon juice and serve hot or cold. (Serves 6.)

STUFFED ZUCCHINI

8–10 zucchini	2 Tbsp. flour
4 Tbsp. butter	½ tsp. lemon peel, grated (optional)
6 oz. Canadian bacon or ham, or 4 Italian sausages, diced	¼ tsp. nutmeg
1 bunch green onions, minced	½ C. heavy cream
2 cloves garlic, minced (optional)	2 Tbsp. pine nuts
	Salt and pepper
	Grated Swiss cheese
	Bread crumbs (optional)

Parboil zucchini for 6–7 minutes, drain, and rinse with cold water immediately. Cut zucchini in half lengthwise and remove seeds, leaving an even shell. Place in buttered baking dish. Melt butter in frying pan, add meat, onions, and garlic, and sauté 3 minutes. Add flour, lemon peel if desired, nutmeg, and cream, and cook till thick. Add pine nuts, salt, and pepper.

Fill zucchini shells with mixture, cover with cheese and bread crumbs. If prepared ahead of time and refrigerated or kept at room temperature, bake in 350° oven 25 minutes. If warm, merely glaze under the broiler for a few minutes.

Cannoli are crispy cinnamon-flavored deep-fried pastry tubes stuffed with ricotta cheese, candied fruit, and chocolate. The pastry is rather difficult to make and you can buy the unstuffed cannoli shells at Italian bakeries. I know this may sound lazy, inauthentic, and reprehensible to cooking moralists. But I am a realist who's seen that people don't make cannoli too often if they have to buy the metal cannoli tubes and practice making the batter and deep frying the shells—which may break after they are removed from the metal tubes—and run the risk of burning their fingers trying to slip the shells out of the tubes.

Italia Coppola has solved the problem in a most ingenious way, by serving the cannoli filling in flaky cream-puff shells. What a refreshing change from the fake whipped cream that one has come to associate with commercial cream puffs!

"CANNOLI" CREAM PUFFS

Choux Paste—Cream Puff, Eclair, or Profiterole Pastry

1 C. water	¼ tsp. cinnamon, optional
5–6 Tbsp. butter	if you are using these for
½ tsp. salt	the cannoli filling
1 C. sifted flour	Egg yolk with water
4 eggs	(optional)

Heat the water with the butter and salt until the water boils and the butter melts. Remove the pot from the heat and beat in, all at once, the flour and the cinnamon, if desired. The dough should pull away from the sides of the pan. Over a gentle flame stir it until it is a nice ball—about another minute. Remove from the fire and beat in, one by one, the eggs. Beat thoroughly at the end. You may use an electric mixer.

Drop spoonfuls of choux paste, like cookies, on a greased baking sheet, or make the puffs with a pastry bag. They can be glazed with egg yolk mixed with a little water before baking, but it is not essential. Bake at 450° for 10 minutes, reduce the heat to moderate (350°), and bake 15–25 minutes more, or until they are puffed and golden. The larger the puff the longer it will take to dry out in the center. Pierce each puff with a knife and leave them in the turned-off oven with the door ajar for another 10 minutes, so they can dry out some more.

Cannoli Filling

1 lb. ricotta cheese	1 C. confectioners' sugar, or a bit more
4 tsp. orange flower water, or part vanilla, part rum	5 oz. semisweet chocolate bits or chopped-up chocolate
1¼ C. mixed candied fruits	

Mix together and use to fill cannoli tubes or large cream puffs. Sprinkle with powdered sugar.

Note: Puffs may also be filled with whipped cream, pastry cream, or ice cream for dessert, with fudge sauce. Or you may use as hot or cold hors d'oeuvre shells for chopped tongue and Swiss cheese and mayonnaise, or crab meat and mayonnaise and seasonings, or whipped cream, parmesan cheese, mustard, salt and pepper.

Cream puffs are also éclairs in another configuration. Push choux paste through a large pastry tube to form the éclairs. Bake at 425° for 10 minutes and 350° for 20–25 minutes more. Fill with:

Basic Pastry Cream Filling for Cream Puffs and Eclairs

2 C. milk	⅓ C. sifted flour
3 eggs	2 tsp. vanilla
⅔ C. sugar	

Optional:

1–2 Tbsp. rum or brandy, if desired, omitting vanilla
For a coffee flavor, add 1–2 Tbsp. instant coffee to the milk

For a chocolate flavor, add 2 squares of melted semisweet chocolate to the milk

Scald the milk. Beat eggs and sugar till pale in color. Add the flour and stir well. Add the hot milk, gradually, still stirring, and return the mixture to the saucepan and stir over moderate heat until it comes to a boil. Remove from heat and add the flavoring. Cool, stirring from time to time to prevent a skin from forming.

Very Rich Chocolate Glaze for Eclairs

4	oz. unsweetened chocolate	4	Tbsp. water
⅔	C. heavy cream	2	Tbsp. white corn syrup
1	C. sugar	1	egg
		1	Tbsp. vanilla

Combine all the ingredients except the egg and vanilla in a saucepan. Stir over low heat till dissolved. Raise the heat and cook till a soft ball is formed, about 225°–230°. Add gradually to lightly beaten egg. Add vanilla.

or

A More Restrained Chocolate Icing

2	oz. unsweetened chocolate	1	tsp. vanilla
3	Tbsp. butter		Pinch of salt
¼	C. hot water, cream or coffee		Approximately 2 C. confectioners' sugar, sifted

Melt chocolate and butter over low heat. Add liquid. When cool add vanilla and salt, and add sugar till the proper spreading consistency is achieved.

The dust is settling a bit on the issue of cooking and sexism. With more and more women working outside the home and many more men getting interested in cooking, things may fall into place. When I first started teaching, I had just a few male students. Some were gay, some apologetic: "I really like doing this more than my wife does, but all she ever lets me do is carve, mix the salad, or barbecue." She didn't want him intruding in her domain for fear of losing control and prestige (how else would she get her share of glory?) or having him find out that it wasn't all that hard or as time-consuming or esoteric as she liked to make out. Over the years the number of male students has increased. And the reasons for taking a cooking class have changed: communal living, divorces, new living arrangements, inflation, restaurant prices, etcetera. Occasionally I'm still asked in hushed tones over the phone if I have a class "For Men Only" (as if it were a secret sin to come out of the closet wearing an apron), or some remedial number for the men who cook but who should not be permitted to mingle with those *House Beautiful* experts. I remind them of Florynce Kennedy's riposte that there are very few jobs that require a penis or vagina, and that all the rest should be open to anyone. I will not support segregation in the kitchen, and find it very rewarding for men, women, and children to be cooking together in a noncompetitive, nonthreatening atmosphere.

In a recent *New York Times* article, Betty Friedan expressed her reborn interest in cooking to get in touch with her female roots. During the early years of the women's movement she had stopped cooking altogether. The women had put their energies elsewhere, "and our rage against the barriers in our way somehow turned off or sapped our willingness or even our ability to cook creatively for those we loved." Lately she's noticed it's been the women who sit around the table discussing politics and "the men who talk about food, show off their growing gourmet expertise and compete as cooks." So we have come almost full circle. Now perhaps she and others can relax and enjoy cooking *when they are in the mood.* As Friedan says, "Why should I deprive myself or be ashamed of the sensuous joy I have been secretly snatching, scrambling eggs for a man I specially love . . . [feeling] unabashed overwhelming love for my son as he ate up every bit of green pasta with eggplant and caper sauce" that she prepared especially for him.

Cooking is now part of the people's liberation process. It can take on whatever role you bring to it, but it is not responsible for the creation of sexist roles in the home or anywhere else in life. Let us hope this will become more and more evident as people cook more for personal pleasure, creativity, and relaxation.

PART THREE:

How Am I Cooking?

Chapter 12

HOW ARE *YOU* COOKING?

It's time to ask "HOW are you cooking?" Well, how are you feeling? How's your mood? Your physical and mental energy? Relaxed and at peace with the world? Tense, troubled, or just plain tired? Do you need cooking as Meditation, to calm you down and relax your mind, to give you some emotional space and renewed vigor? Or do you need cooking to release your High Energy and express your physical power and creative urges?

It is important to draw the distinction between what you are in the mood to *eat* and what you are in the mood to *cook*. They may not overlap. You may crave chicken pot pie but not feel like devoting the slow, Meditative energy that its preparation requires. You may be feeling speedy and need to cook something that is zippier in presentation, like stir-fried almond chicken. Or you may not feel like cooking at all. Honor your feelings. Don't allow guilt to force you into the kitchen.

If you must have chicken pot pie and you are too pooped to prepare it, you have a few options open. If you can afford to go out to dinner, you might find the right restaurant to suit your pot-pie passion. Or you can compromise and heat up one of those frozen pot pies. Or you can say, "Well, I guess chicken pot pie is not in the picture tonight. . . . I'll keep it in mind for an evening when I have more time and energy. Meanwhile I think a cheese omelet might be nice, and then I'll treat myself to a hot bath and a good book." And if your family is craving stuffed chicken breasts en croûte and you're too tired to see your way into the kitchen, it's O.K. to suggest that sandwiches be the menu for the evening and en croûte will be for a time when you too can enjoy the meal and its preparation. Know when to compromise, how to strike a balance between the cravings of your palate and the needs of your body and mind.

That is why it is important to ask HOW am I cooking? The HOW of cooking is you, your feelings, your energy, your being, how you are at that moment. Not next week. Not yesterday. NOW. Because if you are not in tune with HOW you feel *now,* you may be working against yourself. Your venture into the kitchen may be enervating instead of enjoyable.

Your mood affects the pace of the cooking. Usually you get highly energized and speedy behind chopping and dicing, but occasionally you may want to slow down and get *into* the actual physical process, seeing how finely or evenly you can chop the onions, not how fast. There are days when putting in time in the kitchen, *just for the workout,* is more important than the food that results. Recipes are just exercises for you to work out with, like chin-ups or deep breathing. *You* will know what you are getting out of the process, and if people enjoy and recognize the fruits of your labor, that's really nice, but not essential.

I've purposely omitted a *preparation* time schedule at the top of the recipes, and there will be no countdown for you to follow. I won't tell you that a recipe will take twenty-five minutes to prepare because I don't think that cooking should be a game of Beat the Clock. If it takes me twenty-five minutes and it takes you an hour, how will you feel? Will there be a nagging doubt that you've screwed up and done something wrong? Actually, it might take me fifteen minutes one day and an hour the next. The same goes for you. It all depends on mood and energy: Are you cooking to slow down or cooking to speed up? You should set your own pace, not go by mine. Work as fast or as slow as you need to work. I am not talking about *cooking* time. If a recipe says to simmer for two hours, that is pretty accurate. If I suggest that you steam asparagus for five to seven minutes, I don't mean to imply that twenty-five minutes will do (unless you are making soup instead of a vegetable). I am only talking about *preparation* time, how long it takes to organize a dish in order to cook it: *Your* active cooking time, not the recipe's.

Therefore it is possible to choose a recipe just because of the energy it inspires. On days you want to spend a lot of Meditative time in the kitchen, you will select a recipe or technique that is detailed, but not stupefying. The process may be long, but should not be so complicated that you are frustrated rather than totally absorbed in the work.

Some days you want fine results but you want them fast. You want recipes that tap your High Energy, where you get the most mileage out of the least amount of work. Then you will look for recipes that are direct and to the point, simple and quick to prepare, with speed that is not at the expense of quality.

If you are paying attention to HOW you want to cook you will select the recipe to enhance and reflect your mood rather than one that fights you all the way.

Chapter 13

MEDITATION:

"Flow States" in Cooking (The Kitchen Spaceout)

Jane has discovered that she is rarely if ever alone. At the office she is constantly surrounded by people. She works with large groups; there's much talking and joint decision making. At home she is busy with her husband and two children. They are happy to see and be with each other. However, privacy has become a luxury, a rare treat. Jane realizes that she desperately needs some time to be by herself, not exhausted, lying in bed in a stupor watching TV, but alone with her own company and good energy. Sometimes when she has taken a long bath or has gone for a solo walk she remembers how good it feels to be by herself and says, "I should do more of that."

Occasionally Jane likes to have company come for dinner. But when she entertains she wants it to be different from her everyday family cooking situation. Usually her husband and the kids pitch in, but the kitchen is small, and after a while she feels as if she is back at the office, crowded. But she has discovered that on Sunday afternoon, when everyone is out of the house, she has the most wonderful time in the kitchen. She is not rushed. She can really immerse herself in the preparation of the meal, the cooking process. She chops slowly, enjoying the sounds as the knife rhythmically hits the chopping block. She smells the perfume of the pears and oranges as she slices them for dessert. She tastes and stirs the soup or stew. She can hear herself think, can take the time to pay attention to her sensations.

When her husband and kids come home from the park, she is relaxed, smiling, energetic. Dinner is delicious and greatly enjoyed by family and friends because Jane has had the time to enjoy it herself.

Certain aspects of the cooking process have the effect of Meditation upon the psyche. By their very nature of *rhythm, repetition,* and *ritual,* they help you to arrive at a peaceful and relaxed state. Total concentration on physical activities like slicing, chopping, washing spinach leaves, kneading dough, helps you to release tension and free your mind to "spaceout" while your body is absorbed in a seemingly trivial task. Something that could be considered boring, time-consuming, and a drag is turned into creative time spent.

For many the word "spaceout" has negative connotations: "out of it," in dreamland, passive, inattentive. But the Kitchen Spaceout involves concentration of the highest order. You are not mindlessly engaged. You are alert and active. *Your consciousness is opening up while your focus is narrowing down.*

A friend recently remarked that if all that was needed to attain the Meditative state was simply rhythm, repetition, and ritual, then most of the people on the General Motors assembly line would be Zen monks. Obviously, there is a difference between the assembly-line spaceout and the kitchen variety. Instead of trying to tune out the work because it is boring, *you are trying to tune it in.*

In psychological terms the Meditative aspect of cooking can be described as a *"flow"* state. In the June 1976 issue of *Psychology Today,* an article entitled "The Fun in Fun" reports on the research of University of Chicago psychologist Mihaly Csikszentmihalyi (who for obvious reasons is called "Dr. C.")

into "flow" experience. Dr. C. interviewed doctors, athletes, artists, explorers, chess players, who all agreed that when they were engaged in their favorite activity, "flow," or an altered state of being, occurred. Flow is when

> we are completely immersed in what we are doing. In this state a person loses a *self-conscious* [italics mine] sense of himself and of time. He gains a heightened awareness of his physical involvement with the activity. The person in flow finds, among other things, his concentration vastly increased and his feedback from the activity enormously enhanced. . . . The feedback is not an end in itself but rather a signal that things are going well. The person . . . does not stop to evaluate the feedback.

The example from this article that remains impressed in my memory is that of the surgeon who was so engrossed in his work that he didn't notice that some of the hospital ceiling had fallen down till after he had completed the operation!

Dr. C. says that the activity should have some sort of routine and ritual if the flow state is to be achieved. "It should be simple and have non-contradictory rules." If the job is too difficult, then one cannot get into the smooth energy flow space. There should be "an even match between the difficulty of a challenge and a person's ability to meet it. If the demands are too slight, the person feels bored; if too great, he feels anxious."

Flow exists only in the *present,* the *now.* It is the ability to focus on the moment so one can get feedback from the immediate situation.

In the Meditative spaces of cooking we can be totally immersed in what we are doing—slicing, chopping, washing. There is a blending of action and awareness, an altered sense of time. We lose our sense of real time and enter a period of timelessness. "There is an intense centering of attention on the activity; concentration is automatic. We are alert, awake, relaxed but energetic."

Many of the routine kitchen tasks may be considered boring, time-consuming, and insufficiently challenging. But that usually happens because a person is not involved in the physical activity for its own sake. He is thinking of what else he would rather be doing, or what he will do "after this grisly job is over." He doesn't allow himself immersion in the action.

A student of Zen asked his master, "What is the truth (Tao)?" "Your everyday mind," he answered. "When I am hungry, I eat. When I am tired, I sleep." The disciple was puzzled and asked, "Isn't this what everybody does?" The Zen master replied, "Most people are never wholly in what they are doing. When eating they may be absentmindedly preoccupied with a thousand different fantasies. . . . The supreme mark of the thoroughly integrated man is to be without a divided mind."

Centering, centering. Being there *NOW*.

If you are cleaning shrimps, clean shrimps. Get into it.

If you are wiping mushrooms, wipe away.

It is a bit like religious chanting. The repetition, ritual, and confining physical focus that these techniques require open up your mental space.

You don't have to have a mantra or guru to Meditate. There need not be a complex initiation rite or fee for you to achieve that state of inner calm and clarity. If you have a kitchen and a consciousness you can arrive at the Meditative state. Keep your attention *FOCUSED* on what you are doing *NOW*. If you keep centered on the activity, the process will take over.

Again, I would like to differentiate between passive and active Meditation. Obviously, I am not talking about sitting still and counting your breath. But there are active forms as well. Running, aikido, archery, drawing, motorcycle maintenance are all active forms of Meditation. And so is cooking.

You may not be interested in Meditating. Or you may already have a system of Meditation that works for you. This doesn't preclude your reaping the emotional benefits of cooking in the flow state. You can enjoy those activities *for their own sakes*. Instead of rushing through these tasks with one eye on the clock and one foot in the future, *center yourself in the present* and appreciate the tactile, physical pleasures of what you are doing. Since you *are* there, *be* there!

If you do plan to use cooking as a Meditation, there are some precautions you must take. The most important one is *protecting your space.* It is difficult, in fact impossible, to meditate and concentrate if the phone is ringing, the doorbell sounding, people strolling in and out of your work/meditation area. You must see that you are not disturbed. Then you will be able to concentrate on the task at hand, to be fully there, not with part of your mind thinking about the phone, or the door, or others in the house.

Many of the "precooking" activities, such as measuring and slicing, heighten your awareness and increase your energy when you begin to cook. The kitchen processes that may produce the flow state are as follows:

measuring ingredients and laying them out

prep techniques such as cutting, slicing, mincing, chopping, julienning, dicing, peeling fruits and vegetables

washing clams, mussels, spinach, chard, basil and other greens; wiping mushrooms

cleaning shrimp, shelling chestnuts and other nuts

shelling peas, pitting cherries, plums, etc.

assembling, stuffing, layering, (as in wonton, empanadas, moussaka, cannelloni, grape leaves, and other dolmas), forming meatballs—much repetition is involved.

making crepes

buttering fillo dough

rolling out dough, cutting cookie shapes, rolling noodles

kneading yeast dough

stirring and basting

sharpening knives

cleanup in general

Chapter 14

THE "HOUSEWORK" OF COOKING AS A MEDITATION:

Cleaning, Washing, Wiping

I am feeling tense, on edge. I have a mild headache and my hands are not as steady as I would like. I don't feel "in control." Here are three bunches of spinach leaves that are to be washed and made ready for steaming. First I open all the bunches by carefully untwisting the wires; I pay attention not to bruise or tear the leaves. Then I place a colander in the sink, and a deep pot nearby if I plan to cook the spinach, and turn on the cool water in a slow stream. I examine each leaf for traces of dirt. I wash it well; the water flows over my hands. The spinach becomes an intense shade of green. I break off the tough stems and place each glistening leaf in the colander. Greenness, wetness, become one flowing motion. Finally my task is over. I am ready to step out of this action and into the next. The washing took lots of time, unmeasured time. I was able to relax and let the images and feelings flow. I cannot recount all that I thought or felt, all the steps my mind took. If my mind started to drift *too* far afield, I was able to center myself by coming back to

133

the tactile experience of washing the leaves. And when it was all over I may have noticed that my hands seemed surer and my headache had faded.

I am now free to decide what I will do with the spinach after it—and I—am ready. I may choose not to cook it at all—simply make a salad:

SPINACH AND BACON SALAD

2–3 bunches (about 1 lb.) small spinach leaves, well washed and dried

8 slices bacon, rendered, crumbled

Combine with the following:

Dressing

1–2 cloves garlic, minced fine

¼ C. mild wine vinegar or lemon juice

2 tsp. Dijon mustard
Salt and pepper

½ C. olive oil or a bit more

Optional

Croutons or sieved hard-boiled eggs
Chopped mint leaves
Grated parmesan cheese

You may put warm bacon and some fat on spinach to wilt it. In this case, cut down on oil, increase lemon juice or vinegar.

Or you may steam the spinach, drain, rinse, and then cook it in any number of different ways—braised, chopped and creamed, or part of another dish:

BRAISED SPINACH

1½	sticks butter		chopped frozen
1	small onion, minced		spinach,* thawed
2	lbs. spinach leaves,		completely)
	washed well, steamed,		Salt, pepper, nutmeg
	drained; you may chop	2–4	Tbsp. cream (optional)
	it if you like (or 2 boxes	2–4	Tbsp. Madeira (optional)

Melt 1 stick butter in casserole and cook onion till soft. Add drained spinach and stir till butter is absorbed. Add remaining butter and seasoning, and stir till butter is absorbed. You may add cream or Madeira. For spinach Genovese style, add ½ C. raisins, soaked in warm water and drained, and ¼ cup pan-toasted pine nuts.

Incidentally, washing and shredding the leaves of fresh basil for pesto, to be pureed with the oil and garlic, gives you similar feedback to spinach washing. See pesto, p. 244.

Here is another example of Kitchen Meditation:
I've had an unpleasant argument with a friend. In the heat of anger my thoughts were a jumble. There are lots of "I-shoulda-said's" running around in my mind as I step into the kitchen to clean a pound of mushrooms for which I am sure to have little appetite. I dampen a paper towel and dump the mushrooms out of their brown paper bag and onto the counter. I notice that they are almost the same color as the bag. I check to see just how gritty they are; will they need lots of cleaning or just a summary wipe? Then I pick up a round, firm mushroom and proceed to wipe it with a damp towel. I trace its outline with my fingers as the towel picks up the dirt. Each mushroom is in turn caressed and cleaned. Next I trim off the woody stem ends. Some are not so tough. Others crumble a bit in my hands. Finally I consider how to slice them. They are not small and fat. I decide to cut them into thick slices. As I press my knife into each mushroom, there is a slight resistance to the blade, then a

*For a discussion of fresh vs. frozen spinach, see p. 265.

buttery-smooth submission. The mushroom in cross-section reveals its hidden inner anatomy. This has taken lots of time—the wiping, the tracing of contours, estimating the thickness of each slice so that the mushroom pieces will cook uniformly. I have been totally involved in my process. After the slow ritual of cleaning and slicing, I am able to take the time to think about the argument from a calmer perspective. I feel energetic but not speedy. I am free to prepare the mushrooms and will be able to call my friend later.

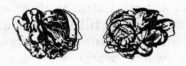

I might sauté the sliced mushrooms and use them as a vegetable:

SAUTÉED MUSHROOMS

| 1½ lbs. mushrooms | Salt, pepper, nutmeg |
| 5 Tbsp. butter | Juice of half a lemon |

Wipe mushrooms with damp paper towel.* Slice or quarter them. Melt butter. Sauté mushrooms quickly, stirring often. Season to taste with salt, pepper, nutmeg, and lemon juice.

If you like, you can vary the recipe by adding 2 Tbsp. sherry or ½ C. cream or sour cream at room temperature, or yoghurt and chopped mint or parsley.

They may become part of a spaghetti sauce:

*It is better to wipe mushrooms clean with a damp paper towel than to immerse them in water and scrub. (They absorb the water too readily.) When they are sautéed all the moisture, juices, and flavor are likely to evaporate. Wiping does take more time but it is worth it for maximum flavor. Because they are so porous, mushrooms—and eggplant—should be removed from plastic packaging and stored in a plain old paper bag in the refrigerator. They won't get spongy, spotted, and slimy, and will keep for about a week. The mushrooms get a bit dry, but will revive when sautéed. Dry is better than funky.

FETTUCCINE VERDI AL FUNGHETTO

2–3 green onions, diced
1 clove garlic, minced
1 Tbsp. oil
6 Tbsp. butter
1 lb. mushrooms, cut in chunks
½ C. dry white wine

2½ C. chopped tomatoes
Salt, pepper, nutmeg
¾ lb. green noodles, cooked al dente
¾ C. grated parmesan cheese

Sauté onion and garlic in oil and butter till tender. Add mushrooms and wine and cook 2 minutes. Add tomatoes and spices and simmer 15 minutes. Serve with green noodles and lots of cheese.

They might appear in soup:

CREAM OF MUSHROOM SOUP

1 medium onion, chopped fine
4–6 Tbsp. butter
1 lb. mushrooms
3–4 Tbsp. flour
3–4 C. beef or chicken stock
1–1½ C. light cream

½ tsp. salt
¼ tsp. white pepper
2–3 Tbsp. sherry or Madeira
Nutmeg, lemon juice (optional)
Parsley, chopped (optional)

Sauté onion in butter for 3 minutes. Add mushrooms and sauté 5 minutes. Stir in flour. Add stock and simmer 20 minutes. Add cream, salt, pepper, and sherry, and lemon juice and nutmeg to taste, if desired. You may sprinkle with chopped parsley. (Serves 6.)

Note: An Italian version of this soup omits the flour and cream. It increases the stock to 6 C. and adds 3 Tbsp. of tomato paste. Just before serving, 3 Tbsp. each red sweet vermouth and Madeira are added and the soup is heated through.

You might mince the mushrooms very finely and sauté them

with green onions to make a mixture called duxelles. Cutting pockets in chicken breasts and carefully stuffing in the duxelles are other aspects of the Meditation.

CHICKEN WITH DUXELLES

Cut 6 whole chicken breasts, boned and skinned, into halves, and carefully cut a pocket in each one.

Duxelles Filling

¾ lb. mushrooms, chopped*

½ C. or more minced green onions (2 bunches)

¼ lb. butter
Salt and pepper

Finely chop the mushrooms and green onions and sauté in butter. Season with salt and pepper, and chill. You may make this filling the day before.

Stuff the chicken breasts with the filling and fold them over it to seal it in. Place in a buttered baking dish.

Sauce

½ lb. butter
2 Tbsp. paprika
Salt and pepper
Juice of 2–3 lemons or

6 Tbsp. bottled lemon juice
Parsley

Melt butter and sprinkle it with paprika, much salt, and black pepper, and add the juice. Pour over the chicken and sprinkle heavily with dried chopped parsley. (You may refrigerate at this point and heat later.) Heat oven to 400° and bake about 45–50 minutes, basting very often so the chicken doesn't get dry. (Serves 6.)

Incidentally, the duxelles makes an excellent omelet or crepe filling.

*Resist using the processor. The mushrooms become grainy, too finely minced, and lose their texture.

CLEANING SHRIMP

For many people the cleaning of shrimp is one of the most tedious tasks in cooking. Before you can turn the activity into a Meditation you must know the easiest way to proceed. Select the routine that works best *for you*. I find it easier by far to clean shrimp *before* they are cooked, rather than after. First, remove all the shells by pulling off the leg pieces first—then the body and tail pieces will fall of easily. Next, cut a slit on the *top* curve of the shrimp to expose the intestinal vein. (There is another, bluish vein at the bottom of the shrimp, but this one does not concern us.) One of the best ways to do this is the Chinese method: Lay the shrimp down on the cutting surface. Hold it flat with one hand and move the knife across the back of the shrimp with one decisive movement—no sawing back and forth, please. Cut the shrimp almost in half; this is called butterflying. The intestinal vein will now be readily visible. Pull it out and pat the shrimp dry with a paper towel. If you break the vein, rinse the shrimp clean with water and dry it *very* well. A wet shrimp will release too much moisture when you cook it and water down the flavor of the sauce. I know that there are books that tell you that deveining is unnecessary, but if you have ever eaten a gritty shrimp you will know what an unpleasant experience it is. What's important is that you can clean shrimp easily and efficiently without resenting the activity or getting bored and therefore coming *out* of your Meditation! So remove *all* the shells, then cut *all* the slits, then remove *all* the veins. Don't do each shrimp separately, because it will take you ten times longer. It will be more of a dance if you can plan your movements rhythmically. You can immerse yourself in the ritual, feel the thinness of the shrimp shell, notice the color of the shrimp, its delicate anatomy, appreciate the sensation of the knife as it cuts the slit in with ease and rhythm. You may find that shelling shrimp is a pleasurable way to spend time in the kitchen without counting minutes.

In the next recipe, after cleaning the shrimp, you can space out on mincing green onions, thin-slicing zucchini uniformly, beautifully.

SHRIMP WITH PESTO

4	cloves garlic, minced	¼	C. dry white wine
2	bunches green onions, minced	¼	C. white wine vinegar
½	C. olive oil	½	C. pesto (see p. 244)
2–3	lbs. shrimp, shelled and deveined	4	small zucchini
			Salt and pepper to taste
			Lemon wedges

Sauté garlic and green onions in oil till soft, not brown. Add shrimp, wine, and vinegar, and stir fry till pink, a matter of moments. Don't overcook! Add pesto.

Cool the shrimp. Add thin-sliced raw zucchini, mix well, season to taste, and chill. Bring to room temperature before serving with lemon wedges. This is best prepared the day before or early in the day so the flavors can mingle. (Serves 6–8.)

Note: For an interesting variation, reduce green onions to one bunch, omit pesto and zucchini. Add 2 tsp. each red pepper flakes, grated ginger root to marinade.

Scrubbing clams and mussels to remove all traces of sand is another Meditative activity in cooking. The water flows over your fingers, the brush rubs back and forth over the hard shells; finally your fingers trace the contour of each shell, testing for sensations of grittiness, any telltale bits of sand that remain.

Once the cleaning process is completed you are free to steam the clams in an inch or two of water or wine. Cover the pan. In about five minutes they will open. Remove open clams and set aside. (Any stubborn ones should be left in the pan and given another chance to cooperate. If they absolutely refuse to open, throw them out!!) When they are cool enough to handle you can remove the clams or mussels from the shells and proceed with the rest of your chopping, mincing, dicing.

I have known many people who had not previously liked clams in any way, shape, or form, but they loved these:

STUFFED BROILED CLAMS

24 clams in the shell, well scrubbed	Salt and pepper
3 Tbsp. butter	¼ C. grated parmesan cheese
4–5 green onions, finely minced	Bread crumbs, sesame seeds
1½ Tbsp. flour	Lemon wedges
½ C. cream	
6–8 pieces of bacon, fried till crisp and crumbled	

Steam the clams till they open. When they are cool enough to handle, remove the clams from the shell and chop them coarsely. Reserve half of the shells. Melt the butter. Add the onions and cook a minute. Add flour, stir well, add cream, and cook till thick. Add chopped clams and crumbled bacon, and season to taste.

Stuff a tablespoon of filling into each half shell. Sprinkle with cheese, bread crumbs, and sesame seeds. Broil till golden brown. Serve with lemon wedges.

I usually serve these as hors d'oeuvres for six, but with salad and French bread they could be dinner for two.

They can be prepared ahead of time and broiled later. They can wait in the refrigerator for a few days before broiling.

Note: When buying clams be sure to get those that are closed and unbroken. A cracked clam or one that doesn't snap shut when you touch it is a dead clam. If the fish dealer gives them to you in a sealed plastic bag, free them, put them in a bowl covered with a wet dish towel, and store in the refrigerator until you are ready to cook them.

Here, you not only get to scrub clams, but you get to clean shrimp too! The prep takes time and is a good relaxer, but the steaming is rapid. Be careful not to overcook the fish.

ZUPPA DI PESCE—Italian Fish Soup

24 clams, well scrubbed
3–4 stalks celery, chopped
1 onion, chopped
3–4 cloves of garlic, chopped finely
1 bay leaf
Pinch of basil
Pinch of thyme
Olive oil
1 1-lb. can of chopped plum tomatoes, or 2–3 fresh tomatoes in season

2 C. dry vermouth or dry white wine
2 lbs. assorted fish, such as snapper, sea bass, cod, cut into spoon-size chunks
1 lb. shrimp, shelled and deveined
1 crab, cracked into 2" pieces
Salt, pepper, parsley
Fried garlic croutons

Steam clams in a separate pot by covering them with a little cold water, bringing to a boil, and steaming till they open. Save the broth.

Sauté celery, onion, garlic, and herbs in oil till softened but not browned. Add tomatoes. Add wine and the clam broth. Add the fish, the shrimp, and the crab. Steam till the fish is cooked but firm—about 7 minutes. Add clams to the soup. Season with salt and pepper, add chopped parsley, and serve with lots of fried garlic croutons (see p. 79n.) to sop up the broth.

Omit fish, add lobster and more shellfish, and you have cioppino.

Chapter 15

PREPARATION AS A MEDITATION:

Slicing, Chopping, Mincing, Dicing

What follow are a few recipes that are mostly prep with very little cooking. If there is any cooking it is of the slow simmering variety which requires little active participation by the cook, who then will have time to get into other things.

How thinly and uniformly can you slice the oranges? the radishes? the carrots? The food processor won't be able to do this for you. So enjoy the power of your hands—not horsepower.

MOROCCAN ORANGE SALAD

Cut 1 lb. carrots in julienne strips,* or soak 2 bunches radishes, for 1 hour, changing water occasionally. Drain and slice thin. Peel 2 oranges and cut crosswise into thin slices.

---

*Julienne means uniform *thin* slivers. See oranges with orange peel, p. 40, and Bigarade orange sauce for chicken or duck, p. 334.

Dressing

	Juice of 1 lemon	1	Tbsp. orange flower
	Pinch of salt		water
1½	Tbsp. powdered sugar		

Mix dressing ingredients. Arrange orange and vegetable pieces on platter, sprinkle with dressing, and chill.

CARROT SOUP

1	stick butter	1	C. milk or cream (or
10–12	carrots, cut in julienne		more)
	strips approximately	½	C. dry vermouth
	¼″ x 1½″	¼	tsp. mace
1	onion, minced		Salt and pepper
2	Tbsp. flour		Parsley, chopped
5–6	C. chicken stock		

Melt butter. Sauté carrots over very low flame for 5 minutes. Add onions and sauté 3 minutes more. Add flour and stir well. Add stock and milk, and simmer 35–40 minutes. Add vermouth and seasonings to taste, and garnish with chopped parsley.

You may do the same with celery and squash.

I rarely puree the carrots in the carrot soup, because I find that puree of carrot soup (crème crécy) is usually too rich for my palate. By keeping the carrots in julienne slices the soup maintains a very delicate, unstarchy texture and the flavor of the carrot is subtle but not too sweet.

A few soups that involve lots of preparation—chopping, dicing, slicing, mincing—and long slow simmering, and are worth the effort for the feedback from the work process and from the people who will enjoy them:

MINESTRONE

Soak 1 C. dry white beans overnight, or boil for 2 minutes and allow to sit for one hour. Bring beans to a boil and simmer 1½ hours, till tender. Drain.

4 strips bacon	1 C. fresh peas
Olive oil	½ medium cabbage, sliced
1 clove garlic, minced	½ C. pasta, small pieces,
1 onion, sliced	or ½ C. rice, uncooked
1 C. carrots, sliced	Salt and pepper
1 C. zucchini, sliced	2 Tbsp. parsley
1 C. potatoes, diced	Basil (1 Tbsp. fresh or 1
½ C. celery, diced	tsp. dry)
2 large tomatoes, peeled,	Grated parmesan cheese
seeded, diced	2–4 Tbsp. pesto (see p. 244)
10–12 C. water and stock (beef	(optional)
or chicken)	

Dice raw bacon and render it in oil. Add garlic and onion, and sauté till soft. Add all the vegetables, except cabbage and peas, and 8 C. water and stock. Simmer for ½ hour to 1 hour, till flavor is rich. Add beans, peas, cabbage and rice or pasta and cook 15–20 minutes more, till all are done. Season to taste and garnish with parmesan cheese. Add pesto if desired.

This soup without beans or pasta will be a vegetable soup, or zuppa di verdura.

VEGETABLE BEEF SOUP

Part I—Basic Beef Stock

3 lb. soup bones, which may be browned in a 400° oven for 30 minutes	3 carrots, diced or left whole, as you prefer
Additional 2 lb. beef brisket	4 stalks celery with leaves
	Parsley
2 onions, chopped	½ bay leaf (optional)
4 leeks, sliced	1 Tbsp. salt
	12 peppercorns
	4 qt. water

Combine ingredients and bring to a boil. Remove scum with a slotted spoon and simmer for four hours, skimming when necessary.

Remove the beef and the bones and dice the meat when cool enough to handle. Strain the remaining stock and chill. Skim the fat, which will have risen to the top and solidified. If you are pressed for time, an ice cube wrapped in a paper towel and skimmed over the top of the pot will pick up fat globules but not as thoroughly as if you had chilled the whole dish.

What you have now is beef stock and some cooked meats. The vegetables will have added their flavor, but will be mushy and not worth saving for the next step, where texture is so important.

Part II—Vegetable Beef Soup

4 Tbsp. butter
1 onion, chopped
2 leeks, sliced
4 stalks celery or more, sliced
6 carrots, peeled and sliced
Beef bouillon from stock recipe (or canned beef stock)

1 C. green beans, cut into 2" lengths
Diced beef from stock recipe (or leftover meat)
1 C. or less peas, frozen or fresh
About 1 C. zucchini, diced or sliced
Salt and pepper

Optional

1 clove garlic, minced
2–4 tomatoes, diced
1 C. rice, lentils, potatoes cut in ½" cubes, or egg noodles
1 bunch Swiss chard, shredded

Additional beef extract such as Bovril or powdered beef broth if the stock tastes watery or weak
Kitchen Bouquet, for color

Melt butter in a large kettle. Sauté onions, leeks, and celery and garlic if desired. Add carrots, beef broth, and tomatoes if desired, and simmer about 30 minutes. You may add rice, lentils, or potatoes at this time. Add green beans and beef.

Simmer 15 minutes more. Add peas, zucchini. Simmer 5 minutes. Add fine egg noodles and shredded chard, if desired. Cook 5 minutes more. Season to taste with salt, pepper and optional beef broth concentrate. You may want to add Kitchen Bouquet for color. (Serves 8.)

Borscht Variation

Heat 1 qt. canned beef bouillon, 1½ qt. meat stock. Add 4 leeks, 6 stalks celery, 2 onions, ½ cabbage, all chopped. Simmer 1 hour. Add 12 peeled beets that have been diced and sautéed in butter for 5 minutes, 1 grated raw beet soaked in ½ C. red wine, and the diced meat from the stock recipe. Simmer 10 minutes more. Serve with sour cream and boiled potatoes.

Here is a recipe you can do the long, Meditative way using fresh spinach and dried beans. Or you can speed up the process by substituting frozen spinach and canned beans. Choose the method to suit your mood.

A tian is an earthenware dish that is used in the south of France. Although a Pyrex baking dish or any ceramic one will do just as well, I still call this recipe:

TIAN

Soak ½ lb. dried white beans overnight in just enough water to cover. Drain, cover with cold water, and simmer, covered, until tender. Just before the beans are finished, add salt to taste. Drain, sprinkle with 2 Tbsp. olive oil, and toss them well. Or use 2 cans white cannelini, rinsed and drained.

Drop 1 C. brown rice into 2 qt. boiling water; boil 30 minutes; drain.

1	large onion or 2 medium onions, diced	fine (or 2 boxes chopped frozen spinach, thawed and squeezed dry)
2	Tbsp. olive oil	Salt, pepper, oregano
6–8	zucchini, diced	Grated parmesan cheese
4	cloves garlic, minced	Bread crumbs
2	lbs. spinach, well washed and chopped	

In a large skillet, sauté onions in 2 Tbsp. olive oil until translucent, about 5 minutes. Stir in zucchini and garlic and toss until zucchini is almost tender—5 or 6 minutes. Transfer the vegetables to a large casserole, leaving the oil in the skillet.

Cook spinach in the oil remaining in the skillet until it wilts. Drain, pressing out as much liquid as possible, and combine with the vegetables in the casserole. Add the cooked white beans and the rice, and season with salt, pepper, and crumbled oregano to taste. Sprinkle the top with a mixture of grated parmesan cheese and bread crumbs. Bake the tian in a moderate oven (350°) until the topping is golden and the cheese is melted. Serve hot or cold. (Serves 10.)

FRUIT COMPOTE—American

1	medium pineapple, peeled, cored, and cut in cubes	Raspberries
		Blueberries if in season
2–3	apples, peeled and diced	½ C. rum or orange liqueur (optional)
2–3	peaches or nectarines, peeled and sliced	Sugar
	Apricots, bananas, melon, papaya (optional)	1 can concentrated orange juice, thawed
	Strawberries	Frozen raspberries, thawed (optional)

Combine fruits and sprinkle lightly with sugar and add orange juice concentrate and frozen berries, if desired. You may add honey, liqueur, and vanilla to taste. Chill 2–4 hours.

For a winter compote try apples, pears, bananas, oranges, grapefruit (and pineapple or papaya if they are available). You may use fresh orange, grapefruit, or lemon juice instead of juice concentrate. Especially good is a compote of only assorted melons—cantaloupe, honeydew, casaba, Persian—flavored with lemon juice and sugar.

Peeling and coring pears, and poaching them, is a slow, repetitious job—why not get into the process and enjoy it for its own sake.

POACHED PEARS WITH CHESTNUTS AND CUSTARD

6	firm but *ripe* pears	12	bottled chestnuts in
2	C. water		syrup, or marrons
2	Tbsp. lemon juice		glacés, chopped
1	C. sugar	2	cups custard sauce
1	1"-long cinnamon stick		Caramel

Peel and core the pears. (I use a melon-ball scooper to remove the core from the underside, leaving the pear intact, stem on.)

Combine the water, lemon juice, sugar, and cinnamon stick in a saucepan and bring to a boil. Add pears and simmer 8–10 minutes. Turn often. Drain and *chill*. When cold, stuff pear hollow with chopped chestnuts. Place standing up in serving dish. Pour the following cold custard around pears and top with caramel. (Serves 6.)

Custard Sauce

1	C. milk	½	C. sugar
1	C. heavy cream	⅛	tsp. salt
6	egg yolks	1	tsp. vanilla

Combine the milk and cream in a saucepan and bring just to a boil. Meanwhile, combine the yolks and sugar in a mixing bowl and beat thoroughly until light yellow and thickened. Gradually pour the milk and cream into the yolk mixture, stirring vigorously with a whisk. Add the salt and vanilla. Transfer the mixture to a saucepan and stir over very low heat. Use a wooden spoon to stir, taking care that it hits all the bottom of the saucepan. Cook, stirring, *without boiling,* until the sauce coats the spoon with an obvious creamy layer. Do not overcook or the sauce will curdle. Let cool, then chill. (Makes 2 C.)

Caramel

Melt ½ C. sugar to caramel stage. Pour caramel over cold pears and cold custard. *Don't assemble till 2–3 hours before serving.*

You may omit custard, chestnuts, and caramel, and poach

pears in syrup. Drain and chill. When *cold*, top with 6 oz. semisweet chocolate melted with 2–3 Tbsp. sweet butter.

Or poach pears whole or halved in:

2 C. red wine
1 C. sugar
   Lemon peel
   Cinnamon

Drain. Reduce syrup by half. Pour over pears. Chill well. You may serve with cold custard sauce above or warm or cold zabaglione (pp. 254–55).

Chapter 16

THE THREE R'S IN MEDITATIVE COOKING:

Rhythm, Repetition, and Ritual

Rhythm, repetition, and ritual are essential to the following recipes. Certain steps are repeated over and over—stuffing, folding, layering. The rhythm should not be speeded up too much if you are using the time to be with yourself and to get feedback from your process.

I'd like to differentiate between two kinds of ritual. One is the ritual you invent for yourself, your particular way of chopping or slicing onions or green peppers. It is the method that works best for you—you know it so well it has become routine or second nature. The other kind of ritual is part of a cultural or historic tradition, for example folding tiropetes, grape leaves, wontons or pot stickers. You could invent your own, but not only does the traditional method work for you, but you enjoy being part of a long-established tradition and merging with the historic continuum of thousands and thousands of people folding wonton or grape leaves in just this ritual manner for centuries.
A Northern Chinese ritual:

151

KUO TIEH—"Pot Stickers" (Pan-Fried Dumplings)

1 lb. pork, finely minced or ground	3 cloves garlic, minced
1 egg	2 Tbsp. dried shrimp, soaked and chopped (or ¼ lb. tiny cooked shrimp)
1 Tbsp. minced ginger root	
1 Tbsp. white wine or sherry	2–3 C. shredded Chinese cabbage (chopped, salted, squeezed to remove excess water)
3 Tbsp. soy sauce	
3 tsp. sesame oil	
⅓ C. peanut oil	
1 tsp. salt, or to taste	6 green onions, chopped finely
6 Tbsp. water chestnuts (8–10)	

Blend thoroughly the pork, egg, ginger, wine, soy sauce, oils, salt, water chestunuts, garlic, and shrimp. Then mix in the cabbage and onion. Put in refrigerator for 15 minutes.

Dough

Put 4 C. flour in a bowl, add 1½–2 C. cold water, and knead till the dough is soft, then allow to stand 20 minutes under damp cloth. Roll dough into 1"-thick ropes with your hands. Cut off 1" pieces. Pat down with your hand. Then roll each out into about a 3" circle, thinner at the edges, a little thicker in the center.

Place 1 Tbsp. filling on each. Close up and pinch dough together. Place so that they can stand up, flattening them a little on the bottom. These must be cooked immediately or the dough will break down.

Heat a few tablespoons of peanut oil in a heavy pan that has a tight-fitting lid. When the oil is hot, carefully place a layer of dumplings in the pan, add ½ C. of water, and cover pan. Steam fry for about 7 minutes, till top of dough is set and bottoms of dumplings are browned. Remove with a spatula. Repeat process till all are cooked. You may then serve with hot oil* and white vinegar.

If you want to prepare these ahead of time you will have to prefry them for about 4 minutes, until the dough is set but the bottoms of the dumplings are not browned. Then repeat the frying process. Just before serving time add more oil and less water and cook until the pot stickers are brown. To cook the amount of dumplings this recipe produces you will have to repeat the frying process about 4 times. (Serves 6 for supper with soup, or 12 for hors d'oeuvres.)

See Wonton, pp. 109–10, spring roll, pp. 234–35, for more of the same Meditation.

Two repetitious and rhythmic dishes with eggplant. (See moussaka/pastitsio, pp. 39–40, for a related dish.) Buy eggplants that are dark purple with no brown bruise spots. They should be *heavy* for their size. The heavier the eggplant, the fewer seeds and air pockets inside.

EGGPLANT PARMIGIANA

2 medium eggplants	2 cloves garlic, minced
Olive Oil	fine
Salt and pepper	1½–2 C. marinara sauce (see
1 C. bread crumbs	pp. 243–44, or use
½ C. grated parmesan	canned sauce)
cheese	Mozzarella or string
1 Tbsp. parsley, chopped	cheese

Peel eggplants and cut into ½"-thick slices. Fry the eggplant in a little olive oil till brown and soft on both sides. Drain on paper towels and sprinkle with salt and pepper. Mix bread crumbs, parmesan cheese, parsley, garlic, and salt and pepper to taste. Open a large can of marinara sauce or make your own. Butter a baking dish. Make a layer of eggplant, a layer of crumbs, and a

*Heat ½ C. sesame oil and ¾ C. peanut oil. Drop in a red pepper flake. If it bubbles and doesn't sink or burn, then add 2 Tbsp. of crushed red pepper flakes to the hot oil, let bubble one minute. Cool. This keeps in a jar for months. If it is not "hot" enough for you add ¼ tsp. cayenne. The strength of the pepper flakes varies. Sometimes they are milder, sometimes lethally hot.

layer of sauce, and keep alternating layers till used up. Top with slices of mozzarella cheese. Bake in 375° oven for 25 minutes. This may be assembled ahead of time and baked later. (Serves 6–8.)

Note: Eggplant is a spongy vegetable. Be sparing with oil or butter when sautéeing. It will drink up every last drop and then release great quantities of grease when heated through.

PATLICAN BOREGI—Turkish Eggplant Stuffed With Cheese

2	long, large eggplants		mixture—about 1 C. in
	Salt		all)
	Oil	3–4	eggs
½	lb. mozzarella, string,	3	Tbsp. chopped parsley
	Monterey Jack, or		Bread crumbs
	Teleme cheese (or a		

Slice eggplants in ¼" slices. Sprinkle with salt and let drain in a colander for 30 minutes. Rinse with cold water and pat dry. Fry lightly in oil till pale in hue and soft. Drain in paper towels. Mash or grate the cheese. Add 2 eggs and parsley and mix well. Spread an eggplant slice with mixture and top with another slice to make a sandwich. Beat remaining eggs. Dip eggplant sandwich in egg and coat with bread crumbs.*
Deep fry 2–3 minutes. Drain. Salt to taste.

LASAGNA VERDE ALLA BOLOGNESE

1	lb. wide green noodles	Salt and pepper
4	C. ragù Bolognese (see	About ½ C. grated
	below)	parmesan cheese

*You may assemble and chill all of these "sandwiches" ahead of time. The deep frying (High Energy) is a last-minute affair (see pp. 232–33 for more on this technique).

Cream sauce

Mix together:

2 C. cream, 2 C. milk (or 4 C. half-and-half)	8 Tbsp. butter 8 Tbsp. flour

Cook noodles al dente, drain, rinse in cold water, set aside on towels.

Place a layer of ragù on the bottom of a buttered casserole. Add some of the cream sauce, sprinkle with cheese, and add a layer of noodles. Continue layering until all the ingredients are used. Top with meat sauce, cream sauce, and lots of cheese. Bake in 375° oven for 25 minutes.

You may use white noodles, too. Freezes well completely assembled and unbaked. This reheats very well, too!

Quick Ragù Bolognese or Meat Sauce

4	Tbsp. olive oil	4	C. (or 2 1-lb. cans) marinara sauce (see pp. 243–44)
1	onion, minced		
1½	lb. ground beef	2	1-lb. cans diced plum tomatoes
2	tsp. minced garlic		
3	Tbsp. minced parsley	½	C. red wine (optional)
1–2	tsp. minced green herbs such as fines herbes or bouquet garni	1	C. sautéed mushrooms (optional)
1	tsp. sweet basil, dried Salt and pepper to taste		

Heat oil. Add onion and ground meat and stir till meat is crumbly. Add garlic, spices, and herbs, simmer one minute, and add marinara sauce and diced tomatoes. Add wine if desired. Simmer anywhere from 30 minutes to an hour; I am not of the school that believes in cooking the sauce for three days. This tastes very fine even after a brief simmer. Add mushrooms for the last 10 minutes. This sauce can be served directly over pasta. It can be stretched by adding diced leftover ham, etc. And it improves in flavor by sitting for a day or so in the refrigerator.

Southern Italian Lasagna

2	C. ricotta cheese	2½	C. tomato sauce
1½	diced mozzarella		Sliced sausage (optional)
	Sautéed mushrooms		

CHICKEN LASAGNA

3	whole large chicken breasts	4	C. broth or broth and cream combined
	Water		Salt, pepper, nutmeg
2	10-oz. cans chicken broth	1	lb. mushrooms, sautéed
		1	lb. lasagna noodles
	Celery stalks and leaves	1	lb. ricotta cheese
	Peeled onion	1	C. grated parmesan cheese
	Parsley sprigs		
8	Tbsp. butter	1½	C. mozzarella cheese, diced
8	Tbsp. flour		

Optional

2	C. marinara sauce (see pp. 243–44)	Green peas (optional)

Poach chicken breasts in 20 oz. broth and just enough water to cover, with celery, onion, parsley, till tender—about 20 minutes. When cool enough to handle, remove the chicken from the bones and shred the meat into strips. Reserve the broth.

Melt butter, add flour, and cook to make a roux. Add 4 C. broth or broth and cream, and cook till thick. Season to taste and add the sautéed mushrooms, the chicken shreds, peas if desired.

Cook the lasagna noodles in quantities of boiling salted water till al dente. Drain, rinse in a bowl of cold water, drain again, and place on towels.

Butter a baking dish. Add a layer of chicken in sauce, a layer of noodles, some dots of ricotta, sprinklings of parmesan and mozzarella, and then more sauce, more noodles, more cheese, etc. You may sprinkle a marinara sauce layer between chicken in sauce and noodle layers if you like. (Serves 8.) Bake in a 350° oven for 35 minutes, or till golden and bubbly.

For a meatless lasagna, omit chicken and use chopped spinach or chard sautéed with onion and garlic and mix with ricotta cheese (see note on cannelloni, p. 170).

Poaching and draining islands of meringue takes time and concentration. Pay attention to texture, lightness of the meringues, creaminess of the custard.

FLOATING ISLANDS

1 qt. milk	1⅓ C. sugar
6 eggs, separated, at room temperature	2½ tsp. vanilla
	Cream

Heat milk till scalded.

Beat egg whites till stiff. Gradually add 1 C. sugar and beat till glossy. Add 1 tsp. vanilla. Form meringue into ovals with tablespoon—push off the spoon into the scalded milk. Poach a few mounds of meringue at a time in milk for 4–5 minutes, 2 minutes on each side, turning once with a slotted spoon. Repeat poaching till all the meringue mixture is used up. Don't let milk boil. Drain meringues on paper towels and keep them dry—change towels if necessary.

Strain the milk and add enough cream to get 3 C.

Beat the egg yolks till pale, and beat in the rest of the sugar. Gradually add a bit of the hot milk, stirring constantly. Then add eggs to milk and cook over low heat till slightly thickened. (If custard doesn't thicken at all, whirl in the blender with some vanilla instant pudding powder, or add 1 tsp. or so arrowroot to 2 Tbsp. milk and heat to thicken—but the texture will be *less silky*.) Add the rest of the vanilla. Strain into serving dish, a deep oval or rectangle. When custard is cold and thickened, place meringues atop custard. Chill well. Can be made at most the day before. You may garnish with raspberries or caramel. (Serves 6.)

Chapter 17

STUFFED GRAPE LEAVES AND
OTHER DOLMAS AS A MEDITATION

The stuffing and rolling of grape leaves is an enjoyable tactile. sensation that you can experience in a Meditative atmosphere. Grape leaves come packed in jars covered with a brine solution. How they roll them up so tightly and stuff them into the jars I will never know. Getting them out of the jar is tricky. You want to pull out each roll of leaves without tearing it into shreds. Be patient. After you triumphantly extricate the leaves from the jar, rinse them to remove the brine, then pat each one dry with paper towels. This is a slow but rhythmic process; your mind can travel while your eyes consider the shapes of the leaves, your fingers feel the dampness of their surface as well as their smoothness. Place them, smooth side down, on the counter. Snip off the stems.

Knead the filling into an oblong shape. It feels crumbly at first, a few grains of rice tumbling out onto the table. Then it comes together and adheres in a cohesive mass. You place some filling on the leaf and proceed with the rolling, tucking, folding, turning. Fold the top part over, fold in the sides, then roll up into the traditional longish finger or cylinder shape.

One leaf follows the next, you reach for the filling, you form it under your fingers and place it on the leaf, you fold and tuck and roll the leaf, pressing just so much till it takes shape under your fingers and an elegant cylinder is formed where once there were grains of rice and flat shiny green leaves. If your attention starts to stray from the task of rolling or if you find yourself getting bored (and out of your Meditation), recenter yourself. Get back in harmony with rolling and folding.

Roll leaf after leaf till the process is completed, the leaves, or dolmas, formed in geometric elegance. Repetition, rhythm, and ritual, Middle Eastern Style. You are breathing rhythmically, your center is calm. You have created something beautiful with your fingers and your eyes.

Now the steaming can begin. Place the leaves seamside down in a single layer in the pan. Cover them with a plate to weight them down and to prevent them from unrolling as they steam. If you make them a day or so ahead of time and decide to serve them warm, you may repeat the steaming procedure, but don't forget to put the plate on top. They can still unroll even though they have been cooked.

Later, if you're feeling "up," you can prepare the avgolemono sauce, beating the eggs rapidly and swirling them quickly into the pan juices. Thus you will have experienced the quiet Meditative space of preparation and the High Energy rush just before serving the leaves and sharing the energy with your friends and family.

Grape leaves are good hot or cold, with yoghurt and lemon juice. The Turks often serve them with tomato sauce and the Greeks make an avgolemono sauce in the pan in which the grape leaves were cooked, using some of the cooking liquids. Here are two excellent recipes, one with meat and one without. You can stretch the meat recipe by increasing the amount of rice. The recipes suggest cooking the dolmas in water, but you could use part chicken broth. Be sure to add about 3 Tbsp. oil to the water in the pot so the leaves won't be dry or stick together. Each recipe makes two large saucepans full—about 40 dolmas.

DOLMAS—Stuffed Grape Leaves

1–2	C. raw rice, washed and soaked for 10 minutes, drained	3¼	cloves garlic, minced
1	lb. ground lamb	1	jar grape leaves, rinsed and drained
1	tsp. allspice	1	tsp. cinnamon
1	tsp. pepper	1	Tbsp. salt
1	onion, minced and sautéed in 4 Tbsp. butter (about ½ C.)	2	Tbsp. parsley
		¼	C. pine nuts
		¼	C. currants, plumped in warm water, drained

Mix filling ingredients well together, place on the grape leaves, and roll into traditional cylindrical form. Place dolmas in a single layer in the pan. Add water or broth and 3 Tbsp. oil to almost cover the dolmas. Weight down with a plate. Cover the pan and steam about 30 minutes.

Alternative Rice Filling

2	C. rice	2	Tbsp. parsley or mint leaves, or both
2	onions, chopped		Salt and pepper
3–4	cloves garlic, minced	1	jar grape leaves
	Butter	1	C. olive oil
2	tomatoes, skinned and chopped		Boiling water or broth to cover
½	C. pine nuts		
½	C. currants		

Soak rice about 30 minutes. Drain.

Sauté onions and garlic in a little butter. Mix in tomatoes, pine nuts, currants, parsley or mint, salt, and pepper. Prepare leaves as described at the beginning of this chapter. Stuff leaves. Place dolmas tightly in a large pan. Pour olive oil and boiling water or broth over them. Put a plate on top. Cover and simmer for about 40 minutes.

Avgolemono Sauce

3 eggs   Juice of 1 lemon

Separate eggs. Beat egg whites till stiff. Blend in egg yolks. Add lemon juice. Beat well. Then *slowly* add some hot broth from dolmas to the egg batter until it is very hot. Pour the sauce over all the dolmas. Remove from heat at once.

As a variation, you might use cabbage leaves. Or you may cook the dolmas in the sweet-and-sour sauce of the stuffed cabbage recipe (pp. 301–2). If you precook the rice, the filling can be put into tomatoes or green peppers and baked, basting with oil, lemon juice, or tomato sauce. In the Middle East any stuffed vegetable, such as zucchini, eggplant, peppers, tomatoes, grape, or cabbage leaves, is called a dolma.

See Claudia Roden's *Book of Middle Eastern Food* (New York: Alfred A. Knopf, 1972), for more information and ideas.

The following recipes are not traditional Middle Eastern dolmas, but the process of stuffing, the rhythm and repetition, are the same.

STUFFED TOMATOES

3–4 large or 6–8 small   2 cloves garlic, minced
     tomatoes   Salt and pepper
     Brown sugar   Bread crumbs
  4 Tbsp. minced onion   Parmesan cheese
  2 Tbsp. minced parsley

Cut large tomatoes in half or cut the blossom end off the small tomatoes. Scoop out the liquid, seeds, and some of the pulp, and put it in a bowl. Leave a good thick tomato shell—don't remove *all* of the pulp. Sprinkle the insides of the tomato shells with brown sugar.

To the seeds and pulp add onion, parsley, and minced garlic. Add salt and pepper and enough bread crumbs to thicken. Spoon filling into the tomato shells. Then top with more bread crumbs and grated parmesan cheese (or grated Swiss, or slices of cheddar or Monterey-Jack). Bake in 350° oven for about 15 minutes. You may brown under the broiler. (Serves 6–8.)

You may also stuff tomatoes with creamed spinach.

POMODORI AL RISO—Tomatoes with Rice

6	large ripe tomatoes	1	Tbsp. fresh crushed basil or 2 Tbsp. pesto (see p. 244)
½	C. olive oil		
2–3	garlic cloves, minced		
¼	C. finely chopped parsley	2	tsp. lemon rind
1	C. rice, uncooked		Salt and pepper
1½	C. hot chicken broth		Grated parmesan cheese (optional)
2	anchovy filets, minced		

Cut a slice from the top of each tomato and scoop out the centers with a grapefruit knife, reserving the pulp and liquid. Stand the tomatoes in a shallow baking pan and sprinkle each cavity with a little olive oil.

In a saucepan cook garlic and parsley in most of the olive oil for a few minutes. Add rice and sauté it, stirring constantly, for about 3 minutes. Stir in hot chicken broth and the reserved tomato pulp and cook the mixture, covered, for about 20 minutes, or until the rice is tender. Add anchovy filets, basil or pesto, lemon rind, salt, and pepper to taste.

Fill the tomatoes with the rice mixture, sprinkle the tops with a little olive oil, top with parmesan cheese if desired, and bake in a moderate oven (350°) for 30 minutes. The tomatoes can be served hot or cold, as a first course or as a vegetable.

An Arabic variation of this dish stuffs the tomatoes with rice, sautéed onion, raisins, almonds, mint, cinnamon, and allspice. The tomatoes are baked, basted with water and honey.

See stuffed zucchini, p. 117.

STUFFED MUSHROOMS

14	medium or large mushrooms	2	Tbsp. flour
	Butter	½	C. heavy cream
1	bunch green onions		Nutmeg, salt, pepper
		½	C. grated Swiss cheese

Preheat the oven to 350°.

Wipe the mushrooms with a damp paper towel and then dry. Chop the stems and 2 of the mushrooms till minced fairly fine.

Mince the green onions, using as much of the green part as possible, add to the butter, and stir fry 1 minute. Add the mushroom pieces and sauté for about 3 minutes, stirring constantly. Sprinkle with the flour, stir well, then add the cream till a fairly thick sauce forms. Season with salt, pepper, and nutmeg.

Stuff this filling into the mushroom caps. Place them in a buttered baking dish and sprinkle the tops of the mushrooms with the grated cheese. Dot with butter. Bake in oven for 15–20 minutes. You can serve this as a first course or as a vegetable dish.

Try these for breakfast one morning:

SAUSAGE-FILLED APPLES

6	Rome Beauty apples	¼	tsp. cinnamon
¾	lb. sweet Italian sausage	¼	tsp. nutmeg
¼	C. chopped onion	1	Tbsp. sugar
¼	tsp. garlic	1	C. water
1	Tbsp. each butter and olive oil	¼	C. calvados (apple brandy)
1/16	tsp. pepper		

Core apples and scoop out extra apple for stuffing. A melon-ball scooper is ideal for this job.

Remove sausage from casing. Sauté onion, garlic, and sausage in butter and olive oil. Add apple pulp, pepper, cinnamon, nutmeg, and sugar.

Stuff apple shells with sausage mixture. Bake in shallow Pyrex dish, add water to pan, and drip approximately 1 teaspoon calvados over each apple. Bake one hour in 400° oven. Baste every 10 minutes. Serve with heavy cream and calvados if you like, but they are good just the way they are. (Serves 6.)

See stuffed baked apples, p. 89, for dessert variation.

Chapter 18

CREPES AS A MEDITATION

The process of making crepes can be a Meditation. There is rhythm, repetition, and ritual. Once you've got the flow state going you hate to interrupt it. Remove the phone from the hook and muffle the droning sound. Ask your housemates not to interrupt you for a while—or set up a time when you are, in fact, alone.

For crepe making you may use *two* sauté pans, preferably Teflon lined: one small—about 6 inches in diameter—and one that is larger, about 8–12 inches in diameter. (Why two pans instead of one? So you don't have to touch the hot crepes with your fingers. Just flip the crepe from the smaller pan over into the larger one—no burnt fingertips, no torn crepes.)

Have a saucepan with melted butter and a pastry brush conveniently located near the stove, and line up the pans, a medium flame under the little one and a very low flame under the bigger one. Remember to *lightly* brush the small pan with the melted butter after every crepe and the big one every ten crepes or so. Have a clear area covered with paper towels where you can flip the crepes out of the pan and stack them as they accumulate. There is no need to put waxed paper between the crepes. The thin layer of butter will prevent them from sticking together.

Remove the batter from the refrigerator. Preheat the pans and place the melted butter nearby. (Incidentally, even if you have one of those electric crepe makers you can still partake of the Meditation; you will just have to adjust your rhythm to that of the machine . . . one more reason to eliminate excess machinery from your life so you can establish your own rhythm and not have to adapt to a manufacturer's energy pattern.)

Then start ladling the batter into the pan, swirl the batter around, let it set, rap the pan lightly, turn the crepe over to set the other side, and then slide it onto a towel or paper towel. Keep an even pace. Once the perfect heat is attained and the right amount of batter is determined in your mind's eye to fill the spoon and film the pan, you can stand there moving slowly, measuring, pouring, swirling, turning. Your body will be engaged in a flowing motion, the crepes will slide out of the pan with ease, and your mind will be calm and relaxed.

CREPE BATTER

1	C. cold water	½ tsp. salt
1	C. cold milk	2 C. sifted flour
4	eggs	4 Tbsp. melted butter

Put water, milk, eggs and salt in blender. Add flour and then butter. Cover and blend till smooth and lump free. Chill for 2–4 hours. (Makes about 20–30 crepes.)

Lightly butter a large and a small Teflon pan. Heat over medium flame.

Ladle about 2 Tbsp. batter into small pan and swirl around till it covers bottom. Cook till set and not shiny, then flip over into large pan. Cook a few seconds.

Turn out onto paper towels. Stack about 12 high. Butter small pan after every crepe, large pan after every 10 crepes.

The batter can be mixed up in the blender and refrigerated for a few days. It can be made up in huge batches. The crepes can be prepared a day or so ahead of time and refrigerated, or they can be stacked in groups of 10 or 12, wrapped with heavy-duty foil, and frozen.

To reheat crepes simply thaw (or remove from the refrigerator if they are not frozen), wrap in heavy-duty foil, and place in a 350° oven with a pan of hot water on the bottom. This will create steam so the crepes will not dry out while heating. They should be warm and flexible enough to roll in about 15–20 minutes. A cold crepe is not flexible and will crack when you fill it and try to roll it into a cylinder.

Some crepes, such as blintzes and cannelloni, can be filled and then frozen. Others with creamed fillings can be filled ahead of time, covered with a sauce or simply dotted with butter and covered with foil, and reheated later. Leave them at room temperature for a few hours, then bake in a 350° oven for about 25 minutes till they are heated through.

Because crepes are bland in flavor, season the filling a bit more spicily than you would if you were going to eat it plain. You don't want its flavor to get lost. Also, be sure that the fillings are thick enough not to leak out of the crepes when reheated. They should not be the consistency that you'd serve over rice; they should be much thicker, because reheating breaks down their flour-butter emulsion and the sauces thin out.

CURRIED CRAB OR SHRIMP FILLING FOR CREPES

4–5 Tbsp. butter
1 onion, chopped
2–3 Tbsp. flour
2 Tbsp. curry powder (or less, to taste)
½ tsp. ginger
1½–2 C. cream, broth, or white wine in any combination

1–1½ lb. crab meat or small shrimp
Diced green pepper (optional)
Diced water chestnuts (optional)
Salt and pepper

Melt butter. Sauté onion till crisp but coated. If raw shrimp are used, sauté them in the butter with the onion till they are pink. Add flour, curry powder, ginger. Add liquids. Cook till *thick*. Add crab if used, and green pepper and/or water chestnuts if desired, and season to taste. You may add cognac or Worcestershire to the sauce. Serve this wrapped in crepes with a thin curry sauce on top, and garnish with chutney.

CHICKEN LIVERS AND MUSHROOMS FOR CREPES
(OR OMELETS)

½–¾ lb. mushrooms, sliced
¼ C. minced green onions
  or onions
4 Tbsp. butter
1½ lbs. chicken livers
2–3 Tbsp. flour
1½ C. beef broth
¼ C. Madeira, sherry, or
  dry Marsala

2 tsp. or more Kitchen
  Bouquet for color
  Salt and pepper
1 tsp. Worcestershire or
  3–4 Tbsp. tomato paste
  (optional)

Sauté mushrooms and onions in butter. Set aside.

Sauté livers but keep them pink in center. Don't overcook. Add flour, then broth. Stir till thick. Add wine and Kitchen Bouquet.

Cut livers into bite-size sections after they are cooked, not before, so they keep their shape and texture and don't get mushy. Add mushrooms and onions. Season to taste with salt, pepper, and Worcestershire or tomato paste, if desired.

To use this as an omelet filling cut recipe in half, omit flour and broth, and stir in ½ C. sour cream at room temperature. That will make enough to fill 2 4-egg omelets.

Some other fillings are:

caviar, sour cream, chopped onions and hard-boiled eggs and creamed spinach, sautéed mushrooms

creamed chicken or turkey

diced ham, green onions, grated cheese

jam or marmalade

or cheese that has been sweetened, as in:

BLINTZES

Fill crepes with a mixture of

2 C. creamed cottage
  cheese
3 Tbsp. sugar
½ C. yellow raisins,
  soaked

½ tsp. cinnamon
1 tsp. lemon rind
1 egg yolk (optional)

Fold crepes and sauté in butter on both sides till golden. Serve with sour cream or powdered sugar. These freeze beautifully! Thaw before sautéeing.

CREPES WITH FRUIT—OTHER SUGGESTIONS

Roll crepes around sliced strawberries or whole raspberries that have been sugared and sprinkled with orange juice and Cointreau and allowed to mellow for a while in the refrigerator. Place the rolled crepes seam side down in a buttered shallow baking dish, allowing 2 crepes per person. Sprinkle with sugar and dot with butter. Bake in 350° oven for about 20 minutes. You may assemble the crepes a few hours ahead and chill. Then allow a few more minutes in the oven.

You may also fill the crepes with poached peach slices, poached sliced pears that have been sprinkled with cinnamon and raisins, or apple slices that have been sautéed in butter and sugar and sprinkled with cinnamon and raisins. Serve with vanilla sauce or sweetened fruit and preserves combined.

QUICK VANILLA SAUCE

1 pkg. vanilla instant
  pudding
1½ C. milk
1 C. cream (any weight)

2 tsp. vanilla
2 Tbsp. brandy or orange
  liqueur (optional)

Combine in blender. Chill. Stir before serving. This is good with fruits, crepes, and as a sauce for soufflés.

The making of the crepes and the assembling of the cannelloni is a double Meditation.

CANNELLONI

3	C. Marinara sauce (see Basic Pantry, pp. 243–44) Filling	squares 4" square or 24 manicotti tubes Béchamel sauce
24	crepes, steamed till warm, or 20–24 pasta	½ C. parmesan cheese

Filling

4	Tbsp. oil	1½ lbs. ground beef
4	Tbsp. butter	2 eggs
1	onion, minced	5 Tbsp. parmesan cheese
1	tsp. minced fresh garlic	Pinch of oregano
1	pkg. frozen chopped spinach, thawed and squeezed dry	(optional) Salt, pepper

Heat 2 Tbsp. each oil and butter. Add onion and garlic and sauté till soft. Add the spinach and stir over heat for a minute or two to evaporate the excess moisture. Put into a bowl. Heat the remaining oil and butter. Add the meat, crumbled, and cook till brown. Add to the spinach and onion. Add eggs, cheese, salt, pepper, and oregano if desired. Chill the filling for a while for easier handling.

Alternate filling

	Oil and butter	2 eggs
1	large onion, minced	Salt, pepper, nutmeg
2	tsp. minced garlic	2 lbs. ricotta cheese
2	pkgs. frozen chopped spinach or Swiss chard, thawed and squeezed dry	½ C. shredded mozzarella cheese (optional)

Cook onion, garlic, and spinach as in meat filling. Add cooked spinach, onion, eggs, and seasonings to the cheeses. Chill the filling.

Cream Sauce (Béchamel)

6 Tbsp. butter
6 Tbsp. flour
Salt, pepper, nutmeg

2 C. milk
1½ C. cream (any weight)

To make the béchamel sauce, melt butter, add flour, add milk and cream and stir till thick.

If you are using crepes (they are lighter than pasta so people may be able to eat more!) make the crepes and stack them; if the crepes have been prepared ahead of time, wrap the stacks in foil and steam them in a 350° oven over a pan of warm water, about 15 minutes, until they are flexible.

If you are using fresh pasta squares, boil them in a huge pot of water to which some oil has been added, stirring occasionally. Drain after 2 minutes. Shake off excess water and then slide into a large bowl of cold water to stop the cooking. Drain on dish towels. (This takes up quite a bit of counter space. You may have to stack the dish towels with the noodles on them if pressed for space.)

If you are using manicotti tubes, boil for 5–7 minutes. Remove with slotted spoon to bowl of cold water.

The Final Assembly!

Pour a layer of marinara sauce on the bottom of a baking dish. Roll up the filling in the pasta or crepes and place the cannelloni atop the sauce. Cover with a layer of béchamel sauce and then dot well with marinara sauce. Sprinkle with parmesan and bake in a 350° oven for 30 minutes. You may freeze these unbaked.

Chapter 19

BAKING BREADS AND CAKES AS A MEDITATION:

Chemistry and Creativity

My mother-in-law, Essie, was one of those people who *hated* to cook but *loved* to bake. While the prospect of preparing a meal or simple hors d'oeuvres for company sent her into a state of mild panic, she was a sea of calm when preparing a chocolate cake. However, I know other people who delight in cooking the most elaborate and complicated dishes but break out in a cold sweat at the thought of having to make bread or apple pie.

Baking is essentially a science founded on principles of physics and chemistry. Precision is required for a modicum of success. You have to be careful not to alter too many basic measurements or you will have a disaster on your hands. Baking is affected by the weather. A buttery crust will be difficult to roll out on a hot day, and meringues will refuse to dry out if the air is damp. Baking soda cannot always be substituted for baking powder.

People who love to improvise, who use recipes as springboards for cooking ideas, are the ones who have the greatest problems

172

with baking. They don't enjoy the exact measuring. They find it inhibiting and mechanical. They resent having to follow directions to the letter because they are unable, due to temperament and an irrepressibly innovative nature, to follow *any* recipe exactly. However, those who are insecure in the kitchen, who are terrified of making mistakes or are confused by the vague directions of many cooking recipes, tend to feel safe with baking.

If you are a freewheeler, don't let the precision required in baking make you tense and rob you of your joy in the process. The last thing you should be is uptight over measurement accuracy. Practice measuring with your hands. Pour a tablespoon of sugar in your hand and memorize what it looks like, how heavy it is. Drop a teaspoonful of salt into your palm. How does that feel? Can you tell a pinch of cinnamon from a half teaspoonful? Loosen up so that you won't have to spend most of your time in the kitchen playing mad chemist, measuring every grain of flour and salt until all the joy is drained out of the baking experience and you feel tense and miserable.

I find that baking is fun and easy if I have preheated the oven and premeasured all the ingredients and set them within easy reach so that when I get to cooking I can really MOVE. I hate to have my rhythm broken by having to stop to find an ingredient on the shelf or to measure something. The flow is all . . . at least, it is for me.

It is important to check your oven for accuracy. Many thermostats are just pieces of sculpture on the front of the stove; the temperature on the dial bears little or no resemblance to what is going on inside. Buy an oven thermometer to check on the reliability of your stove's thermostat. Some ovens run hot or escalate in heat as the cooking time progresses. Some ovens have hot spots. In general, the higher up or farther back you go in the oven, the hotter it is. If you are baking two cake layers on different racks in the oven, it won't hurt to rotate them halfway through the baking time. And if one side of the oven seems hotter than the other, switch things from side to side so that cakes or muffins will rise evenly. If your oven seems to be wildly erratic or the thermostat inaccurate, it will pay to have it professionally calibrated. You owe it to your pastries and to your peace of mind. Nobody likes to go to all the trouble and expense of putting together something potentially wonderful, only to be sabotaged by an inaccurate oven.

Also, be sure that if a recipe calls for an eight-inch springform pan you don't use a ten-incher; the cake will be flatter than a pancake! Have a set of glass measuring cups for liquids and a metal or plastic set for solids. When measuring liquid ingredients, it is usually best to use the glass measuring cup, which you can see through, to judge the accuracy of your measurement. When measuring solid ingredients, metal measuring cups are best. You can fill them to overflowing and then level them off with a knife to get an exact measurement. If you have glass baking dishes instead of metal, lower the oven temperature by 25 degrees.

Just because baking is a precise art doesn't mean that it is not creative; it needn't be *only* mechanical and routine. Baking can be an excellent release of artistic energies once you understand the basic principles behind the techniques. Then you will know when you can add an ingredient or leave one out, when you may double, and when you may substitute one ingredient for another.

Baking has the added advantage of some very physical, sensual gratifications. There are few things in cooking that are as relaxing as kneading bread. The textures of baking ingredients are varied and fun to touch, like whipped egg whites, sifted flour, crushed nuts, smooth melted chocolate. Cutting cookies into different shapes or inventing your own can be an adventure into the world of graphic design. Spreading frosting on ten thin layers of sponge cake is making sculpture of a sort.

Don't be upset if your cakes don't look perfectly "professional." A slightly lopsided or lumpy look will not detract from its homemade goodness. The love and effort it reveals will more than substitute for pastry-tube flowerettes and elaborate decorative icing. Most professional bakers can't afford to use the good ingredients that you will (and still make money).

Personal style affects baking decisions. You can read six different "classic" apple pie recipes and each will be slightly different. All will turn out a "correct" and acceptable pie, but one will be sweeter, one drier, one will add raisins or nuts or cheese. You will have to choose whichever more closely represents your *style* or your *feeling* about apple pie *at that moment*. There are austere bakers (almost a contradiction in terms), who like things mildly sweet, a few raisins here and there, a few stray nuts. Then there are those baroque bakers for whom the idea of creating a sweet becomes an exercise in extravagance. If it's going to be sweet, let's go for broke! Whipped cream with a cake that is already frosted, hot fudge on a sinfully rich chocolate-cake roll. A sweet tooth can be accompanied by a heavy hand or a light one. (I am not a big sweet eater. However, I do serve dessert on special occasions and try to minimize the use of sugar in day-to-day cooking.)

The baking recipes in this book range from the low-key to the mildly hysterical. They all have a place at the table according to your mood and the balance suggested by the rest of the meal you have prepared. Try to follow the recipes exactly the first time, even if it's against your nature. You will then understand how they are supposed to taste, what the textures should be. If you feel like making changes next time, go ahead.

For years I was terrified by the idea of yeast doughs. I was sure that if I were to try working with yeast it would refuse to cooperate, that all my breads would be heavy and inedible. A few years ago I sat in a friend's kitchen and watched her baking some holiday breads. It looked so easy that I knew that I couldn't fail; I realized that it was mind over matter: Since I believed the breads would come out well, they did. For those of you who are still terrified of the notion of yeast doughs and confused by the mystique of how hot is hot, how warm is warm, how to knead and why, there are some excellent publications that ought to banish these fears immediately. May I recommend the following books:

The Art of Fine Baking, by Paula Peck. (New York: Simon & Schuster, Inc. 1961; paper, 1970.)

A World of Breads, by Dolores Casella (New York: David White Company, 1974, also in paper.)

Homemade Bread, by the Food Editors of *Farm Journal*. (Garden City, N. Y.: Doubleday & Co., 1969.)

The Tassajara Bread Book, by Edward Espe Brown. (Berkeley: Shambhala Press, 1970.)

The New York Times Bread and Soup Cook Book, edited by Yvonne Young Tarr. (New York: Quadrangle Books, 1972.)

And if these books don't make you feel confident, ask some friends who enjoy baking if you may watch the next time they are making bread. Seeing is not only believing, it is comforting as well. After seeing, try doing. Experience is part of mind over matter. Once you have success, it sets the tone for future endeavors.

Two favorite breads:

BASIC WHITE BREAD

1 C. buttermilk	½ C. wheat germ
1 C. skim milk	1 cake or envelope yeast
3 Tbsp. sugar or 2 Tbsp. honey	dissolved in ¼ C. warm water with 1 tsp. sugar
2 Tbsp. margarine or butter	added to aid bubbling, to proof the yeast
6 C. unbleached white flour, approximately	

Scald the milks. Add sugar or honey, salt, and butter or margarine, and cool till lukewarm.

Put 3 C. flour and the wheat germ in a mixing bowl. Add the liquids and yeast mix and mix well. Add approximately 3 more C. flour and knead 10–15 minutes until the dough is smooth and elastic. Place in a greased bowl, cover with a dish towel, and let rise in a warm place for 1½ hours.

Punch down and let rise 1 hour. Form into 2 loaves and let rise 1 hour more. Bake in a 400° oven for 35 minutes. (Makes 2 loaves.)

WHOLE WHEAT BREAD

1 C. milk, skim or buttermilk	½ C. warm water
4 Tbsp. honey	1 tsp. ginger
3 Tbsp. margarine or butter	1 tsp. sugar
2 tsp. salt	3–4 C. whole wheat flour
¾ C. water	¼ C. wheat germ
½ C. cracked wheat	2 C. unbleached white flour
2 envelopes or 2 cakes yeast	

Scald milk and add honey, butter or margarine, salt, water, and cracked wheat. Let cool to lukewarm.

Soften yeast in warm water. Add ginger and sugar and let bubble.

In a mixing bowl place 2 C. whole wheat flour and wheat germ. Add the liquids, still warm, and mix well. Add white flour and 1 C. or more whole wheat flour as needed to make a workable dough. Knead for 10 minutes till elastic. Place in a greased bowl, cover with a towel, and allow to rise for 1½ hours.

Form into loaves and let rise one hour, or till double in size. Bake in 375° oven for 30–40 minutes. (Makes 2 loaves.)

A cake with a cookie-dough crust: Patting the thin crust into the pan is a very tactile experience. The filling is really a sweet cheese soufflé—so don't be alarmed when it rises dramatically, then falls upon cooling. It may even crack on top, but you can disguise it if you like with some sweetened sour cream or fruit with a jelly glaze.

FRENCH CHEESECAKE

1 C. flour	4 eggs, separated
1 C. soft butter	¼ C. sweet cream
1 egg yolk	¼ C. sour cream
2 Tbsp. sugar	1 tsp. vanilla
1 lb. cream cheese	¼ tsp. salt
1 Tbsp. flour	1 tsp. lemon rind
½ C. sugar, or a bit more	(optional)

Have all the ingredients at room temperature. Mix flour and butter with fingertips till well blended. Add the egg yolk and sugar and lemon rind if desired and blend again till the mixture adheres and can easily be formed into a ball. Press about half of this pastry into the bottom of a 9″ springform pan. Press the rest inside the rim about halfway up. The crust should be *very thin*. Chill the dough while you assemble the filling:

Cream the cheese till soft. Add flour and sugar, and mix well. Add egg yolks, creams, and vanilla, and beat well. Beat egg whites with salt till stiff. Fold into cheese mixture.

Pour into the pan. Bake in a 350° oven for 50–60 minutes. Cool the cake in the oven with the door ajar. It is best to keep the cake at room temperature. You may refrigerate it if you are making it well ahead of time, but please bring the cake to room temperature before serving. (Refrigeration makes the cake heavier in texture, and I prefer it lighter and creamier.) Incidentally, the cheesecake is delicious when served WARM! In fact, that is the way I usually serve it. Warm in a 350° oven for about 15 to 20 minutes.

For an Italian variation use 1 lb. ricotta cheese. Add 2 Tbsp. pine nuts and ⅓ C. yellow raisins soaked in Marsala, and use 1 tsp. lemon rind, 2 Tbsp. Marsala, in crust.

Another variation: Add ½ tsp. almond extract. Top with ¼ C. brown sugar, 1 tsp. cinnamon, ½ C. finely chopped almonds.

Though it is not my preference, cheesecakes may be frozen.

Thaw, bring to room temperature, and revive in a 350° oven for about 15–20 minutes.

The ultimate meringue dessert:

GATEAU ROLLA—Four-Layer Almond Meringue Cake

5 egg whites	(to prevent the nuts
Salt	from becoming oily,
1 C. sugar	grate in blender with 2
1 tsp. vanilla	Tbsp. sugar)
1 C. finely grated almonds	

Grease 2 large baking sheets with oil. Cut out four 8" circles of bakers' parchment or waxed paper. If you use waxed paper, oil it generously. (Leave the paper a bit larger than the traced circle so you can lift an edge after the meringues are baked.)

Beat the egg whites with a pinch of salt till stiff. Gradually beat in ¾ C. of sugar and beat till stiff and glossy. (To attain their maximum volume and stiffness when beaten, egg whites should be at room temperature and the bowl and beaters free of all water and grease.) Beat in, at low speed, the vanilla and remaining sugar. Then fold in the grated almonds.

Spread meringue mixture within circle outlines on paper—keep meringues uniform in thickness. Bake in a 250° oven for about 60 minutes. Remove the meringues to a rack to cool, and peel off the paper. (Turn page for Frosting.)

Frosting

3 egg whites	2 Tbsp. cocoa
¾ C. sugar	1½ C. softened sweet butter
6 oz. sweet chocolate, melted	

Beat egg whites in the top of a double boiler till they are foamy. Set pan over hot water and gradually beat in the sugar, chocolate, cocoa, and butter. Beat till smooth. Cool till firm enough to spread.

Assemble the 4 layers of meringue with the frosting between layers, and cover the top and sides too. Sprinkle with confectioners' sugar.

This cake is a wonderful excuse for getting rid of accumulated egg whites and satisfies all sweet cravings for days, maybe weeks. It is very rich, and is best if prepared the day before. It keeps for a few days in the refrigerator. It may be frozen.

For dacquoise: Do the same almond meringues with mocha butter cream (see p. 308).
For other cakes see:

p. 100 for chocolate cake roll

p. 306 for chocolate decadence

pp. 307–8 for mocha torte

pp. 307–8 for Sacher torte

p. 309 for chestnut torte

Chapter 20

ROLLING DOUGH AS A MEDITATION:

Pies, Quiches, an "En Croûte," and Fresh Pasta

The preparation of piecrust is Meditative. You measure out the flour, fat, and ice water for the crust and combine them with your fingers. It is a richly tactile experience. Next you proceed to roll out the dough, slowly, carefully, rhythmically. Your mind's eye envisages a circle. Your arms send the energy to the rolling pin, releasing the right amount of pressure to smooth out the dough and help it attain the desired thickness. The crust is lifted into the pan, the edges crimped with your finger or with the tines of a fork.

Piecrusts can be prepared well in advance of baking, so you work when you have some quiet time for yourself. There are some who can prepare a "perfect" piecrust under any circumstances—children running in and out of the kitchen, the phone ringing, the dog tipping over a bowl of water. Midst all this chaos they are relaxed, handling dough, engrossed in the process of patting, pressing, fondling, rocking back and forth, sprinkling flour lightly, seeing a circle. Most people prefer to roll out a crust in relative tranquillity. Know yourself. How do *you* feel when making a pie? Are you mellow and relaxed, or does the process make you tense? Then protect your space. If you need quiet, find a time to be alone with your piecrust, just the two of you, so a dialogue can ensue. If, however, you feel at home with the dough, if the rolling pin is an extension of your hands and natural sounds and noises are merely something you tune out in order to tune in to your work process, you can make your pie at any time.

A few simple things to keep in mind: Do not attempt to roll out piecrusts on a hot day. The butter or shortening will melt and the crust will stick to the board or table.

There are recipes that say chill the dough in the refrigerator before rolling it out. I find that the dough is then too stiff for me to roll out easily. I prefer to roll out the dough and then chill it in the pan if I have time. A compromise is to use ice water to make the basic dough, or to roll out the dough between sheets of wax paper. Chill, then peel the paper off the slightly frozen dough. Also, use instantized flour (Wondra) to flour the board when rolling out the crust. The dough seems to roll more easily on it and doesn't absorb too much extra flour, and the board will be very easy to clean after you've finished.

I rarely roll a pie crust that resembles a perfect circle. That seem to happen only to home economists in TV commercials or in cookbook illustrations. But who knows or cares? Just lift the asymmetrical crust onto the pie plate and trim with a knife to a circle slightly larger than the plate. That is the easiest way of dealing with the problems of pie geometry. If you should tear the crust or get a thin spot, be fearless. Make a Band-Aid of dough; wet it, apply to the crack, and press to seal. That's all there is to it. Once the filling is in the pie no one will be the wiser. If a crack appears on the top crust turn it into a steam-escape hole and decorate the top crust with pastry cutouts. Everyone will think you are Pablo Picasso and the crack will become part of a "careful design scheme."

I discovered that once I made my mind up to be successful with piecrusts I never had a problem again. Just as working with yeast is, it's mind over matter. If you believe that crust is easy and foolproof it will be. This rule of faith works for soufflés, omelets, cakes, breads, and any other area that has been giving you trouble. I know that this advice is mystical rather than culinary, but it is the best I can offer. All practical hints are lost on those who are determined to fail.

BASIC PIE CRUST

Basic Pastry I (for 2 crusts)

2 C. flour	¼ lb. butter or margarine
½ tsp. salt	or 1 C. shortening
1 Tbsp. sugar	½ C. ice water*

For a Rich Pie Crust for 1 Tart Shell

1 C. flour	½ C. sweet butter
1 egg yolk	½ tsp. lemon rind
1 Tbsp. sugar	Ice water to combine*

You may use unbleached flour for piecrusts or part whole wheat flour, part unbleached white.

Put flour on a board or in bowl. Add salt and sugar and lemon rind if desired. Stir with your fingers. Rub in the butter, margarine, or shortening. You can use less if you want. The mixture should resemble cornmeal. Add egg yolk if desired, ½–¾ C. water, as needed, to make a dough that will stick together and form into a ball. Don't handle any more than necessary.

For a baked "blind" pie crust, prick crust with fork, line with foil, weight down with rice or dry beans (red, black, pink, or white—choose your color) and bake in a 400° oven for 15–20 minutes till golden. After 10 minutes you may remove the foil and beans. They prevent the crust from puffing up. (Incidentally, the dry beans may be reused many times. Keep them in their own labeled cannister so you won't get confused and throw them into a pot of soup.)

If you don't feel like making a crust from scratch, or you don't

*In doubling piecrust and bread recipes don't automatically double the liquids. You may find that you need less. Do it by touch and eye.

have the time, it is perfectly O. K. to use a packaged *dry* mix such as Pillsbury or Betty Crocker. The frozen already-rolled piecrusts taste oily to me so I never use them.

BASIC FRUIT PIE—Apple, Peach, Pear, Apricot, or Blueberry

Pie crust Mix—1 box; or pastry for 2 crusts

Mix well:

4–6 C. peeled, sliced tart apples such as Pippins or Granny Smiths; or peaches, pears, apricots, blueberries	1 tsp. cinnamon 1 tsp. grated lemon peel 2 Tbsp. flour ¼ tsp. nutmeg, cardamom, or ginger
½ to1 C. sugar (or part brown sugar or honey) depending on sweetness of the fruit	½ C. raisins or currants, plumped up in water and drained (optional)

Place in pie crust. Dot with butter and seal with second crust. Cut slits for steam to escape. Brush top with cream. Bake in 450° oven for 10 minutes, then turn down to 350° and bake 30–40 minutes; or 375° for 50 minutes.

You may eliminate bottom crust and serve as deep dish pie with only top crust.

Or you may cover fruit with:

Streusel Topping

½ C. flour
¼ C. sugar (brown or white)
½ C. grated cheddar cheese
¼ C. melted butter

} crumbled together

and bake in 400 ° oven for 40 minutes.

Or you may omit top crust and cover with:

1 C. heavy cream	½ C. sugar (white or
⅓ C. flour	brown)

Or with:

1 C. sour cream	2 eggs
½ C. sugar (white or	2 Tbsp. flour
brown)	1 Tbsp. lemon juice

and cover this with streusel if desired.

See also Tarte Tatin, pp. 89–90.

In addition to rolling the crust, here you have the added tactile pleasure of patting the nut-butter mixture over the crust and arranging the fruit in a decorative manner.

PLUM TART

4 tsp. flour	3 Tbsp. butter, softened
½ C. ground hazelnuts,	1 9″ unbaked pie crust
filberts, or walnuts	24 prune plums, halved
⅓ C. sugar	and pitted
Lemon rind	½ C. plum or apple jelly
Cinnamon	

Combine flour, nuts, some of the sugar, lemon rind, cinnamon, and butter, and press on the bottom of the pie crust. Place plums, cut side up, in overlapping circles, on top. Sprinkle with additional sugar. Bake in 400° oven for 10 minutes, then turn down to 350° and bake for 30–40 minutes. Brush with melted jelly glaze.

Another tactile delight:

LINZERTORTE

¼	lb. sweet butter	1½	tsp. grated lemon rind
1	C. sugar	2	C. flour
2	egg yolks	1	Tbsp. cinnamon, or less
1½	C. unblanched almonds, ground finely	½	tsp. ground cloves
		1½	C. raspberry preserves

Heat oven to 350°. Cream butter and sugar well. Add egg yolks and beat well. Stir in the almonds and lemon rind. Sift flour, cinnamon, and cloves together and fold into the creamed mixture. Knead the dough till it is firm and holds together. Grease a pie tin with a removable bottom. Pat ⅔ of the dough into the pan (or a bit less). The layer should be about ½" thick. Spread with the preserves. Roll out the rest of the dough and cut into strips. Roll each strip so it is about ½" wide. (This dough is rich and crumbly. Roll it between sheets of waxed paper, chill well, then cut; or form into lattice strips by rolling ropes of dough with your fingers.) Make a rim about the tart and lattice the top. Bake 40–50 minutes. Cool. Cut into wedges.

See Chez Panisse almond tart, p. 317
Two pies that could be dinner!

Crust

2	C. flour	¼	C. butter
	Cold Water	¼	C. shortening

Prepare piecrust as explained on p. 183. Line a 9" pie plate with half the pastry.

SPINACH PIE

2	lbs. fresh spinach, or 2 10-oz. pkgs. frozen chopped spinach		Salt and pepper
		½	tsp. or more cinnamon
		½	tsp. cayenne pepper
3	Tbsp. chicken, goose, or bacon fat or butter	2	C. ricotta cheese
2	Tbsp. flour	4	hard-boiled eggs, thickly sliced or halved

Optional

1 small onion, chopped	Diced ham
¼ C. pine nuts	
¼ C. currants, plumped in warm water	

Preheat oven to 375°.

Wash and shred fresh spinach, then cook in the water that clings; or thaw and squeeze dry frozen spinach.

Melt chicken fat or butter. Sauté onion, if used, for a minute or two. Add flour and cook till golden. Add spinach and heat it through. Season with spices and add pine nuts, currants and/or ham, if desired. Cool.

Spread the ricotta cheese on the piecrust. Add the spinach mixture and top with sliced or halved hard-boiled eggs. Cover with remaining pastry. Seal and crimp the crusts together, cut a steam hole, brush with cream, bake for 40 minutes or till golden. This is best served lukewarm or at room temperature. You may substitute Swiss chard or beet greens for spinach. (Serves 6.)

PIZZA RUSTICA

Crust

2 C. flour	¼ lb. butter
3 Tbsp. sugar	2 eggs
2 tsp. baking powder	

Filling

½ lb. Italian sausage*	½ C. grated parmesan
½ lb. lean pork, in cubes	½ lb. cubed mozzarella
4 eggs	Chopped parsley
2 lbs. ricotta cheese	Salt, pepper, nutmeg

Optional

Sliced hard-boiled eggs
Cooked chopped spinach
Sautéed onions or minced green onion

*If you can't find Italian sausage, try Polish or Portuguese.

Mix the crust ingredients and allow to rest for 10 minutes. You may need to flour the board well to roll it out. Place half in a Pyrex or metal square baking dish about 9″ × 9″.

Fry the sausage till cooked through. Crumble it. Fry the pork till cooked. Combine the cooked meats (you may use only sausage if you like) with the eggs and ricotta and other cheeses. Add parsley and season to taste. Chopped spinach, sliced hard-boiled eggs, sautéed onion may be added. Pour onto bottom crust dough and cover with the rest of the dough. Seal well; you may brush with egg yolk. Prick the crust for a steam escape. Bake for about one hour at 400°. Cool in the oven.

Cut into squares This is best served at room temperature.

QUICHES

A quiche is also a pie. Unfortunately, along with the crepe, the quiche has become a culinary cliché. I shudder every time I see one on a menu. The quiche has been much abused: made too stringy with melted cheese, given soggy crusts, eked out with fillings that are overcooked, and filled with flour so that it could be prepared ahead of time and frozen. (A true custard, which is what quiches are filled with, contains no flour and cannot survive the freezing process. It separates and becomes watery.)

All the aforementioned disasters can be avoided if you make the quiche on the day you plan to eat it, or prepare it just before serving. It doesn't take to sitting around for days. Quiche is excellent warm or at room temperature. It should not be *so* hot that the custard is still runny. (It firms up as it cools.) Let it sit ten minutes before bringing it from the oven to the table.

The crust should be prebaked for about twenty minutes to help it remain crisp under the weight of a liquid custard mixture. I usually sprinkle some of the grated cheese on the prebaked crust while it is hot so it will melt over the holes and prevent potential leaking. (See basic piecrust, p. 183, for instructions.)

Making the crust is Meditative but assembling the filling can be High Energy.

Essentially, the quiche filling is eggs and cream, combined with any chopped-up meat, seafood, or vegetable you desire, some grated cheese, and appropriate choice of seasoning. It is a good way to dispose of leftover odds and ends that won't feed two or three people well for dinner but will be satisfying to them if cooked in a quiche.

The assembling of the eggs, cream, and filling is rapid and can be adapted to your personal rhythm. You can speed up the filling process by chopping quickly and sautéeing rapidly, or you can do it slowly and deliberately. Determine your pace and flow with it.

ZUCCHINI QUICHE

4	zucchini, sliced ¼" thick	¾	C. grated Swiss cheese
	Salt and pepper	3	eggs
1	9" pie crust (p. 183) prebaked 15–20 minutes at 450°	1	C. heavy cream
		¼	tsp. nutmeg

Parboil zucchini in lightly salted water for 3 minutes; drain.

Sprinkle bottom of pie shell with ¼ C. cheese. Arrange zucchini in decorative circular pattern in the pie shell. Lightly season with salt and pepper.

In a cup, lightly beat the eggs with the cream, salt, pepper, and nutmeg. Pour over zucchini. Sprinkle with remaining grated Swiss cheese, and bake in 350° oven for 35 minutes, or till custard is set.

This quiche can be made with precooked asparagus or spinach, sautéed mushrooms, sautéed onions, and crumbled cooked bacon or diced ham and green onions.

QUICHE OF CLAMS—Clam Pie

Filling

1	9" pie shell	3	eggs
1	7–oz. can minced clams (or baby shrimp or crab)	1	C. heavy cream
2	Tbsp. grated onions or minced green onions	½	tsp. curry powder
		½	tsp. lemon juice
1	Tbsp. finely chopped parsley	½	tsp. Worcestershire

Drain the clams, reserving liquid, and arrange the clams, onions and parsley on the pastry. Beat the eggs thoroughly. Add the cream, clam juice, curry powder, lemon juice, and Worcestershire, and stir. Pour the mixture over the clams, onions, and parsley. Bake at 375° until the custard sets and is golden, about 40 minutes.

This recipe for pork "en croûte" is most unusual because the meat does not have to be precooked before it is wrapped in the crust. I first ate this at the home of artist Beth Van Hoesen. She found the recipe in a French magazine, translated it into English, made a few changes, and passed it on to me. Although it tastes complex, it is very simple to prepare.

BETH VAN HOESEN'S ROAST OF PORK EN CROÛTE

2–2½ lbs. boneless pork loin roast, well trimmed of fat

½ C. Dijon mustard
1 tsp. dried tarragon

Crust:

2–2½ C. flour
1 C. butter

Salt
½ C. water

Prepare dough by putting flour in bowl and mixing in small pieces of butter, salt, water. Roll dough out on a floured board when almost at room temperature, into an oblong slightly larger than the roast. Spread dough with mustard, sprinkle with tarragon, place pork on it, and seal well, wetting dough and pressing down with tines of a fork. Use envelope fold. Place in a shallow buttered baking pan, seam side down. You may decorate with pastry cutouts of leftover dough. (Roast can be refrigerated at this point and baked later.)

Brush dough with beaten egg just before placing in 400°–450° oven for 1 hour and 15 minutes.

Serve with

Mustard-flavored Cream Sauce

3 Tbsp. butter
1½–2 Tbsp. flour
Salt and pepper
3 Tbsp. or more Dijon
mustard

1½ C. milk or cream or
combined (or part
buttermilk or low-fat
milk)

Melt butter in saucepan. Add flour and stir well with a whisk. Gradually add the milk or cream and simmer, stirring, till thickened. For a thinner sauce use less flour or more milk. Add mustard and salt and pepper to taste.

See chicken pie, p. 91, chicken breasts en croûte, p. 92 for similar process.

PASTA

Although pasta takes but minutes to cook and qualifies as genuine Fast Food, the preparation of pasta dough is Meditation pure and simple. The mixing, the rhythmic kneading, feeling the dough go from crumbly to cohesive to elastic and satiny, is quite a tactile experience. Whether you decide to roll it by hand, pulling and stretching the dough over the rolling pin, or in a machine, there is sufficient repetition and ritual to keep you totally centered in the process.

FRESH PASTA

3 C. flour
4 eggs
1 tsp. salt

3–5 Tbsp. water
1 Tbsp. olive oil

Put the flour and salt on a kneading surface. Make a well in the center and stir in the eggs and oil, incorporating a bit more flour with each stir. Add water to make a firm dough. Knead for about 10 minutes. Cover the dough and let it rest for 20 minutes. Separate into 4 parts. Roll each out as thinly as humanly possible, or roll out in a pasta machine. Let pasta sheets rest 10 minutes, then cut to the size noodles you want. This makes about enough pasta for 6.

For green noodles, puree 10 large spinach leaves in the blender with the eggs. Proceed with the green egg mixture in the center of the flour well. (For detailed instructions on pasta making, see Ed Giobbi's *Italian Family Cooking* and Marcella Hazan's *The Classic Italian Cookbook*—details in Bibliography, p. 362.)

Chapter 21

FILLO DOUGH AS A MEDITATION

Working with fillo is a Meditation. There is rhythm, repetition, and ritual. (In fact, sometimes it can seem endless, all those layers and layers of dough, the eternal buttering.) Once you have melted the butter, unwrapped the fillo and cut the sheets to the desired size, and mixed the filling, you can immerse yourself in the process. While your hands are involved in lifting the paper-thin sheets of dough, dipping the soft brush into the liquid golden butter, brushing and stroking, lightly and evenly, your mind is free to flow into other spaces. You are calm, reflective. The dough feels like silk on your fingers, the brush glides over the surface. If you are molding the fillo into particular shapes, such as triangles or cylinders, there are the additional pleasures of working with your fingers to create the traditional forms, the folding, the rolling. Again, if you are easily rattled by lots of noise and diversion in your kitchen, put a note on your door that you are not to be disturbed. Wear a comfortable garment, one that will not restrict your movement. No free-flowing sleeves to flow into the butter. Get in touch with your breathing, your heartbeat, your calm center; then proceed and enjoy the process.

I hear some of you mumbling, All well and good, this sounds like fun, but what the hell *is* fillo dough?

It is a thin pastry that resembles sheets of typing paper and can

193

be found at stores that specialize in Middle Eastern or "gourmet" foods. Don't let the thinness of this dough fool you. It may look incredibly fragile, but you should approach it boldly and with a firm hand. It is almost indestructible. Usually you are building up a series of layers with the dough, so if it tears you can patch it. If one sheet is a bit ragged or short you will never know because it will be concealed under other layers. There are recipes that advise you to cover the fillo with a damp cloth while working. I find that the damp cloth has a tendency to stick to the dough and makes it harder to work with, so I prefer to use plastic wrap. When the fillo is exposed to air for any length of time, if not brushed with melted butter or oil, it will dry out, crack, crumble, and start flying around the room. You'll avoid problems if you take out just as many sheets as you think you can handle quickly and leave the others rolled up and covered with plastic wrap to prevent dryness.

Fillo is very easy to work with if the dough is fresh. However, you may live in a part of the country where the only fillo available is frozen. Don't be discouraged. Persevere. Some brands of frozen fillo are better than others. When you find a good one, you will want to wrap almost everything in fillo. It is light and flaky when baked and entails half the work of puff pastry. You simply brush melted butter between sheets to achieve the flaky effect. No complicated rolling and folding and chilling and rolling and folding. Pastries made with fillo can be frozen *unbaked*. You can also assemble the dishes completely and refrigerate for a few days before baking. The melted butter acts as a preservative. Refrigerating the assembled pastries even for ten minutes facilitates slicing before baking. Once the pastries are baked, however, do not refrigerate them or they will become soggy. All their wonderful crispness will be lost. Just keep them at room temperature, loosely covered. If you prefer to eat them hot, you may reheat them in a 350° oven for 15–20 minutes.

Fillo is so versatile and easy to use that you'll invent a few recipes of your own, I'm sure. It is a wonderful means of presenting traditional foods in a new way.

BOREK—Greek Cheese Pastries (and some variations)

1 lb. feta cheese	4 Tbsp. minced parsley
8 oz. Monterey-Jack or mild Swiss cheese	½ tsp. nutmeg
8 oz. cream cheese	Pepper (optional)
3–4 eggs	1 lb. fillo dough
	1½ C. melted butter

Crumble the feta cheese with your fingers and place it in a bowl. Grate the Monterey-Jack with a hand grater or in the blender.

Put cream cheese and eggs in the blender. Blend till liquefied. Combine the blended eggs with the cheeses. Add the parsley, nutmeg, and pepper if desired.

Cut the dough to the size of your baking dish. (This fills 2 pans approximately 9"x11"x1½".) Layer 11 sheets of fillo in each pan, brushing each with melted butter before placing the next on top of it. Place a layer of the cheese mixture in each dish, then cover with 15 more buttered layers of fillo. Cut into squares or diamonds.

Bake in a 375°–400° oven till golden, 45 minutes or so. This can be frozen unbaked.

For tiropetes (Greek borek), cut dough into 3"x12" strips, butter, place a tsp. of filling at one corner, and fold in triangles, like folding the flag. Take one end corner and fold it diagonally to the opposite edge; then fold the triangular end over the folded edge; repeat till all of the strip is folded up into a final triangle. Variations on borek:

BOREGI—Turkish Borek (Deep-Fried Cheese Pastries)

Filling   Fillo sheets—16"x12"

1 lb. feta cheese, mashed	1½–2 sticks melted butter
fine	2 eggs
2–3 eggs	⅓ C. milk
¼ C. parsley, chopped	

Mix filling ingredients. Brush one sheet with butter. Fold in half (6"x16"). Brush again. Place 2 Tbsp. filling in a long strip, about 3"x½", at the center of one end. Fold pastry edges in by ½" and roll up into a tight cylinder. Brush with beaten eggs and milk. Deep fry at 375° for 3 minutes, or till golden on all sides. Drain.

SPANOKOPITA—Greek Spinach Pie

3 Tbsp. butter	spinach, thawed and
1 large onion, chopped, or	squeezed dry
1 bunch green onions,	1 Tbsp. dried dill or
minced	2–3 Tbsp. fresh
1 clove garlic, minced	cheese filling from basic
2 boxes chopped frozen	borek recipe

Melt butter. Sauté onion and garlic till soft. Add spinach and dill and stir fry till moisture evaporates. Mix with the cheese filling in the basic borek recipe and bake as directed. You may want to increase the nutmeg by another ½ tsp.

See Mrs. Nicholas' Leek Pie, p. 303, for one more variation. Also beef Wellington, pp. 83–84, and meat loaf in fillo, p. 85.

The ultimate fillo pie! This is a great supper with just a salad. It is very rich and aromatic. Have large napkins on hand, because it's a little messy to eat, but well worth every crumb in the lap.

BASTILLA—Moroccan Pigeon Pie

4	lbs. pigeons or squabs, or a 2½ lb. pheasant, or 2 small chickens with giblets and livers, or just 2 large whole chicken breasts. (Pigeons and squabs are very expensive. Therefore I use chicken. You will need about 2–3 cups of shredded cooked meat for the bastilla.) Salt and black pepper	1½	tsp. ginger
		1	tsp. ground cumin, or a bit more
		½	tsp. cayenne
		½	tsp. turmeric
		1½	tsp. cinnamon
		⅛	tsp. saffron
		1	C. water
		7	eggs
		1½	C. slivered, blanched almonds
12	Tbsp. sweet butter	2	Tbsp. sugar
1	C. chopped onions		Fillo dough
2	Tbsp. chopped fresh coriander	8–12	Tbsp. sweet butter, melted
1	Tbsp. chopped parsley	3	Tbsp. confectioners' sugar with 1 Tbsp. cinnamon

Clean birds, setting aside giblets and livers, and rub with salt and pepper. Melt 8 Tbsp. butter in heavy pot and brown birds evenly, turning often. Set meat aside on platter.

To the fat in the pot add the onions, giblets, and livers and cook 5 minutes, until soft. Add all herbs and spices, except ½ tsp. cinnamon, and water, and bring to a boil, stirring constantly. Put birds and their accumulated juices back in the pot. Reduce the heat to low. Cover and simmer 1 hour.

Cool birds and cut meat into 2"x1" strips. Pour 1½ C. of the sauce remaining in the pot into a bowl and set aside. Bring the rest up to a boil and reduce to 4–5 Tbsp. of glaze. Reserve the glaze and return the 1½ C. of sauce to the pot.

Beat the eggs and stir into the hot sauce, stirring till soft curds form. Stir in reserved glaze and set aside.

Melt remaining butter. Add almonds and fry 5 minutes, until lightly browned. Drain on paper towels, then chop coarsely. Mix with sugar and ½ tsp. cinnamon.

Butter a large pizza pan.* Brush 6 sheets of fillo with melted butter and overlap into a circle on the pan. (Some of it will overhang the pan.) Brush 4–6 more folded in the center of the circle. Sprinkle with half the almond-sugar mix. Then spread with half the egg mix. Top with strips of meat, then eggs, then almonds. Brush overhanging fillo on top. Fold over. Add 6–8 more sheets on top, brushing with butter as you go. Tuck edges under or fold back over on top and cover with 3–4 circles of fillo. Can refrigerate at this point for a day or so.

Bake in 350° oven for 25 minutes. Drain excess butter. Bake 20 minutes more till golden brown. Sprinkle with sugar-cinnamon mixture. Serve in 10 minutes, when not too hot to eat with fingers.

Do not refrigerate desserts baked with fillo dough. They will get soggy. Keep them at room temperature, loosely covered.

DRIED FRUIT STRUDEL

Crust

1 lb. sweet butter	1 lb. fillo dough

Filling

1 C. chopped dates	1 tsp. dried orange rind
¾ C. yellow raisins	1 tsp. dried lemon rind
4 C. minced dried apples	1½ tsp. cinnamon
1½ C. chopped walnuts or pistachios	Juice of 3 oranges
	1 tsp. cardamom

Syrup

2 C. sugar	4 Tbsp. orange flower water
1 C. water	
½ C. honey	

*Bastilla is traditionally round in shape. I use a 14" pizza pan with a raised edge. You may use 2 8" or 9" pie pans or square baking pans instead.

Mix filling ingredients. Preheat oven to 350°. Melt butter. Separate fillo dough into three equal parts and cover two parts well until you get to them. Butter about 8 layers of fillo. Place a strip of fruit along one long edge of the stack. Fold in edges and roll up. Repeat twice more. Place the three strudels on a buttered baking sheet and bake 30 minutes, or until brown. Mix syrup ingredients and simmer 10 minutes till thickened. Pour the syrup over the hot strudels.

See Iranian baklava, p. 353.

Chapter 22

PRESERVING AS A MEDITATION

Preserving is a totally Meditative cooking activity. Every aspect of the preserving process involves some sort of rhythm, repetition, and ritual. The fruits and vegetables are to be cleaned, pitted, peeled, sliced, diced, or chopped. The stirring of the preserve is usually done slowly and constantly. You must pay attention to see that the preserves don't burn or get too thick. The jars are to be washed, the lids boiled, the labels prepared.

There has been a rebirth of home preserving and canning in America. After years of eating ready-made, anonymous jams, jellies, chutneys, and the like, we have come to realize that personal choice of flavoring and texture is usually better and more interesting than the mass-produced, middle-of-the-road, watered-down, preservative-laden commercial products.

I never thought that I would be interested in preserving. It seemed so grandmotherly and rustic. How did an urban bird like me get involved in this old-fashioned craft? Nine years ago I was up in Sacramento visiting friends who happened to have an overabundant apricot tree. They had dried apricots, apricot jam, and puree bulging out of their pantry and pleaded with me to take three huge bags of apricots back home. Because I love apricots and had visions of tarts and puddings floating around in my head, I said, "Sure," never dreaming of what a trip this was about to send me on.

When I got home I made a few pies and a mousse, and ate so many apricots I was sure I couldn't face another one till the next summer. There were still two and a half bags of rapidly ripening fruit sitting on my kitchen floor, smelling wonderful and reminding me of their presence. I couldn't bring myself to throw them out. I gave some away, but the fruit seemed to be multiplying in the bags. Finally I decided that I, Joyce of the Subways, would try to make jam. I got the one or two books I could find on the subject (these were the days before the big preserving and back-to-the-kitchen revival, when books on canning and home preserving were few and far between) and read all I could about jam preparation. I bought some canning jars with rubber-lined enamel lids, took my spaghetti pot off the shelf, and got to work. Before I knew it, I was obsessed. I made jam. I made chutney. I invented a sweet-and-sour sauce reminiscent of my childhood days in Chinese restaurants in Brooklyn. If apricots were so easy, why not peaches? And berries?

One year later my basement looked like an emergency food shelter. I had thousands of jars filled with tasty and beautiful preserves. They looked wonderful glowing on the shelves. I admired my handiwork proudly and smiled with delight every time I opened one of my jars of jam. Came the Christmas holidays, instead of making pâtés or cookies for friends, I gave them some chutney and assorted jams. They were delighted. During the year, while I was teaching curry to my students, we opened up some of the chutney to serve with the meal. The next thing I knew I had students begging to learn how to make their own chutneys and conserves.

So when June and July rolled around I found myself with an enthusiastic commune of mad preservers. Like the farm wives of old, we met a few mornings and evenings a week and worked as a team, cutting and chopping fruits, sterilizing jars, measuring and weighing, sealing and labeling. It was great fun and we were incredibly prolific. Having a team to prepare the fruit and do all the tedious and time-consuming chopping was a great help. I thought, too, of those endless hours I had spent in the kitchen cutting up pounds of peaches by myself, and I realized that three of us could do six pounds in about a half hour. Let's hear it for group Meditation!

All this preamble is to encourage you to make some of these goodies for yourself. They are easy to prepare, they keep for years, and they are better than many products you can buy. You will enjoy the process; you may find that there is a friend with whom you would like to share the experience, the work, and the results. You and your friends and family will be enjoying the fruits of your labor for years to come.

For preserving you will need some very basic and inexpensive equipment. You may already have most of it in your kitchen. First and foremost, you will need a large, deep pot, the kind you cook pasta or soup in, and some long-handled wooden spoons for stirring. (Wooden handles will not get hot during the many times you will be reaching down into the pot of hot fruits to scrape the bottom to prevent sticking and scorching.) Also, some long potholder mitts are essential. There is no worse burn than a hot sugar burn. You will need a ladle, some tongs to lift the hot lids onto the jars, and a wide-mouthed funnel for filling the jars without slopping. Most supermarkets today carry a line of canning jars such as Ball or Kerr. You may want to buy a package of gummed labels at the stationery store. That is all the equipment you need, except for the fruit, which you should buy at the peak of its season in bulk. (A crate of fruit is infinitely cheaper than buying by the pound at your local market.) If you are on good terms with the produce man at your market he may save you all the overripe and slightly bruised fruit that he cannot sell. In exchange, give him a jar or two of the goodies you create. You may find him bruising fruit in the back room on purpose to get some more of the loot.

In our city there is a local farmers' market where the small farmers from the surrounding towns come to sell their yield. Much of this fruit is organic, i.e., unsprayed. It is reasonable in price and very fresh. If you have friends with fruit trees, offer them some preserves in exchange for some of the fruits that they won't be able to consume. When a tree is ready and ripe it cannot wait, so you will have more than enough to work with.

One of the most frequently asked questions in the preserving class is "Will we get botulism from the things we make?" Students have visions of themselves and their families lying prostrate on the floor after tasting a jar of homemade apricot jam. So let's put all worries to rest right now. Four things can cause spoilage in preserved foods: enzymes, molds, yeasts, and bacteria. They are all affected by heat. The enzymes are not at all dangerous, but they can change the color and texture of foods and make them look unappealing. They are usually destroyed in the cooking process at 140° Fahrenheit.

Molds are caused by fungi and are usually eliminated at 120°–140°. This doesn't mean that mold won't occasionally appear at the top of a jar of preserves when the jar has been improperly sterilized before sealing. This is a rare occurrence, but if it happens to you, don't panic. The mold is not dangerous, merely unpleasant in taste. Very often the food underneath is unaffected by its presence. Simply spoon it off and taste the remaining preserve. If the flavor or aroma of the mold is all-pervasive, chuck the jar of preserves. If not, the preserve is safe to eat.

Yeasts are also fungi, and they cause fermentation, like the fizziness in beer. But fizziness is not what you want in banana jam or apple butter. Yeasts are destroyed at 140°–190°, and will affect foods that have been improperly sealed. They will not hurt you, but they spoil the food.

Finally, there are bacteria, of which the botulism germ is an example. Most are destroyed under very high heat, about 250°. The botulism germ *can* grow in the sealed airless container, and its spores are very resistant to heat. However, *high acid foods*, while they may allow molds and yeasts, *do not promote the growth of heat-resistant bacteria*. The more acid in a fruit or vegetable, the more impossible it is for germs like botulism to occur. Low acid or nonacid foods like meats, fish, and certain vegetables are likely to promote the growth of the heat-resistant germs, and these are the ones I avoid. The only foods I preserve are high in acid and will *not* foster the growth of botulism.

For further information on botulism and germs in general, may I recommend the U.S.D.A. Consumer Service Home and

Garden Bulletin #162, "Keeping Food Safe to Eat," which you can get from the U.S. Government Printing Office in Washington, D.C. This ought to set your mind at ease.

To sterilize the canning jars before filling them, you can put them through the hottest cycle of your dishwasher, if you have one, and keep them hot, or you can pour boiling water into each jar, let it sit for about two minutes and pour it out, and then fill the jars with the hot preserves. Boil the lids for about five minutes, to soften the rubber. Then with the tongs lift the hot lids onto the clean jar tops and screw on the rims tightly. Wait till the jars cool and then test them for a perfect seal. Usually you will hear a chorus of "pings" as the vacuum forms inside the jar (as the contents of the jar cool, they contract, literally sucking down the lid to fill the vacuum) to let you know that the lid has sealed. To be sure, after the jars have cooled, unscrew the rims; if the lid stays down you will know that the jars are perfectly sealed. If by some chance a few have not sealed (and this may occur if the jars and the lids were not hot enough), then reboil the contents and the lid and resterilize the jar and start again. There is no need to throw out the jam or chutney. If only one jar out of a batch failed to seal, then eat it quickly or keep it in the refrigerator. There are no chemicals or preservatives in home products, therefore once opened they will not keep forever. Unopened, they will keep for years. Some jams and jellies will darken in color as they age, but they will still taste very good and will be perfectly safe to eat. As a matter of fact, I think that the chutneys and sweet-and-sour sauces improve with age. I advise people to wait at least six months to use a batch of chutney so that the kick from the vinegar dies down and the chutney flavors have a chance to mellow and harmonize.

The only exception to all this information pertains to the dill pickles, which are *cold packed*. The jars are filled with cold water and the lids do not seal. The pickles are fermenting in the brine solution and cannot spoil as long as you keep them closed. They are ready to eat in about six weeks, and to get them crisp, the jar should be opened first, then closed and placed in the refrigerator for one day so that the pickles will firm up.

One more technical term before you can get cooking, and that is "hot-water bath." This means putting the *sealed jars* in a deep pot, covering with boiling water, and covering the pot and simmering for the amount of time specified in the recipe. This kills bacteria and perfects the seal. This advice is given on only a few of the recipes, mostly those involving vegetables.

The test for jam and jelly readiness is the plate test. It is really very simple. While simmering the preserves, keep a stack of plates in the freezer. When you think the jam is thick enough, drop a spoonful or two on the cold plate. If it firms up a bit and doesn't continue running, the jam is ready to seal in the jars. Blueberry and blackberry jams should be sealed when they are still a little runny because they are very high in natural pectin and seem to get very thick and hard if cooked too long.

I hope that all this talk of jars and germs and sterilizing, and tongs and potholders, hasn't scared any of you off. Actually, preserving is so easy and so much fun you will get hooked before you know it. There is incredible satisfaction that comes from opening a jar of chutney or jam that wasn't thickened with artificial pectin and filled with preservatives in some factory. The aroma of ripe fruits of summer will make you feel that all is well with the world.

For more on preserving, freezing, and drying, see:

The Complete Book of Home Preserving, by Ann Seranne. (Garden City, N.Y.: Doubleday and Company, 1953.)

Putting Food By, by Rita Hertzberg, Beatrice Vaughan, and Janet Greene. (Brattleboro, Vt.: The Stephen Greene Press, 1973.)

Home Preserving Made Easy, by Vera Gewanter and Dorothy Parker. (New York: The Viking Press, 1975.)

Fine Preserving, by Catherine Plagemann. (New York: Simon and Schuster, 1967.) Not just basic recipes and techniques, as in the other books. Here you'll find some really unusual recipes.

For toast, crepe, and cake fillings:

STRAWBERRY PRESERVES

Put equal amount of berries and sugar in pot, stir to coat, and let sit 24 hours. Bring to boil. Let boil 5–7 minutes. Remove berries with slotted spoon. Distribute equally in hot jars. Boil syrup to jellying point, adding lemon juice to taste and excess liquid from berries (As the berries sit in the jars they will release additional juices.) Add syrup to jars. You may want to add a bit of honey to each jar. Stir to distribute berries. Seal and store.

RASPBERRY HONEY JAM

4 C. raspberries	Lemon juice
3 C. sugar	Honey

Let raspberries and sugar sit for a few hours. Cook till thickened. You can strain through a strainer to remove the seeds. Add lemon juice and honey to taste. Put in jars, seal, and store. (Only 4 half-pint jars, alas.)

APRICOT JAM

4 lb. apricots (about 8 C.)	4 Tbsp. lemon juice
6 C. sugar	

Pit and quarter the ripe apricots. (You should let them sit 12–24 hours before cooking so they can release some of their juices.) Add sugar and lemon juice. Stir and bring to boil. Simmer till thick jelly syrup forms (about 220°). You may want to remove apricots with slotted spoon and cook syrup down. Seal and store. (Makes 8–10 half-pint jars.)

For apricot-orange jam, add 1 orange ground in the blender with the lemon juice.

PEACH JAM

12 C. peaches, peeled and chopped
¼ C. lemon juice or more

9 C. sugar
Almond extract, at least 2 tsp.

Mix peaches, lemon juice, and sugar, and simmer till thick, stirring often. Add almond extract to taste when done. You may want more lemon, too. (You may cook with 6–10 oz. chopped candied ginger for a variation and serve over ice cream.) (Makes 10–12 half-pint jars.)

You may do this with pears and ginger, adding 2 C. yellow raisins and 1 Tbsp. grated lemon rind for a variation.

SPICED FIG JAM

Juice of 1 orange
1 lemon—rind and all
5 oz. preserved ginger
5 lb. purple figs, chopped fine
2 tsp. Five Spices powder

(if you don't have this add ½ tsp. powdered cloves.)
2 tsp. cinnamon
7 C. sugar

Combine orange juice, lemon, and ginger in blender. Add to other ingredients in cooking pot. Cook till thick. Pour into jars and seal. (Makes 10 half-pint jars.)

For plum conserve, grind 2 whole oranges and 1 lemon in blender. Omit ginger and Five Spices, and cut cinnamon to ½ tsp.

BAR LE DUC

4 C. honey
10 C. sugar

6 C. water
14 C. fresh currants

Boil honey, water, and sugar till quite thick. Add currants and simmer one or two minutes. Remove currants with slotted

208

spoon and keep warm in the jars. (Distribute currants equally; place jars in pan of hot water.) Reboil syrup till quite thick (use plate test) and taste: You may want more honey. Pour over fruit. Stir once and seal. Use excess syrup as glaze for tarts. If berries overcook or get too runny, you may add 2–4 boxes of rasberries and cook until thick. Eat with cream cheese on crackers for dessert. (Makes 18 ½-pint jars.)

PRESERVED PEARS OR QUINCES

4	lb. pears or quinces		Cinnamon stick
1	bottle rosé wine	1	tsp. cardamom
8	C. sugar		(optional)
2–3	C. water (optional)		

Peel and core fruit, cut in slices or chunks or halves. Poach in syrup of other ingredients, till clear. Add cardamom if desired, and reduce syrup if necessary. Cook 1 hour, let sit 12 hours, cook 1 hour more.

A few chutneys. These are excellent with the traditional curries and roast meats. They also make great sandwiches when combined with cream cheese.

MANGO CHUTNEY

2	large onions	3–4	C. brown sugar
4	cloves garlic	2	tsp. salt
1–2	limes	1	Tbsp. cinnamon
3–4	C. Cider vinegar	1	tsp. allspice
8	oz. preserved ginger	1	tsp. cloves
5	lb. mangoes, peeled and sliced	¼	tsp. cayenne
2	firm papayas, peeled and sliced	1	C. raisins

Combine onions, garlic, limes, vinegar, and ginger in blender. Add to all other ingredients in cooking pot, and boil gently 1 hour, stirring often. (Makes 6–7 pints.)

PEACH CHUTNEY

⅔ C. preserved ginger
1 onion
2 cloves garlic
1 qt. cider vinegar
4 lb. peaches
½ lb. raisins

1½ tsp.–1 Tbsp. red chili
powder or 1½ tsp.
cayenne
2–3 Tbsp. mustard seed
1 Tbsp. salt
1½ lb. brown sugar

You may chop ginger, onion, and garlic in blender with vinegar. Combine with other ingredients in cooking pot and simmer slowly for 1 hour, stirring often. Seal and store. (Makes 5 pints.)

PEAR CHUTNEY

10 oz. preserved ginger
2 large onions
4 oranges
3 C. cider vinegar
5–6 lb. (16 C.) sliced Anjou
or Comice pears, firm
2 lb. light brown sugar

2 boxes yellow raisins
2 tsp. cloves
2 tsp. cinnamon
1 tsp. salt
1 tsp. cayenne
1 large can pineapple
chunks

In blender, puree ginger, onions, oranges, and vinegar. Combine with other ingredients in cooking pot and simmer till thick. (Makes 8 pints.)

Less chunky than chutney and smoother—and equally delicious:

PLUM OR APRICOT SWEET-AND-SOUR SAUCE
(For Chinese roast pork, roast chicken, turkey)

2	large onions	2	C. yellow raisins
5–10	oz. preserved ginger	4	C. brown sugar
8	cloves garlic	2	tsp. cinnamon
3	C. cider vinegar	1	tsp. cloves
12	C. apricots or red or blue plums, pitted and chopped	1	tsp. allspice
		3	tsp. salt
		1	tsp. cayenne pepper

Puree in blender the onions, ginger, garlic, and vinegar. Combine with other ingredients in cooking pot, and simmer till thick. If the plums are too soupy after 1 hour, add 1–2 packages of dried minced apples and cook 20 minutes more. (Makes about 8 pints.)

SAM ESTERKYN'S DILL PICKLES

12	lb. small pickling cucumbers, scrubbed and soaked in ice water	1	bulb garlic
2	large bunches dill		Pickling spice
			Kosher salt
			Celery, optional

In each jar place:

	Cucumbers	1	tsp. pickling spice
2	sprigs dill	1½	Tbsp. salt
2	cloves garlic, smashed		Piece of celery

Fill jars with cold water. Boil lids. Fasten rims tightly. Let sit at least one month; best 5–6 months later. You can do this with green tomatoes and chili peppers. (Makes about 12 quarts)

CARROT PICKLES

16 medium carrots, scraped and sliced into julienne strips (4 C.)
1 onion, peeled and sliced thin (½ C.)
¾–1 C. sugar
½ tsp. salt
¼ tsp. celery seed
1 Tbsp. vegetable oil
2 C. white vinegar
¼ tsp. whole cloves
1 Tbsp. fresh sliced ginger root
½ tsp. cinnamon

Toss carrots and onion together and pack into hot sterilized jars. In 4-qt. enamel pot, combine the rest of the ingredients. Bring to a boil and simmer 3 minutes, stirring till sugar dissolves. Ladle over vegetables. Seal. Process 10 minutes in hot-water bath. (Makes 2 quarts)

CATHERINE PLAGEMANN'S PAPAYA PICKLE

1 C. white sugar
½ C. white wine vinegar
½ C. water
1 small bay leaf (optional)
12 cloves or more
2 cinnamon sticks, broken up a bit
2 Tbsp. papaya seeds
2 large papayas, not too ripe

Bring all the ingredients to a boil except the papayas and cook for a few minutes. Add the papayas, cut into chunks. Simmer for about 15 minutes. Put it into freshly cleaned jars and seal. Good with curry, roast chicken, or turkey. You may do this with cantaloupe. 1 med. large cantaloupe = 2 papayas. (Makes about 3–4 half pints.)

A final frivolity—for garnishing cakes, desserts:

CANDIED FLOWERS

QUICK CANDIED FLOWERS

Roses, violets, orange flowers, mint leaves, etc.

1   egg white, beaten till   Superfine granulated
    foamy   sugar

Stem the flowers and wipe the petals clean. Brush each petal with egg white (use a paint brush) and then swish in a bowl or bag of fine sugar. Set out to dry on a dish covered with more sugar. Keep in a warm spot till ready to use. These will hold up for a few hours.

NOT-SO-QUICK CANDIED FLOWERS

1   lb. flower petals   2   C. sugar
1   C. cold water   Pinch of cream of tartar

Wash the petals in ice water. Dry on towels, carefully wiping up the excess moisture. Put them on baker's parchment or paper towels to air. Combine water and 2 C. sugar in a deep pot till dissolved. Add the cream of tartar and cook the syrup till 240° (soft ball). Remove the syrup from the heat and submerge the flowers in the syrup, pushing them down with a wooden spoon. Bring back to a boil, remove from the heat immediately, then pour the flowers and syrup into a cold bowl. Let sit overnight.

In the morning remove the flowers with a slotted spoon and place them on a rack with waxed paper beneath. Add the ½ C. sugar to the pot, add the syrup, and stir till dissolved over high heat. Cook again to 240°. Add the flowers, remove from heat, and let set again overnight in a bowl in the syrup.

The next day drain the petals on a rack, bring the syrup up to a boil, and add the petals. Remove from heat and stir the petals till the syrup starts to get grainy. Have sheets of unglazed white paper (baker's parchment, typing paper, etc.). Pour the flowers and the syrup on the paper. Shake the flowers to separate them and leave them to dry. Store them in an airtight jar or tin cannister with sheets of white paper separating the layers. These will keep for months.

Chapter 23

FAST FOODS:

High Energy Cooking, Physical and Mental

Just recently I offered a class entitled "Fast Foods," a course for those who would like to eat well but who don't want to spend ten hours in the kitchen, and whose every meal need not be a production number. The response was most enthusiastic but a little perplexing. I was amazed to find out how many people were embarrassed and defensive about signing up for such a class. Many expressed feelings of guilt for not taking a "gourmet" cooking class, but they didn't have a lot of time at their disposal, etc. . . . They seemed to believe the equation Food = Love, and if they wanted to cook quickly, they must love less. I tried to explain that love for others is not measured by time spent. Sometimes we must learn to love *ourselves* and conserve energy and time. Let's be realistic. There are days when we don't have a great deal of time for ourselves, and there are places we'd rather be than in the kitchen. We owe it to ourselves to pay attention to *all* the aspects of our lives, not just the culinary ones. Perhaps there is a concert we'd like to attend, a play to see, friends to visit. With only so many hours in the day, it's easy to see that cooking might not always take first place, or even third. So that is where Fast Foods and High Energy Cooking come into your life. If you are in a rush to make that eight-o'clock movie or you have energy to burn and can't find a partner for tennis, step into the kitchen, my friend, and get ready to MOVE!

Actually, you don't have to be pressed for time in order to want to cook Fast Foods. Sometimes you're just in the mood to tap that kind of energy. I love the tempo of short-order cooking because it releases some of that speedy High Energy that I enjoy. I stir, I shake the pans, I bend slightly at the knees, adjust the height of the flame, lift the pan, flip things out onto the platter, and have a hell of a time. That is why the kitchen is in the center of my home. It is not closed off at the end of some corridor. People pass through on their way to someplace else. They can linger if they like, get a hit off my energy, watch, help out, taste and run, or stay and savor.

High Energy cooking falls into two basic categories. The first is Physical High Energy. Certain cooking techniques produce quick body movements, tap speedy energy, and send us soaring around. We need to move quickly and with ease if these techniques are to be effective.

The Physical High Energy techniques include stir frying, sautéeing, deep frying, pan broiling, and what I call "assembly jobs." The latter are dishes that are very fast to put together once the basic ingredients are collected and measured. "Assembly jobs" include soufflés, omelets, sauces and certain soups, vegetable, meat, and fish dishes which may involve steaming, broiling, baking. The initial preparation is rapid and there is not too much time involved in the cooking process—at least, not *active* time on the part of the cook. Some of the assembly jobs may use canned and frozen foods and take advantage of time-saving equipment such as mixers, blenders, and the like.

The other kind of High Energy cooking is more mental than physical. Usually it's improvisational cooking: creating new dishes, thinking on one's feet, taking risks, salvaging disasters, dealing with failure on a noncosmic level. It involves split-second decisions. You start to make a soup and you find out that you are missing three of the basic ingredients. What do you do? You have half a pound of ground round and three friends have dropped by unexpectedly. What can you cook that will feed the four of you? You've burned the roast. Too bad. Can you save the good meat and add it to yesterday's vegetable soup?

Creative (Mental) High Energy cooking usually implies cooking without recipes, as opposed to Physical High Energy cooking, which uses recipes effectively and well. You may, in fact, use many of the same physical cooking techniques, but there is the element of the unknown, the challenge of making it up as you go along. Now this kind of cooking is not for everyone. Some people are too insecure to wing it. But there are others who hate to follow recipes, and use cooking as free-play time in their day.

Lori goes to school in the morning. After school she picks up her son from the baby-sitter, plays with him, reads him a story, does some homework while he naps. After school and studying, the last thing she wants to do is open a cookbook and read a recipe.

Ina teaches photography when not doing her own exacting work in the darkroom. She is new at cooking but doesn't want to have to follow a recipe every time she wants to cook. And she doesn't have time to run around to three different markets to collect all the ingredients the cookbook recipe requires.

Bob is a busy lawyer. After reading briefs all day or planning courtroom tactics, the last thing in the world he wants to do is make himself even tenser by adhering to a recipe format, simple or elaborate. He needs to get up, move around, relax, throw things together.

What Lori, Ina, and Bob have in common is a need to loosen up in the kitchen, follow their creative energy and get free of linear, verbal thinking.

After a full week of teaching when I am obligated to follow the recipes (after all, my students paid to learn how to make chocolate mousse and coq au vin) I too need a break from routine. When I cook for myself I love improvisational cooking, where my imagination and creative powers are as revved up as my body.

Occasionally, you too may feel as if you are in some sort of a rut, as if your cooking is falling into a predictable pattern. Even your dog is bored with leftovers. You know you should be trying new recipes, but you don't feel like reading another cookbook, or taking a class, or bothering a friend for her latest jazzy recipe. How about trusting your sensations? How do you feel? How is your energy, your mood?

Close your eyes for a while and try to imagine WHAT you would like to eat if you had your choice. What textures do you need? What sensation—hot? cold? creamy? crispy? sweet? All right. Now let's see what we have in the pantry that fits some of those needs. . . . Some celery. Walnuts. Sour cream. Apples. Potatoes. Well, how about chopping up the onions fine and the potatoes into small cubes. Apples too. Melt a little butter and let them cook for a while. Want to add any leftover meat, some bacon? How about a fried egg on top? No hash tonight? O.K., how about a soup—sort of a Senegalese? All right. How about apples, onions, and celery. Topped with toasted walnuts. Is that more like it? Soup, perhaps chicken stock with a few embellishments to make it seem special. Apples, celery, curry, egg yolks. A meal in a bowl. Interesting, exotic. Perfumy to the nose. Pretty to the eyes.

HASH

3–4	raw boiling potatoes, finely diced	3	Pippin apples, finely diced (optional)
2	medium onions, finely diced		Celery, diced (optional)
	Bacon fat, chicken fat or butter, or all three		Salt and pepper
			Worcestershire or hot sauce
1½	C. ham, roast beef, or corned beef, finely diced		

Sauté potatoes and onions *slowly* in the fat or butter. When almost done, add meat, and apples and celery if you are using them. Cook about 10 minutes more. Season to taste with salt, pepper, and Worcestershire. For a variation, add caraway seeds.

SENEGALESE SOUP

6 C. chicken broth
4 egg yolks
1½ C. heavy cream
Salt and pepper
2 tsp. or more curry
powder
½ tsp. ground ginger
Grated lemon rind
(optional)

1 C. cooked chicken
breast meat, diced
2 small apples, diced
Green onions, minced
(optional)
Diced avocado
(optional)

Heat chicken broth. Combine egg yolks with cream and spices. Gradually add hot broth to yolks and cream, then return all to the pot. Heat till thickened. Chill well. Serve garnished with diced chicken meat, bits of tart green apple, and green onions or avocado if you like. (Serves 6.)

If you come home from work feeling wiped out, cooking without recipes might make you even *more* tired and tense. Know yourself. Pay attention to the kind of cooking that really relaxes you. What do you actually *want* from the experience? Do you need to unwind or do you want to rev up? Do you need the security blanket of a recipe, with its precise proportions and predictable results? Or do you want to be free from rules and exactitude? Will improvisational cooking give you what you want or will it make you crazy? How will you feel if your dinner is less than perfect? After all, you are working in an area where there are no set formulas, no guidelines to follow. Anything goes. And sometimes it goes on for too long. You may make mistakes. The final choice of how much, how long, and when to stop is up to you. Sometimes a dish will be "done" way before you finish it. When I was studying painting there were times when I stopped the painting too soon; the concept or image had not yet fully emerged. Sometimes I overpainted and lost the image I was trying to express.

Recently I taught a seminar called "Cooking Without Recipes," an improvisational cooking class where we all decided how we might like to deal with the ingredients on hand.

However, "Cooking Without Recipes" was more than just a cooking class. It was an exercise in risk taking. The majority of my students, who usually wanted to learn fancy party food and foolproof family meals, didn't sign up for these lessons. After all, some dishes might not "come out." But fortunately there was a little band of adventurers willing to break with cooking formulas and discard old food hang-ups. We had a wonderful time!

Sometimes we planned well and stopped while we were ahead. Occasionally we got carried away, wanted to please too many palates at the same time, and added just one more thing and ruined the dish. Or we changed it so drastically from our original concept that it became something else that we didn't want at all. We certainly had our share of disasters! There was the mysterious rhubarb soufflé that rose dramatically in the oven and then slowly evaporated before our eyes. There was the time that Bob C. added chocolate to a pie that was already so sweet our teeth cringed when we bit into it. The rum we poured with great panache into the tangerine compote was so overwhelming that the tastes of lemon rind and cardamom were lost to us forever. Not bad. Just didn't taste like tangerines anymore. One night a dried-fruit-and-rice pudding curdled so hideously that all of the Grand Marnier and whipped cream in the world could not bring it back to life. Bob L.'s ingenious cooking solution? "Let's go to Baskin-Robbins!" And he was right.

We learned to think on our feet. We learned not to lose our sense of humor although we had lost the dish. And we found out a great deal about each other, how we thought, how differently things tasted to each of us. We could taste something and say, "It needs more tartness," but not know or agree on how to get there. Lemon juice? Vinegar? Wine? The answer depended on the cook's personal palate and cooking experience.

Improvisational cooking is not only fun, but it is very economical. What better way to use up all the leftovers in the refrigerator? Open up all those plastic containers and assemble the mysterious fragments into a soup, a stew, some rare mélange, that only-happens-once kind of dish. Leftovers can inspire you to create new dishes that are so outstanding you may go out of your way to re-create them again and again.

If the lettuce in your refrigerator has wilted and, it's too late for that cool and crispy salad, don't throw it out; how about lettuce soup?

If you have some leftover mashed potatoes, how about a soufflé, or a pancake? If there is leftover ham or roast beef and you are tired of hash or bean soup, how about inventing a great spaghetti sauce or incorporating the meat in a salad? Leftovers, instead of being the bitter end, can become new beginnings.

CREAM OF LETTUCE SOUP

1½	C. chicken broth	1½	C. milk
4	small heads of lettuce (Bibb, Boston, or butter), trimmed and coarsely chopped	1	C. sour cream or yoghurt
			Croutons
			Salt and pepper
3	Tbsp. butter		Chives or nutmeg or mint
3	Tbsp. flour		

Bring the broth to a boil. Steam the lettuce in it for 5 minutes, remove the leaves with a slotted spoon, and puree them coarsely in the blender. Melt the butter; add the flour and then the milk; cook till thick. Add the sauce and the sour cream to the lettuce and whirl in the blender a few seconds. Heat the soup and add as much of the reserved chicken broth as needed for texture and flavor. Season to taste and serve with croutons (p. 79n.). (Serves 6.)

ALI BAB'S POTATO SOUFFLE

1½	lb. baking potatoes (3 large Idaho) or 2 C. leftover mashed potatoes	¾	C. heavy cream
		1½	tsp. salt
			Pepper
4	Tbsp. sweet butter		Grated parmesan cheese, chopped chives or green onions (optional)
	Flour		
4	eggs, separated		

Preheat oven to 425°. Scrub potatoes and bake on the middle level of the oven for 40 minutes, or until done. Remove from oven (but leave oven turned on) and let cool a bit while you butter and lightly flour a 1½-qt. soufflé dish and mix egg yolks and cream. Halve the potatoes and, with a spoon, remove the flesh from the jackets and quickly put it through a potato ricer into a saucepan. Add the remaining butter to the potatoes in the saucepan, mixing vigorously with a wooden spoon over low heat for a few minutes.

Remove from the heat. Then add the salt, pepper, and the egg yolks and cream. Mix thoroughly.

Beat the egg whites until they are stiff but not dry. Add half the egg whites to the potatoes, folding them in with a large spatula. Then fold in the rest of the egg whites, and the grated cheese, green onions or chives if desired. Pour into the soufflé dish and put into the oven. Bake for about 30 minutes. The soufflé will rise quickly, then sink a little as it solidifies.

Another great way to use up leftover mashed potatoes.

ROY DE GROOT'S POTATO PANCAKES

6	green onions	2	lb. potatoes, boiled and
2	Tbsp. minced parsley		mashed
2	Tbsp. butter, melted	½	C. Wondra flour
½	C. cottage cheese		Salt and pepper
2	egg yolks		Olive oil

Preheat oven to 450°. Chop the green onions. Add chopped green onions, parsley, butter, cottage cheese, egg yolks to potatoes. Work in enough flour to make a firm dough, while seasoning to taste. Press into patties, lightly brush with oil, and place on a cookie sheet. Bake 15–20 minutes till crispy outside, soft inside. You may just place in a casserole and not shape into patties, but bake longer.

PASTA WITH HAM AND ZUCCHINI

Oil and butter, about 2
Tbsp. each
1 onion, chopped
3 cloves of garlic
1 lb. perciatelli or
spaghetti
1 C. diced raw or cooked
zucchini

1 C. leftover ham, diced
2 C. diced tomatoes or 1
C. tomato sauce, 1 C.
diced tomatoes
Salt and pepper

Melt butter, add oil. Sauté onion 2 minutes. Add garlic and raw zucchini and cook 2 minutes. Add ham, cooked zucchini, tomatoes and mushrooms if desired. Simmer 5 minutes. Add salt, pepper. Pour over cooked and well drained spaghetti and mix well.

What is important for both kinds of High Energy cooking, physical and mental, is a well-filled Basic Pantry (more about this to come)—and an open mind. It is helpful to have easy access to all the ingredients and equipment so that your basic cooking energy is not interrupted while you are groping around for missing components of the dish. Concentration is of the utmost importance but it is not rhythmic, repetitious, and ritualistic. Rather than following rules, you invent your own, thinking up new ideas that you may never repeat again.

O.K., you're sold. When can you get into this Fast Food business? You've always had a fantasy about yourself as a snazzy short-order cook in a three-star diner. There you are, just knocking out one masterpiece after another. Perfect timing. What bravado! What style!

What follow are the recipes that could set you on the road. First the Physical High Energy recipes, then the assembly jobs that can be assembled from the Basic Pantry, the key to Fast Foods and wild times.

Chapter 24

PHYSICAL HIGH ENERGY COOKING:

Body Language in the Kitchen

Most of the basic frying techniques require High Energy. Sautéeing, deep frying, stir frying, and pan broiling (which is sautéeing without extra fat in the pan) are physically demanding. And agility is essential if you are juggling a few pans at one time. You must pay attention to see that things are not getting too brown too fast, and to decide when things need to be turned. You just cannot walk away to answer the phone and forget about what is happening on the stove. The moment you turn your back it can be all over: The food goes from done to overdone to disaster.

SAUTEEING

SCALLOPINE DI VITELLO AL MARSALA

1½ lb. veal scallops, sliced thin*
Butter and oil
Seasoned flour: flour, salt, pepper, garlic powder, nutmeg

½ lb. mushrooms, sautéed in 3 Tbsp. butter
Juice of 1 lemon
⅓ C. dry Marsala

Dredge the veal scallops in seasoned flour and sauté in half butter, half olive oil till brown on both sides. Set aside on heated platter. To the juices remaining in the pan add lemon juice and sautéed mushrooms and stir, scraping up all the brown bits. Add Marsala. Reduce over very high heat. Pour over veal. (This is known as "deglazing the pan.")

Piccata Variation

Omit mushrooms. To the pan juices add 4 Tbsp. lemon juice, 4 Tbsp. capers, and 3 lemons sliced thin, and heat them through. Pour capers, lemons, and sauce over veal. You may add ¼ C. white wine or beef stock to the pan.

Saltimbocca alla Romana

With a toothpick, thread a slice of prosciutto and a sage leaf to each slice of veal. Do not roll up. Sauté in butter and oil till golden on both sides. Remove veal to a heated platter. Add ½ C. white wine to the pan, scraping up all of the pan juices and brown bits. Reduce the liquid to about ¼ C. and pour over the veal.

*Veal scallops should be cut from a solid piece of meat and sliced thin. Pounding thick cutlets to thinness is relatively ineffectual. When the pounded veal hits the pan it shrinks almost to its original size and thickness. If you can't afford veal or can't find it at your market, you may use boned chicken or turkey breast in these recipes.

Milanese Style

Dip veal in flour, then beaten egg, then bread crumbs, and sauté in butter till golden. Sprinkle with parsley and garnish with lemon wedges.

Bolognese Style

Same as above, but topped with prosciutto, a slice of cheese (Gruyère or Emmenthal) and a dot of tomato paste.

BISTECCA ALLA PIZZAIOLA—NEAPOLITAN STEAK

Oil	1 tsp. oregano
1 tsp. garlic, minced	Parsley
2 C. peeled tomatoes, chopped	Enough steak for 4–6 people
Salt and pepper	

Heat 2 Tbsp. oil in pan. Add garlic but don't brown. Add tomatoes, salt, pepper, oregano, and cook over high heat for about 7 minutes Pan broil steak to proper doneness. Cover with sauce. Sprinkle with chopped parsley.

For Carne Asado, a Mexican variation, top the steak with a sauce of:

2 onions, sliced	1 8-oz. can Ortega chopped green chilis
4 fresh tomatoes, sliced	Salt and pepper
2 cloves garlic, minced, sautéed in oil	

Don't forget steak au poivre as another super High Energy Dish, p. 354.

PAN BROILED LAMB STEAKS

	Oil or butter, just a drop or two to grease the pan	2	tomatoes, sliced thin
6	lamb steaks, lean as possible	1½	tsp. oregano
2	cloves garlic, minced fine		Black pepper, freshly ground
1	large onion, sliced thin		Lemon juice
			Red wine, about ½ C.
			Salt

Heat the pan. Add the oil or butter and sear the meat quickly on both sides. Top with garlic, onion, tomato, oregano, and pepper, and cover the pan. Cook till meat is pink, the tomato and onion slightly wilted, about 5–7 minutes.

Remove the meat to a heated platter. Add lemon juice and red wine to the pan juices, swirl in a bit of butter, if desired, and pour over the meat. You may serve with lemon wedges. Salt to taste after cooking.

Fish is best when not overcooked. So sautéeing is a "natural" to preserve its moistness and delicate texture.

LENGUADO ALLA NARANJA—Sole With Orange

2	lb. filet of sole	⅓	C. dry white wine
	Flour	1	Tbsp. finely grated orange rind
	Butter		
	Salt and white pepper	2	large oranges, peeled and segmented
4	Tbsp. finely chopped onion		Parsley
⅔	C. orange juice		

Coat filets lightly with flour. Sauté in butter until well browned on both sides and flake easily when tested with a fork. Sprinkle with salt and pepper to taste, transfer to a heated serving platter, and keep warm.

In the butter remaining in the pan, cook onion until it is soft. Stir in orange juice, wine, and orange rind. Season the mixture

226

with salt and pepper to taste and simmer it for 3–5 minutes. Add the orange segments and heat them through

Arrange the orange segments over the sole and pour the sauce over them. Serve hot. Sprinkle with parsley.

Sole Amandine Variation

Dredge filets in seasoned flour. Sauté quickly in butter till golden on both sides, turning once.

In a separate pan, sauté slivered, blanched almonds in butter till golden. Pour over sautéed fish. Sprinkle with chopped parsley and serve with lemon wedges. (Serves 6.)

STIR FRYING

Stir Frying is sautéeing speeded up, like a 33⅓ rpm record played at 45 or even 78 rpm. It may require some practice on your part to set your pace and determine the best working rhythm. The vegetables, meat, or fish are in the pan or wok just for a few seconds. You can't stop and start, or redo. Stir frying requires a great deal of organization on the part of the cook. The slicing and mincing and chopping can be done in a more Meditative space. But the actual cooking is super High Energy.

Incidentally, stir frying can make you tense and crazy if you are not in the mood for the rapid roadrunner pace. When I teach Chinese cooking I often advise the students to ignore the written recipe while in class and *watch* me cook. It is important to pay attention to the rhythm of preparing the dish, the body's action. In much of Oriental cooking, whether it is three tablespoons of diced green pepper or ten is less important than *when* it goes into the pan, *how long* it stays there and *how often* it is stirred. That is something that you must learn from doing, feeling, and seeing. It cannot be accurately described with words: "Take one onion. Slice. Stir fry briefly. Remove from pan. Add beef. Stir fry till almost done. Return onions to pan. Stir a few minutes till cooked." It is through written (or spoken) language that we must *describe* the cooking action, but it is in terms of body language that we finally *understand* it.

For *Stir Fry* (Chinese) cooking: Put on your apron and your

Adidas. Arrange the vegetables on a platter in order of cooking time. Have the marinated meats in a bowl, the sauces mixed.

(The "work" in Chinese cooking is in the advance preparation, the slicing—which you can get faster and faster at if you practice. The cooking takes but moments. Many of the ingredients can be sliced and refrigerated hours ahead of time, and the dinner assembled rapidly at the last moment.)

Heat the wok or high-sided frying pan. Cook the vegetables first, till they are almost done but still crisp. Set them aside on a warmed platter, reheat the wok and cook the meat. Then combine the vegetables with the meat and heat all of them through.

Incidentally, smashing garlic with a cleaver and then pulverizing it into tiny fragments, or doing the same thing to a slice of fresh ginger root, can be a wonderful release of physical energy. For a few more stir fry recipes, see the shrimp recipes (pp. 229–30) and sweet-and-sour pork and shrimp (p. 249).

OYSTER SAUCE BEEF WITH ONIONS

1½	lbs. sliced flank steak	2	cloves garlic, minced
2	Tbsp. soy sauce	1	C. sliced onion
2–4	Tbsp. sherry	3	Tbsp. cooking oil
1	Tbsp. cornstarch	1	tsp. sugar
½	tsp. salt	½	C. beef stock
2	thin slices ginger, minced	4	Tbsp. oyster sauce
		½	tsp. pepper

Marinate beef in soy sauce, 2 Tbsp. sherry, cornstarch, salt, ginger, and garlic.

Stir fry onion in oil and set aside. Stir fry beef; add onions, sugar, stock as needed. Add oyster sauce and additional sherry and pepper to taste.

GINGER BEEF

1 lb. flank steak	Peanut oil for frying
2–3 green onions, sliced in 2" lengths	1 C. preserved ginger,* julienne sliced
1 onion, sliced	

Meat Marinade

2–3 tsp. cornstarch	1 tsp. minced fresh ginger
2 Tbsp. soy sauce	
2 Tbsp. sesame or peanut oil	

Slice the steak thin and marinate.

Heat and oil the wok or frying pan well. Sauté onion in oil till crisp and transparent; set aside. Then stir fry the beef. When the beef is half done, add ginger, onion; stir fry till done and serve.

FRIED CHICKEN WITH GREEN PEPPER

½ lb. chicken, boned	½ C. chicken soup or water
1 onion, diced	
Oil	½ C. peanuts, raw
2 green peppers, diced	
1–2 hot peppers (dried red or fresh green hot ones)	

Marinade

2 tsp. light soy sauce	1 egg white
2 tsp. cornstarch	½ tsp. salt
1 Tbsp. ginger juice	
2–4 stalks green onion, minced	

*I use half preserved ginger in syrup and half Japanese pickled ginger for a sweet-and-sour flavor contrast.

Dice the chicken into walnut-size cubes. Marinate for 15 minutes.

Stir fry first the onions and peppers for 4 minutes, set aside. Heat oil and stir fry the chicken and hot peppers, adding broth or water as needed. Return onions and green peppers to pan. Heat briefly. Garnish with the peanuts that have been pan toasted.

ALMOND CHICKEN

2 C. raw chicken meat, diced small
2 Tbsp. light soy sauce
1 Tbsp. sherry or vermouth
1 Tbsp. cornstarch
1 egg white
1 tsp. ginger root, minced (optional)
Garlic (optional)

1 C. onion, diced
1 C. diced celery
3 Tbsp. peanut oil
1 C. chicken soup
1 C. button mushrooms
1 C. frozen peas, thawed
½ C. diced water chestnuts
Salt to taste
½ C. almonds

Marinate chicken in soy, oil, wine, cornstarch, and egg white. Minced ginger and garlic may be added to the marinade.

Stir fry onions and celery in oil 2 minutes. Remove and set aside. Stir fry chicken, adding stock as needed. Add all of the vegetables for the last 2 minutes. Salt to taste.

Sauté almonds in separate pan and put on top of the chicken.

These shrimp are Meditative to clean but very quick to prepare—Mediterranean stir fry cooking.

SHRIMP PIQUANTE

4 Tbsp. butter
2 Tbsp. olive oil
3 cloves garlic, minced
2 bunches green onions, chopped, using most of the green
¼ C. dry vermouth
Juice of 1 lemon

1 C. marinara sauce (see pp. 243–44) (canned is fine)
Dash Worcestershire sauce
Salt and pepper to taste
2 lb. shrimp, shelled and deveined

Heat the butter and oil in a large sauté pan. Add the garlic and green onions and sauté about three minutes, till softened but not brown. Add the vermouth, the lemon juice, the marinara sauce, Worcestershire, salt and pepper. Simmer for five minutes and season to taste. (You may stop the sauce at this point and stir fry the shrimp at the last minute.)

Add the shrimp and cook just till they turn pink. This is a matter of moments; *do not overcook* the shrimp or they will be tough. Note: Shrimp do not reheat very well. They lose some of their crisp texture. You may prepare the sauce ahead of time, but not the shrimp. This is excellent served over rice, or just with French bread to sop up the delicious juices. If you want to serve this over pasta, double the amount of marinara sauce and increase the seasonings. Pasta is bland and needs a spicier sauce.

For Shrimp à la Grecque variation add:

¼	C. minced parsley	2	C. peeled chopped
1	Tbsp. fresh dill or 1 tsp.		tomatoes
	dry	1	C. crumbled feta cheese.

Heat till cheese melts. You may use onions instead of green onions, and substitute ouzo or brandy for vermouth.

For Scampi: omit vermouth and tomato sauce, and increase the garlic to taste.

Though these are *not* Chinese recipes, they do involve the use of the stir-fry technique and the same physical High Energy.

CHINESE/ITALIAN ASPARAGUS

1½	Tbsp. peanut oil	1	Tbsp. fresh ginger,
2	lb. Italian hot sausage,		grated
	sliced in julienne strips	3	cloves garlic, chopped
2	lb. asparagus, sliced		Water
	diagonally		Salt

In a large skillet or wok heat oil and sauté sausage. Remove and set aside. Add asparagus, ginger, and garlic to skillet and water as necessary until asparagus is cooked (a combination of sautéeing and steaming). Put sausage back in skillet to heat through. Salt as needed.

Variations

Use chicken broth instead of water.
Omit ginger and use parmesan cheese.
Include onions and/or celery.
Instead of asparagus, use broccoli or cauliflower (these must be blanched first), or zucchini.
Serve over a medium-weight pasta or noodle.

STIR FRIED GREEN BEANS

To prepare the beans: Cut about 1½ lb. beans into 2"–3" lengths. Boil in a large quantity of salted water until crisp, about 3–7 minutes. Drain and spray briefly with cold water to set the color and stop the cooking. (This may be done earlier in the day),or just drain and proceed with the following:

Fagiolini All'Aglio

Melt 2 Tbsp. oil mixed with a bit of butter. Add 3 cloves garlic, minced. Don't brown. Stir fry with the beans till warmed through. You may add a bit of onion, if desired, or diced prosciutto.

Green Beans with Celery and Almonds

Sauté ½ small onion and 4 stalks celery, thin sliced, in butter till crispy tender. Add beans and heat through. Sprinkle with salt and pepper. Sauté blanched almonds in butter in another pan till golden, and add to beans and celery. You may add diced ham to this dish.

CHERRY TOMATOES IN CREAM

1	box cherry tomatoes	2–3	Tbsp. brown sugar
2–3	Tbsp. butter		Freshly chopped parsley
	Salt	¼	C. or more heavy cream

Sauté tomatoes in butter. Season lightly with salt and add brown sugar. Cook, stirring occasionally, shaking the pan, till sugar melts and tomatoes are tender, about 3–5 minutes. Add cream to pan and heat briefly. Sprinkle with freshly chopped parsley. This is so good you may want to serve it in a separate bowl so you can spoon up the sauce instead of letting it run all over the plate. You may use honey instead of brown sugar. For a variation try mint leaves instead of parsley.

DEEP FRY

Although there is some repetition and routine to the deep frying process, deep frying is High Energy cooking. You *have* to keep moving quickly. You cannot afford to space out and allow your mind or body to wander, because you might miss the moment when the morsel is golden brown and ready to emerge from the bubbling oil. You must be alert to the temperature of the fat, not letting it get too low so the hors d'oeuvres cook too slowly and absorb too much oil. You must put in just the right number of pieces to keep the fat temperature steady and be able to turn them, flip them onto the paper towel and again onto the awaiting platter without too much time elapsing and without splattering yourself with hot oil. If you do not like to "perform" in public, this may not be the best kind of cooking experience for you unless you have a concealed cooking area and roller skates to get the goodies to your guests on time. Keeping them warm (the hors d'oeuvres, not the guests, although that is important too) on a hot platter in a low oven is one possible solution, but something is lost in translation. They are never quite so crisp and delectable. If you'd like to practice cooking in front of friends and family, deep frying is a good exercise in sharing your space and energy in the kitchen. They'll enjoy watching you prepare the food, marvel at your proficiency, and anxiously await the munching as the aromas waft in the air. If you are a ham, and like your moment on stage, then this can be a bravura performance for you, master of the deep fryer, creator of golden morsels that bubble in the pan and crackle on the tongue.

The following hors d'oeuvres are deep fried. You don't need a special pan for deep-fat frying. I use my wok because it requires less oil than the traditional deep-fat fryer; however, a large high-sided frying pan will work perfectly well. To test the oil for readiness I dip in a wooden chopstick. When bubbles appear around the stick the oil is ready, approximately 375°. Be sure to have lots of paper towels spread out to drain the food as soon as it is golden in color. You will need a slotted spoon or a wire basket spoon to lift the morsels out of the hot fat.

PAKORAS—Indian Potato Hors d'Oeuvres

½	C. chick-pea flour*	1	small onion, sliced thin
¼	tsp. baking soda	½	C. diced raw potatoes
5	Tbsp. cold water	3	Tbsp. fresh coriander,
1	tsp. salt		chopped cilantro, or
½	tsp. ground cumin		Chinese parsley
½	tsp. ground red pepper		

Mix chick-pea flour, baking soda and water. Stir in the rest. Drop in hot oil 1 Tbsp. at a time. Deep fry till golden. (Makes 10–12.)

INDONESIAN CORN FRITTERS

1	8-oz. can corn niblets, drained	2	Tbsp. scallions, minced
1	clove garlic, minced	3–4	Tbsp. flour
2–3	beaten eggs	½	tsp. salt
3	Tbsp. celery, diced	¼	tsp. pepper
		2–3	Tbsp. crushed almonds

Mix and drop into hot fat, 1 Tbsp. at a time. Turn if needed. Drain and serve hot.

*Available at health food stores

SHRIMP BALLS

1½ lb. shrimp	1 tsp. grated ginger root
15 water chestnuts	1 tsp. garlic, minced
4½ tsp. cornstarch	2 tsp. sherry
4 Tbsp. green onions, minced	1 large egg, lightly beaten
	Salt

Shell and devein shrimp and chop fine. Chop water chestnuts very fine and combine with shrimp. Add green onion, cornstarch, ginger, and garlic and mix well. Add cornstarch, sherry, egg, and salt to taste. Work the mixture together thoroughly and shape it into balls about 1" in diameter. Fry them in hot, deep fat (375° to 380°) until they are golden brown. Remove the balls with a slotted spoon and drain them on hot paper towels. Serve them very hot with hot mustard (below) or sweet-and-sour sauce (pp. 210, 249) or chutney (see pp. 208–9).

Hot Mustard

Into ¼ C. dry mustard stir enough water or beer to make a thin, smooth paste. Let the paste stand for about 15 minutes to develop flavor.

SPRING ROLL

½ lb. pork strips, julienne cut ¼" - 1", or ¾ lb. ground pork	2 tsp. cornstarch
	⅓ lb. tiny cooked shrimp, minced
1 Tbsp. wine or sherry	1 tsp. ginger root, minced
1 Tbsp. soy sauce	8 water chestnuts, minced
2 Tbsp. oil	Salt, pepper
½–1 C. bamboo shoots, cut in strips	3 cloves garlic, minced
4 stalks celery, stripped	30–40 spring roll pancakes or egg roll wrappers, about 2 lb., purchased at Oriental specialty store or at market.
4–6 dry mushrooms, soaked, cut in strips	
½ lb. bean sprouts	
2–3 spring onions, cut 2" long (6–10 Tbsp.)	

Marinate the pork in wine and soy sauce. Fry in oil. Add the bamboo shoots and celery and mushrooms and cook one minute. Add bean sprouts. Combine with the rest of the ingredients and cool. Put about 1 Tbsp. of filling on each egg roll wrapper. Fold in ends and then roll up. Seal with a solution of a little cornstarch mixed with water. You may fry these in two stages. Dip in hot fat for a minute to set the dough, then drain and set aside. Then finish the deep frying just before serving time. Or you may make these and fry them immediately. Serve with hot mustard and sweet-and-sour sauce.

Forming spring rolls, wontons, etc., can of course be a Meditation. There is tactile enjoyment, geometry, repetition, ritual. Much time can elapse till the work is done, and you can profit from lost sense of "real" time by letting your mind flow in a space where there is suspended time, the "now" awareness of the process of folding, rolling, fondling.

ORIENTAL FRIED CHICKEN

6 boneless chicken breasts, soaked in milk to cover, with 1 tsp. grated ginger root (or more to taste), 1 tsp. lemon rind, and garlic and soy sauce if desired

Flour mixed with salt, pepper, nutmeg, garlic powder, ground cloves, ginger to taste

Vegetable oil for deep frying
Lemon wedges

You may remove the skin from the chicken if you like. Marinate 2–6 hours. Dredge chicken in seasoned flour and deep fry till golden brown. Drain on paper towels. Serve with lemon wedges. Serve with rice, fried bananas if you like, orange slices.

Chapter 25

THE BASIC PANTRY:

Its Role in High Energy Cooking

Sautéeing, deep frying, stir frying are all cooking methods. The next category of Fast Foods or High Energy cooking is what I call the assembly jobs. They may involve the use of a variety of cooking techniques like steaming, broiling, baking, frying, and their combinations, but what makes them High Energy cooking is that once all the ingredients are laid out and measured, the actual time and energy involved in preparation is brief and to the point. Some dishes involve a quickly prepared stage and lots of slow cooking—others require assembly of basic ingredients.

Organization is the key. Have all of your ingredients and equipment on hand. Then set your own comfortable pace. Incidentally, don't forget the quiches and crepes in the Meditative cooking section. They are also assembly jobs, because once the crusts and the crepes are ready, the final preparation can be High Energy.

An essential for assembly job cooking is a well-stocked pantry. At the opening session of a cooking class series I give the students a list of ingredients that I call the Basic Pantry. If you have some of these staples on hand dinner is but moments away. When someone drops in on you unexpectedly or if you've been unable to get to the market for a major shopping expedition you will be able to put together a tasty meal.

One evening after a class in Improvisational Cooking, we were sitting around the table discussing the dinner and our cooking experiences. One of my students, Queenie, who had always hated cooking, said, "Joyce, when you first gave me the Basic Pantry list I looked at it and thought, Here is a list of my enemies. Now when I look it over I'm not so threatened. They might even become friends." You don't have to have everything on the list. *Select only the ingredients that reflect your personal palate.*

THE BASIC PANTRY

Dry staples

flour (unbleached white, whole wheat, Wondra, cake, or pastry type)

cornstarch or arrowroot (potato starch, too)

sugar (white and brown)

piecrust mix

bread, bread crumbs

rice (long grain, short grain, brown and white)

whole rye, whole-wheat berries, cracked wheat

pasta and noodles, assorted shapes

dried lentils, peas, beans

nuts: walnuts, almonds, pecans, pine nuts

coconut flakes

raisins, currants, dates, assorted dried fruits

cocoa, instant coffee, baking chocolate (semisweet, unsweetened)

gelatin, instant pudding mix

cookies like Amaretti, gingersnaps, graham crackers, etc.

238

powdered broth mixtures

coffee, tea

"Wet" staples

honey, maple syrup, molasses, or Karo syrup

olive oil

cooking oil: peanut, corn, safflower

vinegar, red and white

soy sauce, oyster sauce

teriyaki sauce (see recipe, p. 241)

ketchup, chili sauce

Worcestershire, Tabasco, and hot sauce

Kitchen Bouquet, Maggi, or Bovril

barbecue sauce (see recipe, p. 242)

mustard (Dijon preferred)

salad dressings (see recipe, p. 240)

mayonnaise (see recipe, p. 245)

sesame tahini (sesame seed paste with oil)

canned soups: chicken and beef broth, onion, tomato, mushroom or celery or cheese

canned tomato sauce, tomato paste, puree, Las Palmas red sauce, Marinara (see recipe, p. 243–44)

canned diced tomatoes, plum tomatoes

canned beans, white or red, chick-peas

canned chili peppers

canned clams, baby shrimp, tuna

olives, black or green

canned almond paste, chestnut puree, marrons in syrup

canned fruits like apricots, grapes, pitted cherries

currant jelly, orange, lemon, or ginger marmalade, apricot, strawberry or raspberry jams, etc., (see preserves, pp. 206–12)

chutney (pp. 208–9) sweet-and-sour-sauce (see recipe, pp. 210, 249)

green peppercorns

vanilla extract; orange, lemon, almond too

Spices

salt, pepper, cinnamon, nutmeg, ginger, cloves, coriander, cumin, curry powder, chili powder, cayenne, paprika, mustard powder

optionals: cardamom, allspice, mace, turmeric, saffron

Herbs

oregano, basil, thyme, tarragon, rosemary, mint, chives, dill, bay, mixed green herbs

optional: marjoram, savory, sage, etc.

Refrigerator

eggs

butter or margarine

milk, cream, buttermilk, etc.

assorted cheeses like parmesan, Swiss, cream, ricotta, cottage, mozzarella, cheddar,

sour cream, yoghurt

pesto (see recipe, p. 244)

refrigerator biscuits or rolls

bacon, Canadian bacon, sausages, ham slice

Italian sausage, Polish sausage, chorizo

oranges, lemons, apples, pears, etc.

(onions, potatoes, garlic, bananas may be stored at room temperature)

Freezer

Frozen dough, patty shells, etc.

chopped spinach or chard, peas, whole baby carrots, beans

orange juice concentrate

frozen berries

pound cake, lady fingers

ice cream

Liquor cabinet

dark rum

dry (white) and sweet (red) vermouth

sherry, Madeira, port, Marsala—fortified wines that come "sweet" or "dry"

Amaretto—an almond liqueur, like crème de noyaux

calvados—an apple brandy

cognac—a brandy from the town of Cognac (in cooking, brandy and cognac are interchangeable)

framboise—a raspberry liqueur

Grand Marnier—an orange flavored brandy similar to Cointreau and curaçao

Kahlúa—a coffee liqueur

kirsch—a cherry liqueur.

red and white wines

beer

SALAD DRESSING "VINAIGRETTE"

1 C. olive oil	Salt and black pepper
2–3 Tbsp. white or red wine vinegar	1 clove garlic, finely minced
2 Tbsp. lemon juice	
1 heaping tsp. Dijon mustard	

Combine in blender 20 seconds. Good over mixed greens,

endive and watercress salad, cooked vegetables. May be added to the following

Green Salad

- *Hard-boiled eggs
- *Grated parmesan cheese
- *Drained, canned white beans
- Raw sliced mushrooms
- *Black or green olives
- Diced celery
- *Diced cooked bacon
- *Diced apple and walnuts
- Minced green onions or chives
- Cooked potatoes, sliced
- Cooked broccoli, zucchini, green beans, asparagus

The dressing keeps 1–2 weeks in pantry and much longer in the refrigerator, but bring to room temperature before using.

The following sauces may be prepared in huge batches and kept in well-closed jars on the pantry shelf. They keep for ages and make nice gifts for friends.

TERIYAKI SAUCE

½ C. sweet sake (mirin)	4 Tbsp. brown or white sugar
½ C. sake	
¾ C. soy sauce	2 Tbsp. light corn syrup

Combine all ingredients and bring to boil. Be careful to put in a *deep* pot so it doesn't bubble over. Reduce heat. Simmer about 1 hour, till thickened. Keeps on shelf in pantry for 1 year. For broiled steak, chicken or fish.

For Steak

Pan broil steak on high heat to brown both sides. Dip steak in teriyaki sauce and return to pan and burn slightly on both sides (1–2 seconds). Serve with some of the sauce poured over steak.

*all in Basic Pantry

For Salmon

Sauté on both sides. Cook till done, Top with freshly grated ginger root and then add teriyaki sauce as you would with the steak.

For Yakitori (Broiled Meat on Skewer)

Beef filet, cubed to bite size
Chicken breast, cubed
Mushrooms, sliced

Onion, sliced
Green pepper, sliced
Teriyaki sauce

Alternate meat and vegetables on bamboo skewers. Broil over charcoal or under broiler, or pan broil to your liking, and baste at last minute, since sauce made with soy sauce burns easily. Serve with some sauce over the skewer.

(For variety, use grated ginger, grated sesame, or red pepper in teriyaki sauce.)

BARBECUE SAUCE

¾ C. ketchup
⅓ C. or less cider vinegar,
2 Tbsp. Worcestershire
½ C. brown sugar or honey
(or less to taste)
1 Tbsp. dry mustard

2 Tbsp. chili powder
½ tsp. ground ginger
1 clove garlic, minced
2 Tbsp. butter or oil
2 Tbsp. lemon juice or
1 tsp. lemon rind

Combine ingredients and simmer till smoothly blended.

Barbecued Spareribs

Sprinkle 3 racks of back ribs (cracked) with salt, pepper, and garlic powder. Either broil 20 minutes on each side or bake in 400° oven for 45–60 minutes. Cover with barbecue sauce the last 5–10 minutes.

Flank Steak

Broil 3–5 minutes on each side and serve with sauce on side.

Chicken

Broil 10–15 minutes on each side and baste with barbecue sauce the last 5 minutes.

CHINESE ROAST PORK MARINADE

Combine in blender:

1	clove garlic	2	Tbsp. soy sauce
1	walnut-sized piece of peeled ginger root	2	Tbsp. ketchup
2	Tbsp. brown sugar	½	C. beef broth

Marinate a 2-lb. boneless pork loin roast (or 2 1-lb. pork tenderloins) for 2–6 hours. Bake in 350° oven for 1 hour, basting often with marinade and turning once. When done, roll in a mixture of thick soy* and ketchup. Serve with hot mustard, apricot chutney, or sweet-and-sour sauce. This is excellent served hot or cold. One 2-lb. roast serves 4–5 for dinner, 8 for hors d'oeuvres. This marinade is excellent with chicken —marinate 2–6 hours, broil, and baste with marinade. You may add orange juice concentrate.

These sauces can be prepared in large batches and frozen for 6 months or longer. The tomato sauce can be refrigerated for a week. The pesto can be kept in the refrigerator for 3–6 months if the top of the sauce is filmed with olive oil.

MARINARA SAUCE

1	large onion, chopped	chopped, or canned plum tomatoes
3	Tbsp. olive oil	Salt and pepper
2–3	cloves garlic, minced	Pinch of sugar
1	stalk celery, diced (optional)	Tomato paste for flavor (optional)
2–3	leaves basil	
2	lb. tomatoes, coarsely	

*Thick soy can be purchased in a store specializing in Chinese condiments. It has the consistency of molasses. If you cannot find it, combine 2 Tbsp. molasses, 2 Tbsp. soy sauce, and 2 Tbsp. ketchup for the final glaze.

Sauté onion in oil till soft. Add garlic and cook 2 minutes. Add the rest and simmer 30–40 minutes. Strain or puree in a blender for smooth texture, or leave small pieces and don't puree.

For pasta and meats. For pizzaiola sauce add:2 additional tsp. minced garlic, 2 tsp. oregano.

PESTO ALLA GENOVESE

2 C. fresh basil leaves,* tightly packed	2 Tbsp. pine nuts or walnuts
½ tsp. salt	½ C. parmesan cheese
2 tsp. finely chopped garlic (or more)	½ tsp. black pepper
	1 C. olive oil

Combine ingredients and puree in blender or processor. If too thick add about ½ C. more olive oil, or more if needed. Store in jars. Film top with thin layer of oil.

Serve with lightly *buttered* pasta (fettuccine, trenette, linguine). The pesto should be at room temperature and the noodles drained, buttered, and aerated a bit before adding the pesto to the pasta. Add 2 Tbsp. pasta cooking water and mix well. Do not let the pesto "cook" or it will turn brown.

This is a remarkably versatile sauce. A few tablespoons added to soup or stirred into the melted lemon butter for fish or vegetables and the dish is transformed—for the better. I smear it on broiled steak or chicken in place of an herbed butter. When fresh basil is out of season, I mix pesto into my vinaigrette salad dressing to pour over sliced tomatoes and mozzarella cheese or just greens. I would never be without a jar of pesto in the refrigerator and a stash in the freezer.

*Fresh basil is minty, spicy, and aromatic. It has about a six-month season and tastes nothing like the dried.

Chapter 26

ASSEMBLY JOBS

Fast Sauces For Fast Foods

The following sauces are quick to assemble from ingredients in the Basic Pantry and go well with Fast Foods—foods prepared with High Energy techniques such as sautéeing, steaming, broiling.

Mayonnaise made in the blender is almost foolproof. Have the ingredients at room temperature. And be sure that you add 1/4 C. oil to the yolks in the blender jar to guarantee the emulsion. Add the rest of the oil very gradually and stop pouring when the desired thickness is achieved. If you don't feel like making mayonnaise and have the bottled version on hand, many of the variations suggested can be done with the commercial product, doctored up for flavor.

MAYONNAISE

2 egg yolks	2 Tbsp. lemon juice, or
¼ tsp. salt	more to taste
½ tsp. dry mustard	¼ olive oil
(optional)	¾ C. mixture of *good olive*
Cayenne or black	*oil** and salad oil
pepper to taste	

Combine all ingredients in blender except for the ¾ C. oil. Blend a few seconds. With the blender still whirring, gradually beat in the remaining oil.

Rémoulade Mayonnaise

Add capers, minced onion, parsley, tarragon, salt, and pepper to mayonnaise. (Minced pickles are optional.) Good with cold salmon, shrimp, crab, cooked celery, hard-boiled eggs.

Curry Mayonnaise

Add 2–3 tsp. curry powder and 2 more Tbsp. lemon juice.

Mustard Mayonnaise

Add 3 Tbsp. prepared Dijon mustard or more to taste. You may add ½ C. sour cream if desired.

Green Mayonnaise

Add 1 bunch chopped sorrel or watercress.

Aioli Mayonnaise

Add 3 cloves minced garlic when starting the mayonnaise.

---

*A flavorful, fruity oil distinguishes homemade mayonnaise from the commercial product. Some olive oils are so bland you won't even notice that they are there. Try this with a Sicilian, French, or California oil that is aromatic and greenish-golden in color.

BLENDER HOLLANDAISE SAUCE

3–4 egg yolks
2 Tbsp. lemon juice

Pinch of salt
1½–2 sticks hot melted butter

Have all the ingredients except the butter at room temperature. In the blender combine the egg yolks, lemon juice and pinch of salt. Cover the container and put the blender on high speed for an instant, turning the machine on and off immediately. Put the switch on high again, remove the small plastic insert in the cover, and gradually add the butter in a thin, steady stream. Serve at once.

Maltaise Sauce

Add 1 tsp. orange rind, 4 Tbsp. orange juice. This is also delicious with lime rind and lime juice.

Béarnaise Sauce

Cook 1 Tbsp. chopped shallots or onions, 1 tsp. tarragon, ¼ C. white wine, and 2 Tbsp. tarragon vinegar till reduced and only about 2–3 Tbsp. remain. Add to hollandaise sauce made by any method you choose, eliminating lemon juice.

Another technique for

HOLLANDAISE SAUCE

Melt 2–3 Tbsp. butter in a pan. Add 3 egg yolks and 2 Tbsp. lemon juice. Mix well with whisk. On very low flame, keep stirring and add gradually about 1½ sticks of *cold* butter, in about 1″ chunks. Stir constantly and remove from heat if separation occurs. Keep whisking, and when smooth return to low heat. When all the butter is absorbed, remove from heat and season with a bit of cayenne, pepper, and a bit of salt.

This sauce is good on steamed vegetables, grilled meats, grilled or poached fish.

POACHED FISH

Whole fish, approximately 6 lb. salmon or bass	6–8 Peppercorns Onion, halved Parsley, sprigs Tarragon (optional)
Equal parts water and white wine to cover ⅔ of fish	1 Tbsp. salt

Place fish on a long piece of heavy-duty foil and then place on rack. (It is easier to work with foil than cheesecloth, especially for turning fish onto the platter.)

Bring the liquids and seasonings to a boil and simmer 10 minutes. Add the fish and poach about 7–9 minutes per inch of thickness. This is a more accurate method for timing than by weight. A thick 6-lb. fish will take longer to cook than a 6-lb. thin and flattish one. I check for doneness by poking the fish down to the backbone with a chopstick. If the stick pierces the flesh easily the fish is done. Lift the fish on its piece of foil, and slide it off the foil onto the platter.

Remove the top layer of skin and drain any liquid that may collect on the serving platter. Garnish the fish with cucumber slices and parsley. Serve with hollandaise sauce if it is to be eaten warm, or with a flavorful mayonnaise if it is to be eaten cold.

POACHED FISH FILLETS

White wine or vermouth, about ½" to cover bottom of pan

1 piece fish per person: sole rolled into a spiral ("turban") and skewered with a toothpick, salmon steaks, or other	Salt and a few peppercorns Herbs added to bouillon (optional)

Bring liquid to a boil. Add the fish and cover the pan. Poach till done, about 6–8 minutes. Check often.

You may stuff the fillets with crab meat or chopped shrimp and herbs.

CHINESE SWEET-AND-SOUR SAUCE

½ C. wine or cider vinegar
½ C. brown sugar
½ C. ketchup
½ C. water

1½ Tbsp. cornstarch mixed
    with 4 Tbsp. water for
    thickening

Bring ingredients to a boil. Add starch mixture gradually. Taste and adjust seasoning.

Fish

To the sauce add 2 Tbsp. (preserved) or 2 tsp. (fresh) minced ginger and (optional) ½ C. Chinese preserved cucumber. Flour the fish and deep fry. Drain and pour the sauce over the fish.

Shrimp

Clean and devein 1 lb. shrimp. Sauté 1 onion cut in chunks, 1 green pepper, 1–2 stalks celery until crispy cooked. Set aside. Heat shrimp in sauce until pink, stirring often. Don't overcook! Add reserved vegetables, pineapple chunks, drained, and add a bit of the juice to the sauce. Heat through.

Pork

Deep fry pork cubes that have been dipped into cornstarch or flour mixed with Five Spice powder and a bit of ground ginger. The pieces should be very small so the pork cooks quickly, or you may dip each piece of pork in and out of the oil, pausing a few seconds between dips to cook it more slowly. This way the pork will remain juicy and not turn into charred, dry bits. The pork can be fried earlier in the day. Anyway, the countdown for the pork is to stir fry one onion, and one diced green pepper for a minute or two, add optional pineapple cubes or tomato wedges. Add the sweet-and-sour sauce to the pan, add the cooked pork cubes, and cook till the pork is heated through.

TARATOR SAUCE—Tahini With Walnuts

½ C. chopped walnuts
2 cloves garlic, smashed
4 Tbsp. chopped parsley
4 Tbsp. tahini (sesame paste)*

Juice of 2 or more lemons
Salt

Combine ingredients and puree in blender. You may need a bit of water to make the blender move easily. Season to taste. This is an Arabic all-purpose sauce for cold boiled shrimp, mussels, fish, and vegetables.

This variation on "tarator" sauce was invented by my Cooking Without Recipes class:

TURKISH ASPARAGUS

2 bunches medium-sized asparagus
4 Tbsp. butter
¼ C. onion, chopped
½ tsp. garlic

4 Tbsp. tahini
4 Tbsp. lemon juice
¼ C. filberts (hazelnuts)
½ C. chicken broth
Salt

Peel and steam asparagus. Test for doneness by placing a knife point in the thick part of the stalk.

Melt butter in a frying pan, add onion and garlic, and sauté. In blender, combine tahini, lemon, and nuts. Add to pan and add chicken broth and a pinch of salt. Heat through.

Drain asparagus and pour sauce over. (Serves 6–8.)

*Found in health food stores or stores that specialize in foods of the Middle East.

SAMAK BI TAHINI—Lebanese Fish With Sesame Sauce

4 lb. red snapper filets
Salt and pepper
Olive oil
3 onions, chopped and
sautéed

Juice of 3 lemons
1 C. tahini
1 C. white wine

Clean, wash and dry snapper. Rub all over with salt, pepper, and olive oil. Bake in preheated 400° oven for 25 minutes. Reduce heat to 350°, cover with mixture of onion, lemon juice, tahini, and wine, whisked together till light, and bake for about 20 minutes. Place fish on platter and decorate with lemon slices, black olives, radishes, nuts, pimento, parsley, etc.

The following meat and fish recipes take time in the oven (but that time is generally unsupervised—not much for you to do). Yet they take but seconds to prepare for cooking. Many of the sauces are right out of the Basic Pantry, but the final taste is anything but basic.

LEG OF LAMB WITH JULIA CHILD'S MUSTARD SOY GLAZE

4½–5 lb. leg of lamb, trimmed
of excess fat—at room
temperature 4 hours

Insert many slivers of garlic all over lamb. Cover with the following glaze:

½ C. Dijon mustard
3 Tbsp. soy sauce
¼ C. olive oil beaten in a
bit at a time

1 tsp. rosemary or
oregano or Italian
seasoning (optional)

Bake in 350° oven for 1½ hours for rare lamb; 1¾ hours for pinkish lamb. Restrain yourself from overcooking the lamb. It is so much better when it is pink and juicy.

ORANGE-GLAZED PORK LOIN

5–6 lb. pork loin roast, cut into chops and tied, or boneless, tied
Garlic slivers
Salt and pepper
1 can (or a bit more) frozen orange juice concentrate, thawed
¼ C. honey
¼ C. soy sauce
½ C. ginger marmalade, or small jar preserved ginger pureed in blender
¾ C. bitter orange marmalade
Orange slices
Orange liqueur (optional)

Insert slivers of garlic in loin roast. Rub lightly with salt and pepper and roast in 350° oven, fat side up, for about 1½ to 2 hours. Baste with orange juice, honey and soy sauce. Add marmalades and roast another ½ hour, for a total of 20–25 min. per pound. Serve with orange slices, orange juice, and degreased pan juices. You may add a bit more marmalade to sauce if needed, and some orange liqueur. (Serves 6–8.)

If you are in the mood for a cooking workout, eager to spend all day on a recipe for a stuffed leg of veal, you could turn to Julia Child's four-page recipe for stuffed leg of veal Perigordine. On a day when you have less time you might attempt a similar presentation with half the culinary effort.

I used to buy leg of veal already stuffed with prosciutto and mortadella from my butcher in Rome. When I realized that I was coming back to this country and wouldn't know how to reproduce this dish at home, I spent the morning with him while he was preparing the roasts that he called:

ROLLÉ DI VITELLO—Roman Stuffed Leg of Veal

Unroll a 4-lb. leg of veal roast and stuff with 6 slices of mortadella, 6 of prosciutto, a few grindings of nutmeg, and a sprinkling of rosemary. Roll up and tie, inserting slivers of garlic in meat and more nutmeg and rosemary on top. Brush with oil and top with some butter. Place in a heavy casserole with a lid, covered, in a 325° oven for almost 2 hours, till tender, basting with white wine about every 20 minutes. You may add chopped vegetables such as carrots, onions, tomatoes, celery to pan and use natural meat gravy for sauce. (Serves 6.)

A few practical hints about shopping for and cooking fish and shellfish: A fish market that carries FRESH fish does not smell fishy. If you walk into your local market and the aroma is overpowering, walk out.

Also, fish is truly a Fast Food. If you overcook fish it falls apart. Not too appealing to scrape up all those little shards on your plate. And when you overcook shellfish they turn rubbery and resentful. So watch out! Also remember that the flavor of these fruits of the sea is delicate and subtle. Therefore, don't drown them in heavy and complex sauces. One night I ordered a seafood coquille at a "gourmet" restaurant. After gingerly lifting up a half-inch-thick crust of melted cheese, I found a few tired pieces of something that used to be fish. I couldn't taste it under the gummy sauce, and its texture was all but annihilated under the leaden blanket of rubbery cheese. Just remember to cook fish and seafood with a light touch. They will love you for it and so will the diners at your table.

IKAN BANDANG PANGGANG—Indonesian Baked Fish

2–3 lbs. of fish filets, such as snapper or ling cod
2 tsp. salt
1 tsp. pepper
3–5 cloves of garlic, minced finely

Basting liquid

½ C. melted butter
3 Tbsp. lemon or lime juice
½ tsp. crushed chili pepper
½ C. Indonesian soy (Ketjap Manis) or dark soy mixed with 2 Tbsp. molasses

Rub the fish with a paste of the salt, pepper and garlic. You may want to score the top of the fish with a knife if the filets are very thick, so that the flavor may penetrate better and the basting liquid absorb easily. Bake in a 400° oven for 5 minutes.

Combine basting ingredients and pour half of the liquid over the fish. Bake 10 minutes more. Pour on the rest of the sauce and bake an additional 10 minutes. Serve topped with the pan juices.

HUACHINANGO À LA VERACRUZANA
—Red Snapper, Veracruz Style

3 lb. snapper filets
Salt and pepper
3 Tbsp. butter or oil
2 onions, sliced
5 cloves garlic, minced
2 green peppers, cut in strips
2–4 chopped canned green chili peppers
2 tomatoes, sliced, or 1 can of chopped tomatoes

1 tsp. each oregano, basil, and ground cumin
1 crumbled bay leaf
2 tsp. chili powder (Gebhardts is excellent. Do not confuse this with chili pepper!)
Boiled potatoes
Sliced black olives

Salt the fish filets and place them in a baking dish. Sauté the onions, garlic, peppers, chilis, and tomatoes for 5 minutes. Add the spices and herbs, simmer 2 minutes, add salt and pepper to taste and pour over the fish. Bake in a 400° oven for about 30 minutes. Garnish with the olives and boiled potatoes.

Zabaglione is the ultimate virtuoso High Energy dessert. It may be served as a sauce over berries or peaches, but it is quite delicious and sensual served by itself.

ZABAGLIONE

6 egg yolks
Salt
½ C. sugar

Grated rind of 1 lemon
¾ C. dry Marsala (sweet if you prefer).

Beat egg yolks with a pinch of salt, sugar, and lemon rind till very light and fluffy. Place in top of double boiler over medium heat. Gradually beat in ¾ cup of Marsala, beating CONSTANTLY till quite thick. This will take about 5–7 minutes. Serve warm.

To turn this into a cold sauce, you may fold in 1 C. heavy cream, whipped, with 1 Tbsp. gelatin dissolved in ¼ C. cold water and melted, when basic zabaglione is cool.

Or, for a

QUICK COLD ZABAGLIONE SAUCE

for baked fruits or fresh fruits like berries, peaches:

Combine in blender:

1 pkg. vanilla instant pudding	½ C. cream (any weight)
1½ C. milk	Grated rind of 1 lemon
	½ C. dry Marsala, or more

A UNIQUE ZABAGLIONE TORTE

1 envelope gelatin softened in ¼ C. cold water	1 C. heavy cream, whipped
4 eggs, separated	3 pkgs. lady fingers
1 C. sugar	Macaroon crumbs (crushed Amaretti)
1 C. sweet Marsala Grated rind of one lemon (optional)	

Dissolve the gelatin over low heat.

Beat the egg yolks and sugar till thick in the top of a double boiler. Beat in the Marsala and keep beating till thickened. Beat in gelatin, and lemon rind if desired.

Beat the whites till stiff. Fold whites and cream into yolk mixture.

Line a springform pan with lady fingers. Pour in half the custard. Sprinkle with crumbs. Add another layer of lady fingers.

Add the rest of the custard. Add the crumbs and top with lady fingers. Chill well. Unmold. You may serve with more whipped cream and berries. This fills an 8" or 9" pan. (Serves 6–8.)

A few desserts that can be assembled using only ingredients from the Basic Pantry:

CHARLOTTE MALAKOFF

Lady fingers to line 1-qt. mold
½ C. sweet butter
½ C. sugar, superfine
¾ C. ground blanched almonds
½ tsp. almond extract
¼ C. kirsch
1½–2 C. heavy cream, whipped

Oil 1-qt. mold and place a buttered waxed-paper circle on bottom.

Line sides with lady fingers. (You may line bottom with lady fingers, too.)

Cream butter, gradually adding sugar, and beat till light and fluffy. Add almonds, almond extract, and kirsch. Fold in whipped cream. Pour into mold. Chill 6–7 hours. Unmold. Decorate top with whipped cream. You may decorate with strawberries or raspberries. (Serves 8.)

ZUPPA INGLESE

Three layers of sponge cake or pound cake (Sara Lee
Frozen is excellent, sliced horizontally)
Myers dark rum
Apricot or raspberry jam
Vanilla custard filling (1 C. milk, ½ C. cream, 1 pkg.
instant pudding, mixed and chilled till thick), mixed with
½ C. chopped candied fruit*
Whipped cream, about 1 C. sweetened with 2 Tbsp.
confectioners' sugar, 1 tsp. vanilla
Chocolate shavings

Butter a mold or loaf pan. Place in it one layer of cake and
sprinkle generously with rum. Spread the cake with jam, then
add a layer of custard. Then another layer of rum-sprinkled cake
spread with jam, then more custard. Finally the last layer of cake
with lots of rum. Chill well. Then unmold. (You may place in
freezer for easier unmolding). Frost with whipped cream and
decorate with chocolate shavings. (Serves 6–8.)

TORINO PUDDING

8	Tbsp. sweet butter	2	Tbsp. vanilla
4	oz. semisweet chocolate	¼	C. Myers dark rum
1	1-lb. can unsweetened	4	egg yolks
	chestnut puree	2	packages lady fingers (or
½	C. sugar		pound cake)
¼	tsp. mace		

Melt butter and chocolate in the top of a double boiler.
Put the chestnut puree in a mixer bowl and beat in the sugar,
vanilla, rum, mace, the butter and chocolate mixture, and the
yolks, one at a time. Pour into a standard loaf pan lined with

*If you hate candied fruit, substitute fresh berries, chopped marrons, or
raisins soaked in Marsala.

rum-sprinkled lady fingers or pound cake slices. Chill 6 hours or overnight. (This freezes very well and holds up for days in the refrigerator.) Unmold and serve in thin slices. You may accompany this with whipped cream, but it is staggeringly rich as it is. (Serves 6–8.)

Chapter 27

VEGETABLES AS HIGH ENERGY COOKING:

Bigger Is Not Better

Although I am not a vegetarian, I am a lover of vegetables. I need to eat them every day. Many a meal is served without the presence of meat at our table, but rarely a meal without vegetables. I try to respect their inherent nature and do all I can to cook them with inspiration. Sometimes I like vegetables served simply, with just lemon juice or melted butter. Other times I enjoy the richness of a hollandaise or more complex sauce, the constrasting textures of hot and cold, smooth and crunchy.

Vegetables are beautiful to look at, varied in shape, texture, and color. But often they have been badly treated by well-meaning, unskilled cooks. The vegetables come to the table overcooked, limp, and faded. I'm sure that is why many children refuse to eat cooked vegetables but will quite cheerfully take carrot and celery sticks in their school lumchboxes. Never have I had to tell my children that if they eat their spinach they will be as strong as Popeye. And they have never replied, like the little kid in the Hoff cartoon, "I say it's spinach and to hell with it!"

Perhaps the American obsession with size is one of the reasons that vegetables are overcooked. We often confuse bigness with quality. Vegetables and fruits are grown so large that they must be cooked longer to become tender; and the line between tender and limp is a thin one.

When I go to the supermarket and look at the produce I often get angry. The stands are filled with huge asparagus, gigantic strawberries, immense and shiny tomatoes, monumental waxed apples and cucumbers. If the produce had been grown to be used in a Dutch still-life painting, I could appreciate its giant proportions aesthetically. But these pretty-to-look-at vegetables and fruits are tasteless. They are filled with cellulose and air pockets. Watery in texture, they lack the sweetness and delicacy of flavor found in the smaller, less visually impressive variety.

One doesn't have to read E. F. Schumacher to know that "small is beautiful"—and flavorful. Fruits and vegetables are most succulent and at the height of their flavor in the beginning of the season, when they are small in size. Quickly they reach the point of no return, where taste is sacrificed for scale. In Italy tiny spaghetti-thin asparagus are valued for their flavor. They are the "primizie," the first of the season. They are awaited eagerly from spring to spring, eaten avidly for weeks, and then are gone. The Italians don't wait to pick the asparagus when they will be more impressive in size because they know that the larger the stalk, the more waste and the less flavor.

Are we powerless in the face of the available produce, the diminishing quality of our fruits and vegetables? We have a few options open to us. We can grow our own. We can try to shop at markets which carry organic produce (but don't be shocked at the prices—the smaller, more fragile, unsprayed produce is costly because of rapid spoilage and damage which may occur when handling ripe rather than green produce). We can shop directly from the small farmer, the one who does not spray his produce, has a smaller yield, and will deal directly with the consumer rather than through the huge wholesale produce markets; or we can join community consumer groups sometimes called "food conspiracies." They shop for produce in quantity at local farmers' markets or go directly to the small farmer. Then the families divide up the food and save in price and profit in flavor from the group's bulk purchase. Our local farmers' market will sell one pound of cherries to a single person just as happily as they will sell three crates of fruit to a "conspiracy" or commune.

The back-to-the-garden movement is booming. Why? For a number of reasons, and they are not only economic. In fact, home gardening can become an expensive hobby, not always a way to save money. But the cost seems worth it because of the flavor and the possibility of picking things when they are ripe, not when they are best able to be shipped. This gardening renaissance is also responsible for the recent canning and preserving revival.

Also, many have discovered that gardening, like cooking, is creative, meditative, and food for the soul as well as for the body.

If you do not plan to grow your own, if there is no local farmers' market in your area and you are not able to deal with this problem by going to the source directly, then the best you can do is *complain* at your market.

You have the power to accept or reject because you are paying. The market wants you to be satisfied so you'll come back. If enough people say they want thin asparagus, or the smaller, more flavorful berries instead of the mommoths now available, perhaps a choice could be made possible. If there are some people who still want size as opposed to flavor, fine, let them have it. But there ought to be a few options open to those who have tried the grandiose and found it wanting.

While their preparation is usually Meditative—washing, peeling, mincing, chopping—most vegetables are Fast Foods. They do not profit from long cooking. What follow are a few High Energy vegetable recipes.

ASPARAGUS

Trim the asparagus to relatively equal lengths, either breaking them off at the most tender point or trimming the white ends off with a knife and leaving only the green. If they are thin, there will be no need to peel them. If they are larger than your finger in width, then peel them with a potato peeler from the bottom to some point midway up the stalk.

Place them in a vertical steamer basket (or in a double boiler with the top part inverted over the bottom pot so that the asparagus will cook standing up, the thicker ends in the water, the frail tops just in the steam). Steam till tender but crisp (about 3–8 minutes, depending upon the thickness of the stalks). Test with the point of a knife at the bottom part of the stalk.

Asparagus are easiest to eat with fingers. Relax and enjoy them. Dip in:

Butter Parmesan Sauce

Melt butter in a separate pan till it is bubbly. Drain the asparagus stalks and sprinkle with grated parmesan cheese. Pour hot butter over the cheese and the stalks. The heat of the butter will melt the cheese.

Or serve with lemon juice or hollandaise sauce (see pp. 247–48)

Or whipped cream flavored with salt, pepper, and lemon rind.

Roy de Groot's Pecan Butter Sauce

¼	lb. butter	1–2	tsp. white vinegar or
¼	C. chopped pecans		tarragon vinegar

Sauté pecans in butter. Add vinegar. Heat and serve.

See Chinese/Italian asparagus (pp. 230–31), Turkish asparagus (p. 250), asparagus with prosciutto (p. 355).

BROCCOLI

Separate broccoli into stalks of about the same size and peel the stems. Steam about 5 minutes, till tender-crisp, when the point of a knife pierces the stem easily. (The peeling of the stem permits the thicker stalk to cook in the same amount of time as the flowers.) Serve with lemon butter, hollandaise (p. 247), or garlic butter and sliced black olives. Or rinse with cold water, chill, and serve with vinaigrette sauce (p. 240).

Brussels sprouts are really tiny cabbages and can be crisp and delicate if not boiled to a soggy pulp. Here is a recipe that combines the techniques of stir frying and steaming. A little liquid is all it takes.

BRUSSELS SPROUTS PARMESAN

Wash and trim 2 pt. of sprouts. Halve them lengthwise. Melt ½ C. butter in a large skillet and add 1–2 cloves minced garlic. Add the sprouts and 2–3 Tbsp. chicken stock. Cover the pan and steam the sprouts over low heat, 10–12 minutes or till tender. Sprinkle the sprouts with salt, pepper, and ½ C. grated parmesan cheese. Stir till cheese blends with butter.

When steaming cauliflower or cabbage, place a piece of lemon in the water to eliminate the cabbagy smell.

CAVOLFIORE PIEDMONTESE

Steam a whole head of cauliflower, or break into flowerets, till done but crisp. Pour over it the following sauce:

4 Tbsp. butter	2–3 Tbsp. wine vinegar
1 small onion, minced	¼ C. stock
1 clove garlic, minced	Minced parsley
2 anchovy fillets, minced	Salt and pepper

Sauté the onion and garlic in the butter till soft. Add anchovies, vinegar and stock, parsley, salt, and pepper, and simmer 1 minute.

If you have always hated cabbage because it was limp and waterlogged, please try the following recipe. It may change your mind about cabbage forever.

SIMPLE STEAMED CABBAGE

Take a green cabbage and tear it into pieces. Fill a huge bowl with cold water and toss in a handful of salt and a handful of sugar. Soak the cabbage in this for at least 4 hours.

Shortly before the meal begins, put about 1½ C. water in a deep pot. Add a piece of lemon peel and 2 or 3 whole peppercorns. Add a pinch of salt and a pinch of sugar. When water boils, drain cabbage and put into pot, lower fire a little, and let cook 5 minutes. Test with fork for degree of doneness. It is essential to avoid mushiness. When crisp cooked, drain well, add butter and pepper generously, and serve immediately. Top with a sprinkling of crumbled crisp bacon and toasted pine nuts. (Serves 6.)

ZUCCHINI, YELLOW AND GREEN SUMMER SQUASH

Clean zucchini and cut into 1" slices or long strips. Steam till crisp done (2–3 minutes). Serve with butter, garlic, optional onions or chopped tomatoes. Or with plain lemon butter.

Or with

Walnut-Garlic Sauce

1 tsp. salt	1 C. chopped walnuts,
6 Tbsp. butter	toasted in oven or frying
2 Tbsp. oil	pan
2 tsp. minced garlic	

Melt butter and oil and sauté garlic till soft and golden, not brown. Add walnuts and salt. Heat briefly, then pour over the squash and serve immediately.

Or with

Green Onion and Sour Cream Sauce

Melt 4–6 Tbsp. butter in pan. Add 4 Tbsp. green onions and cook a few minutes. Add ½ C. sour cream, which is at room temperature,* salt, and pepper, and mix with the squash.

---

*To prevent curdling and separation, warm sour cream and yoghurt slightly before adding them to hot soups and sauces. You may do this by placing the container in a bowl of warm water for a while.

TOMATOES

Cut 3 large tomatoes in half or remove blossom end of 6 small tomatoes. Cover with Dijon mustard, salt, pepper, and cheddar cheese. Bake in 375° – 400° oven for 12–15 minutes.

Or top with the following mixture:

1 C. bread crumbs
2 cloves garlic, minced
1 Tbsp. parsley, chopped
5 Tbsp. lemon juice

5 Tbsp. olive oil
Salt and pepper
Basil (optional)

Broil 10 minutes or bake 15–20 minutes in a 400° oven.

See cherry tomatoes with cream (pp. 231–32) and dolmas section (pp. 160–61) for more tomato recipes.

For Fast Food-High Energy cooking we may use shortcuts like canned or frozen food.

It is easy for us on the West Coast, with our abundant and readily available produce, to turn up our noses at people who use frozen chopped spinach. Of course fresh spinach is different from frozen and does not taste the same. However, it may not be available at your market. And after having seen what passes for fresh in some stores, I would say the average shopper may be better off buying the frozen! For example, during the past few summers the fresh green peas have been terribly starchy. Even after many minutes of steaming with lettuce, sugar, and onions they still tasted like nothing and their texture was mealy, not juicy like the frozen ones. This winter, with fresh spinach at 39 cents a bunch and frozen spinach 24 cents for a package that is the equivalent of two bunches, I may well select the frozen, especially when the recipe calls for spinach that is chopped. If the green beans are limp, or the carrots tough and starchy, I will reach for the frozen package of beans or whole baby carrots every time.

While frozen vegetables are a little less nutritious than fresh (but more nutritious than canned and without those chemical

266

preservatives), they can still taste wonderful. Better to eat a revived frozen vegetable than no vegetable at all . . . or a fresh one that has been cooked to death.

The secret with frozen vegetables is how to cook them so that they will *taste* as good as the fresh. The first thing to remember is to *ignore*, totally, *all the instructions on the package!* I always *thaw* the vegetable *before cooking*, so I won't have to resort to boiling for it to thaw. I leave it at room temperature for a few hours or in the refrigerator overnight. All frozen vegetables have been "blanched" (cooked for a few minutes in boiling water and then rinsed with cold water to set the color and stop the cooking); therefore, there is no need to boil them again. Take the thawed vegetable and proceed with the recipe as if the vegetable were fresh. For peas, thaw, put in the pot with butter, and steam for about 3–5 minutes, till tender. For beans, thaw and stir-fry in a little butter or oil, with garlic or onion if you like. They will be "done" when they are heated through. For spinach or chopped broccoli, thaw and squeeze all the extra moisture from the leaves. Then heat through in butter or in an already-cooked cream sauce. Baby carrots should be thawed, then heated with butter and a little broth or water, perhaps a dash of brown sugar or honey, till they are tender, about 5–10 minutes, depending on the thickness of the carrots.

If you've substituted canned broth for homemade stock or frozen peas in place of fresh in a recipe, don't feel guilty for having taken a shortcut. That the soup tasted good and was enjoyed by those who ate it is what matters. Maybe you had other things to do with your time that day. You *did* cook the meal and didn't send out for Chicken Delight, so stop letting the purists bum you out! Cooking is not a morality and endurance test.

A few recipes using frozen vegetables:

CREAMED SPINACH

2 pkgs. frozen chopped
  spinach (or chopped
  Swiss chard or chopped
  broccoli)*
3 Tbsp. butter
3 Tbsp. flour

½ C. cream (any kind)
¼–½ C. sour cream
  Salt and pepper
½ tsp. nutmeg
½ tsp. garlic powder

Thaw two packages of chopped spinach and drain well. Melt butter and add flour. Add cream and stir till thick. You may want a bit more cream if too thick. Add sour cream, salt, pepper, grated nutmeg, garlic powder, and spinach. Stir well. Adjust seasoning. (Serves 6–8.)

See spinach pies (p. 186 and 196) and spinach Genovese style or braised, (p. 135).

PEAS À LA FRANÇAISE

2 pkgs. frozen peas,
  thawed, or 3 lb. fresh
  peas, shelled
1 bunch scallions, minced
1 small head of Bibb or

  Boston or butter lettuce,
  shredded
6 Tbsp. butter
1–2 Tbsp. sugar
1 tsp. salt

Place all ingredients in a heavy kettle with a bit of water. Bring to a boil, cover, and simmer 3–5 minutes for frozen peas, about 10–15 minutes for fresh, depending on tenderness and youth of the peas. If there is too much liquid, let a little boil away at the end. (Serves 6.)

*You can use grated fresh zucchini, too.

PISELLI CON PROSCIUTTO—Roman Peas

6 Tbsp. butter, or a bit more	½ C. chicken stock, or a bit more
⅓ C. finely chopped onions	4 oz. prosciutto, cut into strips
2 pkgs. frozen peas, thawed, or 3 lb. fresh peas, shelled	Salt and pepper

Melt 3 Tbsp. butter and sauté the onions for about 5 minutes, till soft but not brown. Add the peas and the chicken stock, cover, and simmer till the peas are done (2–5 minutes for frozen peas, or 8–15 minutes for fresh, depending on the size of the peas). Sauté prosciutto strips in remaining butter till they curl, stirring often. Add to the peas. Season with salt and pepper. (Serves 6.)

GLAZED BABY CARROTS

2 pkgs. frozen baby carrots (or 14–16 fresh ones)	Salt Nutmeg or cinnamon Grated orange or lemon rind (optional)
½ C. dry white wine	
8 Tbsp. butter	Mint leaves, crushed
4 Tbsp. brown sugar	(optional)

Thaw frozen carrots (or peel and cut fresh ones into uniform 2–3 inch lengths and parboil about 5–7 minutes). Cook in wine with butter, sugar, and seasonings, till tender.

See Moroccan carrots (p. 341–42).

Two soups using frozen vegetables:

PEA SOUP

2 pkgs. frozen peas, thawed (4 C.)
1 chopped onion
3 C. chicken broth
1 C. water
3 Tbsp. butter
2 Tbsp. flour
Salt and pepper
2 egg yolks
1 C. light cream or buttermilk
½ tsp. fines herbes (optional)

Cook peas and onions in broth and water. Puree when tender. Melt butter and add flour. Add the puree and cook till thick. Season to taste.

Combine egg yolks and cream or buttermilk. Gradually add some hot soup, then add this back to soup. Heat, but don't boil.

For an interesting variation, use 1 pkg. frozen chopped spinach, 1 pkg. frozen peas.

CREAM OF SPINACH SOUP

4 Tbsp. butter
1 small onion, finely chopped, or 4 Tbsp. dried minced onion
3–4 Tbsp. flour
6 C. chicken broth
2 pkgs. of frozen chopped
spinach, thawed and squeezed dry
Salt and pepper
¼ tsp. nutmeg
1¼ C. heavy cream
2 egg yolks (optional)

Melt butter in deep kettle. Sauté fresh onion briefly. Add flour and mix till blended. Don't brown. Add chicken broth. Bring to a boil, stirring occasionally. Add the spinach (and dried minced onion). Simmer 3–5 minutes. Add salt, pepper, and nutmeg to taste. Puree a bit at a time in the blender along with 1 C. cream. (Soup may be frozen or refrigerated at this point.)

Just before serving bring to a simmer and add 2 egg yolks mixed with ¼ C. cream. This step is optional. You may just want to add more cream and nutmeg. Garnish with drop of sour cream, sprinkle of nutmeg. Keeps about 4 days in refrigerator and freezes well. (Serves 6–8.)

When homemade soup stock is not available, canned potato soup, canned beets, canned broth help make these quick soups possible:

QUICK WATERCRESS SOUP

4 bunches watercress	About 1 C. heavy cream
3 C. canned potato soup or vichysoisse	Salt and pepper

Steam the watercress over lightly salted water. Puree a bit at a time in the blender with the soup and the cream. Chill well. Adjust seasoning.* Garnish with shredded watercress leaves. (Serves 6.)

CREAM OF BROCCOLI SOUP

3 C. fresh broccoli, chopped into 2" pieces, or frozen chopped broccoli, thawed	Salt and pepper
	1 C. or more heavy cream
	1 can potato soup
	1–1½ Tbsp. curry powder**
4 C. or more chicken broth	Sour cream
4 Tbsp. dried minced onion or 1 small fresh onion, diced	Chopped green onions

Steam chopped fresh broccoli in broth with onion and salt. When tender, puree in blender with 1 C. cream. Add potato soup, a bit more cream if needed, and salt, pepper, and curry powder while blending. Garnish with sour cream and green onions. Freezes well and keeps about 4–5 days in refrigerator. When heating, you may want to add egg yolk-cream enrichment.

*If a dish has been seasoned when hot but is to be served cold, be sure to taste it just before serving. You will probably have to add a bit more salt and pepper.

**Curry powder and paprika may be warmed in a dry pan over low heat for a few moments if they are not heated during the cooking process. This revives their flavor, as they tend to go flat in the jar or can.

If this soup is too thick, dilute with more chicken broth. Be sure to puree the curry powder and cream with some of the broccoli so you mix the spices well into the soup and don't have any "hot spots." (Serves 6.).

QUICK COLD LITHUANIAN BORSCHT

1   1-lb. can beets with the juice
2   C. buttermilk
1   heaping Tbsp. sour cream
    Bowl of sour cream (optional)
2   hard-boiled eggs, chopped

½   fresh cucumber, peeled and diced
⅛   tsp. sugar
4   Tbsp. minced green onion tops
2   Tbsp. minced fresh dill (if available)

Puree beets and juice in blender. Chill thoroughly. When beet mixture is very cold, mix in buttermilk, sour cream, eggs, cucumber, and sugar. Sprinkle with minced onion and dill. May serve with additional sour cream. (Serves 4–6.)

Some "embellished" canned broths:

ZUPPA PAVESE

6   C. "rich"* chicken stock
12 rounds of bread
2   Tbsp. butter

6   eggs, or just yolks
    Parmesan cheese
    Dab of tomato paste (optional)

Bring stock to a boil. Sauté bread rounds in butter in a separate pan. Put 2 bread rounds in each bowl, and 1 egg. Pour in boiling soup to partially cook the egg. Garnish with cheese. You may dot each bread round with a dab of tomato paste. (Serves 6.)

*Add 1 tsp. powdered chicken soup, 1 Tbsp. white vermouth.

STRACCIATELLA ALLA ROMANA

6 C. "rich" chicken stock	Salt and pepper
3 well-beaten eggs	Minced parsley
3 Tbsp. parmesan cheese	(optional)

Bring stock to a boil. Mix eggs, cheese, and seasoning. Stir into the hot soup. Garnish with parsley. (Serves 6.)

Potage Germiny variation

Cook 1 C. chopped spinach or sorrel leaves in 6 C. hot stock for 3–5 minutes. Add 4 egg yolks (or 2 whole eggs) beaten till pale, first gradually warming them with some of the hot broth. (If egg batter is not hot enough before it is mixed with chicken broth, the eggs will curdle.) Heat and add sherry.

AVGOLEMONO—Greek Egg-Lemon Soup

6 C. chicken broth	½ C. precooked rice,
Juice of 1 large or 2	noodles, or any type of
medium lemons	pasta (optional)
3 eggs, well beaten till	
foamy	

Heat chicken broth. Add some hot broth very slowly to the eggs with lemon until egg batter is almost as hot as the broth. Then pour all together into the chicken broth. Add whatever pasta or rice you want in the soup. (Serves 6.)

Chapter 28

PRONTO: PASTA!

High Energy Cooking all'Italiana

To the average American the word "pasta" suggests starch served with a tomato or meat sauce that has been simmering on top of the stove for hours, days. Or an elaborate preparation like cannelloni or lasagna. However, the Italians know that pasta is Fast Food. Most of the sauces are assembled at the last minute and the pasta itself can take as little as three minutes for fresh and ten minutes for dry to prepare. High Energy is needed to coordinate the sauce and the pasta so that they are simultaneously ready to be assembled and served instantly. This may take a little practice, but I guarantee you that the results will be worth it. Does this sound like Pasta Propaganda?

All right, if the truth be known, I am a pasta maniac. Not only that, but my family has inherited my mania. If given a choice on any night of the week, on any occasion, when asked what they would like for dinner, everyone will say, "Pasta." It doesn't matter that we had it the day before, or two days before, or even for lunch. We just never seem to get enough. It is my solution to

273

the economic crisis. A pound of pasta easily feeds four to five Americans inexpensively and deliciously (only three Italians). It is the ideal Fast Food and can be prepared on the spur of the moment. If someone drops in on you for dinner you can always whip up something wonderful if you keep a few packages of dried pasta, some parmesan cheese, and canned tomato or marinara sauce on the pantry shelf. For simple High Energy cooking follow a recipe, but if you want to tap your Mental Energy, you can invent sauce combinations at will, using leftover meats and vegetables.

My pasta mania got started when I was living in Italy. I gained twenty pounds trying all the pastas I could find in my travels up and down the countryside. My American metabolism was not accustomed to such massive doses of starch. But the pounds were easily vanquished upon my return to the U.S.A. and those inevitable meat and salad dinners. Now I seem to have it under control. I can indulge in my weakness at least once a week without the demon fat coming to get me. I think the difference is that in Italy pasta is the first course and the bulk of the meal. Meat and vegetable portions are very small and come *after* the pasta course. Pasta is served in one form or another twice a day: in soup *(in brodo)* or "dry" *(pasta asciutta)* with a sauce. Now when I serve pasta for dinner I usually have just a salad accompaniment and call it a night. I do not follow it with a meat and vegetable course. And I don't have those three-hour lunches to linger over or nap after. Nothing can put the pounds on faster than a big plate of pasta, some meat, a vegetable, some fruit and cheese and wine, and then a siesta! I don't know if I could give up pasta even if threatened with increasing corpulence. It just satisfies too many personal taste cravings. And it is so versatile that I constantly feel challenged when I cook the sauce of the day.

If you feel Meditative, have time and rolling-pin expertise, and take pleasure in the process of rolling dough (or a pasta machine), you would do well to make your own. If you are fortunate enough to live in a city with a large Italian population like San Francisco, Chicago, or New York, you can probably buy fresh pasta at your local Italian delicatessen. If you use dried pasta try the imported brands like Da Cecco and Agnese and Star. These are better than most of the domestic products. But just be sure that whatever pasta you cook is made with *durum wheat semolina* or it will not attain the perfect texture, "al dente," that elusive quality that means "to the tooth." The pasta must be cooked so it is still a bit firm when you bite into it. When you look at a strand in cross-section you will see a tiny white dot of barely cooked pasta in the center—a dot, not a glob.

Test a strand every minute or so after the pasta boils so that it does not overcook and become a soggy disaster. Remember to cook the pasta in quantities of boiling water, *at least* 2 qt. per pound, adding salt and 1 Tbsp. of oil to the water *after* it boils. The oil prevents the pasta from sticking together, but it doesn't hurt to stir once or twice for added no-stick insurance. Start testing for al dente-ness after a few minutes: 2 minutes for fresh pasta, 5 for dried.

Many cookbooks' advice to the contrary, you should NEVER rinse pasta. Just drain it in a colander, shake it to get the excess water off, and pour the noodles into a serving bowl that has a little butter or oil in it. To incorporate the butter, mix the noodles briefly, so they won't stick to each other. (The exception to this rule is when cooking lasagna noodles or cannelloni pasta squares. Drain in a colander. Put into a bowl of cold water to stop the cooking, then spread out on dish towels.)

The Italian way is to mix the sauce *with* the pasta, not slop a spoonful on top. The sauce and the noodle must combine for that perfect balance of sauce to starch. For every size and shape of noodle there is the proper thickness for the sauce. A broad noodle can take a heavy sauce like Bolognese, a medium-size noodle takes a medium-weight sauce like Amatriciana, and a delicate egg noodle or very thin pasta should get the lightest of sauces such as pesto, butter, cream, and cheese. An overly heavy sauce will annihilate a fine noodle, and a light sauce will get lost if mixed on a heavy pasta. That is why there are traditional blends like "spaghetti alla carbonara," "trenette al pesto," etc.

Most of the following selection of High Energy quick pasta recipes can be assembled from the staples in the Basic Pantry and don't require elaborate last-minute shopping.

SPAGHETTI ALLE VONGOLE (Neapolitan)

1 lb. pasta (spaghetti, linguine, etc.)
1 onion, chopped
2 cloves garlic, minced (or more)
¼ C. or more olive oil
Pepper
24 small clams, steamed

open, with juice, or 1–2 cans clams, chopped or whole
3 Tbsp. parsley, minced
2 C. marinara sauce (optional)
Pesto to taste (optional)
Oregano (optional)

Sauté onions and garlic in oil till soft and not brown. Add clams and their juice, parsley, and marinara sauce if desired. Simmer a few minutes to combine flavors. Add pepper to taste. You may add pesto or oregano if desired, too. While sauce is being prepared, boil pasta in salted water for 9–10 minutes, till al dente. Mix with drained pasta. (Serves 6.)

You may make a similar sauce for shrimp, crab, or steamed mussels.

SPAGHETTI WITH BACON, CLAMS, AND PESTO

1 onion, sliced
2–4 cloves garlic, minced
1 lb. pasta (spaghetti or linguine)
½ lb. bacon, cut in small dice

Parsley, pesto to taste (about 2 Tbsp.)
2 small cans minced clams
Lots of ground pepper

Sauté onion and garlic in oil. Add bacon and simmer 7 minutes till soft and cooked. Add parsley and clams and cook till flavors mingle. Season with pepper. Add pesto and heat through. Boil pasta al dente, drain well and mix well with the sauce.

SPAGHETTI ALL'AMATRICIANA

1 lb. pasta (spaghetti, penne)
1 large onion, sliced thin
5 Tbsp. oil
½–1 tsp. red pepper flakes
Water
½ lb. lean bacon cut into tiny strips

4 Tbsp. dry white wine
1 lb. fresh tomatoes, peeled and diced, or 1-lb. can
Salt and pepper

Sauté onion in oil till soft. Add red pepper and 2 Tbsp. water and cook 2 minutes. Add bacon strips. Let it cook for a few minutes till almost crisp, then add wine and let the wine reduce. Add tomatoes and simmer 5 minutes. Add salt and pepper. Boil pasta al dente, drain well. Mix sauce with pasta and garnish with cheese. (Serves 6.)

For a spicier pasta—"all'arrabiata," or "angry"—increase the crushed red pepper flakes.

SPAGHETTI ALLA CARBONARA

1 lb. spaghetti
2 Tbsp. butter
4 Tbsp. olive oil
¾ lb. thick-cut lean bacon, cut in julienne strips
½ lb. julienne cut Canadian bacon

4 eggs
8 Tbsp. grated parmesan cheese
2 tsp. black pepper

Boil spaghetti al dente. While pasta is cooking, sauté bacon and Canadian bacon in butter and oil. Don't overcook, but cook till tender and bubbly in pan. In the serving bowl mix eggs and parmesan cheese. Add *lots* of ground black pepper. Drain bacons and mix immediately with eggs and cheese. Drain the spaghetti and mix well with the sauce. The heat of the bacon and pasta cooks the eggs! (Serves 4–6.)

SPAGHETTI SOLERI—Carbonara Variation

1 lb. pasta—spaghetti or
  perciatelli
  Butter and oil
1 onion, sliced thin
½ lb. thick-cut bacon
3 Italian sausages,
  crumbled

1 C. frozen peas, thawed,
  or fresh peas, cooked
1 C. sautéed mushrooms
3 eggs mixed with 6 Tbsp.
  parmesan cheese
  Pepper

Boil pasta al dente. While pasta is cooking, melt butter with oil. Add onion and cook till soft, about 5 minutes. Add bacon and sausage and cook till soft but not brown and not crisp. Add peas and mushrooms and heat through. Add to the eggs and cheese and drained pasta and mix well. Add freshly ground black pepper. Mix with drained al dente pasta. (Serves 6.)

Omit eggs and cheese and you have Spaghetti all'Abbruzzese.
Omit eggs and cheese and add 2 C. tomato sauce, and you have spaghetti alla zingara.

SPAGHETTI CARUSO

1 lb. spaghetti
1 medium onion, chopped
1 lb. chicken livers, cut
  up
4 Tbsp. butter
½ C. sautéed mushrooms
  (optional)

½ C. Marsala or white
  wine
½ C. chicken stock
  (optional)
1 C. tomatoes, diced
  (optional)
  Salt and pepper

Brown onions and livers lightly in butter. Add cooked mushrooms and wine and simmer till absorbed. Add chicken stock if needed, and optional tomatoes. Season with salt and pepper. Boil spaghetti al dente. Drain and mix with sauce.

The following recipe calls for cream that is lightly whipped. Italian cream is heavier than ours and does not turn watery and thin when the hot pasta hits it. To prevent this thinning out, it is advisable to whip the cream till it is the texture of stirred yoghurt.

PAGLIA E FIENO

½ lb. white noodles
½ lb. green noodles (same thickness—linguine or fettuccine)
½ lb. prosciutto

Butter
1 C. heavy cream, lightly whipped
½ C. parmesan cheese
Pepper

Cook the two pastas together till al dente. Mix with prosciutto that has been sautéed in butter a few minutes. Mix with the heavy cream and lots of parmesan cheese. Pepper to taste.

Sautéed mushrooms may be added to the prosciutto, or crumbled Italian sweet sausage may be used instead of it.

Chapter 29

OMELETS AS HIGH ENERGY COOKING

Omelets are very easy to make. I will not give you a spiel on how many years of continued practice are needed before you can turn out the "perfect" one. If it is not precisely symmetrical when you fold it, so what? Try again. If it browns ever so slightly it will still taste delicious. But really, what's the big deal? The only practical advice I can give is to tell you not to make the omelets too big. It is tricky to fold a six-egg omelet, but a two- or three-egg omelet practically turns itself. Be sure that the pan is large enough for the eggs to cover the pan in a thin layer in order to set quickly.

A frittata is an omelet that has had the filling stirred into the eggs rather than folded into its center. It is a bit heavier and more firmly cooked than an omelet and a little less difficult to prepare because you do not need to fill, fold, turn, and flip onto a platter. Heat the filling, beat in the eggs, stir to combine the two, and cover the pan a minute to set the frittata, then unmold.

I do not believe in special pans for omelets or crepes. I have an assortment of Teflon-lined pans, a few heavy aluminum sauté pans and some cast-iron skillets as well. I grab whichever seems handy at the time, one that is the *right size* for the *number of eggs* I have stirred up.

Omelets are very versatile in the kinds of energy they evoke in the cook. Some are virtuoso productions, like the omelet for one or two which is whisked together in a second and flipped out of the pan moments later, creamy on the inside and firm and golden on the outside. The cooking rhythm is smooth but rapid. However, omelet making can be slowed down, as in the frittata mode, where the fillings are prepared in the pan, the eggs stirred in and cooked slowly till set. These involve a more laid-back action than the in-and-out-of-the-pan number. Get in touch with how you feel, your body rhythm: If it's to be a quickie, then see how smoothly you can regulate the action, even if it takes but a second to create the dish. Have everything within easy reach, preheat the pan, have the platter nearby, then go!

You may chose to chop the filling components with quiet Meditative precision, carefully laying out all of the ingredients. Then change tempo gradually. Sauté the filling, melting the butter and stirring slowly, keeping a quiet but watchful eye on the pan and a spoon in hand. When the vegetables have reached the desired consistency (and you control this by adjusting the heat on your stove and how often you stir), pour in the eggs, lower the heat, and quickly stir till they are set, or cover the pan and let the eggs firm up slowly.

The technique you select is determined by the texture you want to feel on your tongue when you bite into the omelet. If you like it creamy, stir slowly but constantly. If you want it firm and chewy, then use the lid and an even, low heat. Texture, technique, and your energy are interdependent. So do not attempt a flashy bravura omelet if you are feeling tense and tired. Your efforts will be counterproductive. Tune in to your tempo and follow where it leads. Then cooking will be a supportive experience rather than one more hassle in your day.

BACON, POTATO, AND ONION OMELET

2 Tbsp. diced bacon
½ small onion, diced
1 small boiled potato, diced
3 Tbsp. grated Swiss cheese

Salt, pepper
Chopped chives or parsley
3 eggs, beaten lightly

Render bacon. Add onions and potatoes and cook a few minutes. Add cheese, salt, pepper, and chives or parsley. Then stir in the eggs and keep stirring till they are soft but set. Serve at once. (Serves 1.)

DADAR DJAWA—Indonesian Omelet

2–3 eggs	1 small tomato, sliced
½ small onion, sliced	¼ C. shredded ham
¼ tsp. crushed chili peppers	2 Tbsp. chopped parsley Butter
¼ tsp. salt	2 Tbsp. soy sauce

Beat eggs well and set aside. Mix all other ingredients except soy, and sauté in butter. Add eggs and cover pan. Lower heat. Cook until set. Serve with soy. (Serves 1.)

An extravagant but delicious

CAVIAR OMELET

1 stick butter	8 eggs, lightly beaten
1 onion or 6 green onions, minced	8 oz. caviar Sour cream

Melt butter and stir in the onions. Cook till crisp but cooked. Add the eggs and stir well. When they start to set add some of the caviar. Fold the omelet and turn out onto a platter. Slit the center and add the sour cream and the rest of the caviar. (Serves 4.)

Other omelet fillings:

Sautéed mushrooms (p. 136)

Chicken livers and mushrooms (p. 168)

Ratatouille (p. 331)

Creamed spinach (p. 267)

Diced ham, green onions

Grated assorted cheeses

Grated Monterey-Jack cheese and chopped chilis

Not as firm as a frittata, but just as good:

OJJA BIL MERGAZ—Tunisian Sausage Omelet

¼	C. olive oil, or a bit more	2	tsp. paprika
1	lb. hot sausage or chorizo, in 1" chunks	1	tsp. harissa, or hot sauce (optional)
4	small potatoes in ½" cubes (optional)	3	peeled tomatoes, quartered
3	cloves garlic, minced	½	C. water
1	tsp. caraway seed	4	green peppers, sliced
	Salt and black pepper	10–12	eggs

Heat oil in a heavy skillet. Add sausages, and potatoes if desired. Add spices and harissa if desired and cook till sausage is light brown and potatoes are golden. Add tomatoes, water, and peppers, and cook rapidly till most of the liquid has evaporated and tomatoes are a puree. Beat eggs in a bowl. Add to sausage mixture and stir till soft curds form.

HARISSA (HRISA)—Moroccan Hot Sauce

½	C. ground red hot pepper	2	tsp. salt
¼	C. ground cumin	6	Tbsp. oil
		2	Tbsp. boiling water

Mix ingredients well. Store in cool, dark place.

Chapter 30

SOUFFLES—HOT AND COLD, AS HIGH ENERGY COOKING

While soufflés may take twenty or thirty minutes in the oven, their preparation is High Energy Fast Food cooking. Once the soufflé ingredients are assembled, it should take no more than six to ten minutes to put together! Butter is melted, flour whisked in, milk added and stirred evenly but briskly till the cream sauce base is formed, a matter of moments. Then the soufflé base is poured gradually but swiftly into a bowl that holds the egg yolks. Next the flavorings (melted chocolate, grated cheese, chopped cooked vegetables, etc.) are stirred in. The whites are beaten till stiff, again a rapid process, and then folded lightly but quickly into the base. The mixture is poured into the soufflé dish and placed in the oven. It is a dance that requires quick but flowing movements.

The measuring of the ingredients can be done well ahead of time in a quieter more reflective space, if you choose. The eggs can be separated slowly, cheese grated, onions diced with precision, or you may get speedy with the process. The prep time can have its own rhythm, reflecting or contrasting with the assembly energy of the soufflé.

Unfortunately, soufflés have an unwarranted reputation for trickiness. They have had a bad press, and are really very easy,

284

almost foolproof. You will have success with a soufflé if you remember a few simple points. A little soufflé insurance: Always preheat the oven. Always have the ingredients at room temperature. Always have at least three more egg whites than yolks, and have a souffle dish that is the right size for the capacity of the recipe. A one-quart soufflé will rise nowhere near the edge of a two-quart dish.

There are two schools of soufflé making—the French, which likes the soufflé to be runny in the center, and the American, which likes the soufflé to be dry throughout. I lean toward the runny school myself. When folding whites into the soufflé base, be sure to stir in one third of the whites with a whisk and then quickly and lightly fold in the remaining two thirds, leaving some tiny islands of whites visible. The whites are the leavening agent, so don't be too zealous and deflate them by overfolding them into the soufflé mixture. Baking may be speeded up a bit by raising the oven temperature in a given recipe or, conversely, slowed down by lowering the temperature to prolong the cooking time. With practice you will get to know each recipe and its time variables by heart. You will then feel free to play with the timing and the temperatures for your convenience. Just remember that basically most soufflés are simply a cream sauce base thickened with egg yolks and leavened with egg whites that have been stiffly beaten. When you have done one soufflé you have done them all. And yes, you may peek at the soufflé in the oven to see how it is doing if you look quickly and refrain from slamming the oven door. A soufflé must be served immediately or it will sink rapidly. Then it will taste good, but you will have to call it a pudding, serve it with cream or some related sauce, and smile. Be fearless. The laws of physics are on your side. Heat expands things, therefore the air bubbles in the egg whites increase in size and the soufflé rises. You can't fail.

CHEESE SOUFFLE

3 Tbsp. butter	½ C. minced cooked ham
2 Tbsp. flour	or Canadian bacon
1 C. cream or milk	Salt and pepper
4 egg yolks	¼ tsp. nutmeg
1½ C. grated Swiss cheese	¼ tsp. cayenne
¼ C. green onions, minced	7 egg whites

Optional

sautéed mushrooms	diced chilis
crumbled bacon	
¼ C. shredded parmesan cheese	

Preheat oven to 400°. Add flour, stir, then add the cream. Stir over heat till thickened. Lightly mix the egg yolks in a large bowl. Gradually add the hot sauce. Stir well. Add cheese, green onions, and ham, and season to taste.

Beat the egg whites till stiff. Stir one-third into the cheese mixture, then fold in the rest lightly. Pour into a well-buttered 1½- or 2-quart soufflé dish. Bake 30–35 minutes. (Serves 6). Incidentally, the cheese cake (p. 178) is really a *sweet* cheese soufflé in a cookie crust.

Corn and Cheese Soufflé

Add 2 C. corn niblets and 2 C. creamed corn, and reduce cheese to only ½ C.

Spinach and Mushroom Soufflé

Sauté 3 Tbsp. minced onion in 5 Tbsp. butter. Add 1 package frozen chopped spinach, thawed and drained. Fold into soufflé base along with ½ C. sautéed mushrooms. Omit all cheese, ham, etc.

The cake roll below is a horizontal soufflé that has been baked in a jelly-roll pan instead of the usual soufflé dish. It is then stuffed, rolled, and served at room temperature with the caviar filling, or warmed in a 350° oven for about 15 minutes with a duxelles (p. 138), creamed chicken à la king (p. 92), curried seafood (p. 167), or creamed spinach filling (p. 267).

CAVIAR CAKE ROLL

4	Tbsp. butter		Pepper
½	C. flour	1½–2	C. milk
½	tsp. salt	5	eggs, separated

Preheat oven to 350°–375°. Butter, line with waxed paper, and butter again a 10" × 15" jelly-roll pan.

Melt butter in saucepan. Add flour, salt, and a dash of pepper, and gradually add milk. Cook one minute till very thick. Mix the yolks with a fork and add gradually to hot sauce. Beat whites till stiff and fold into the sauce. Spread the batter in the pan and bake about 35–45 minutes, till puffed and browned. Cover with damp towel and chill in refrigerator 5–10 minutes. Unmold and spread with filling. Roll up onto board or platter. Serve with additional sour cream. (Serves 8.)

Filling

| 8 | oz. inexpensive red caviar* | 2 | Tbsp. sour cream |
| | | 4–6 | oz. cream cheese |

Mash cheese, cream, and 6 oz. of the caviar with fork. Fold in remaining caviar.

A classic dessert soufflé:

*Don't use the black lumpfish caviar; its dye will run and stain the filling a ghastly purple.

CHOCOLATE SOUFFLE

3 oz. or squares of semisweet chocolate	4 egg yolks
1 C. milk	1 tsp. vanilla or 2 Tbsp. brandy, Grand Marnier,
½ C. sugar	Kahlúa, kirsch, or crème
⅛ tsp. salt	de menthe
4 Tbsp. butter	6–7 egg whites
3 Tbsp. flour	

Preheat the oven to 350°.

Chop the chocolate with a knife into smallish slivers. They are easy to pick up if you do the chopping on a piece of foil or waxed paper. In a small saucepan heat the milk, sugar, salt, and chocolate shavings, stirring occasionally, till the chocolate is melted.

In another pot melt the butter, add the flour, and stir till smooth. Add the chocolate milk and cook till thick and lump free. Add this gradually to egg yolks which have been lightly beaten in a large bowl with a whisk or fork. Add vanilla or liqueur.

Beat the whites till stiff. Stir one third of the egg whites into the chocolate mixture. Carefully and lightly fold in the rest of the whites. Pour into a buttered and sugared 1½-qt. soufflé dish. Bake 35 to 40 minutes. Serve with Quick Vanilla Sauce (pp. 169–70) or sweetened whipped cream.

Variations: Pour half of the soufflé into the dish, add a layer of chocolate-covered cherries, chocolate mints, nuts, etc., then top with the remaining soufflé.

For a mocha soufflé, omit melted chocolate, and add 2 Tsp. instant coffee and 2 Tbsp. cocoa to the hot milk.

For a vanilla or almond or liqueur soufflé, omit chocolate and increase vanilla extract or liqueur of your choice. You may add grated lemon or orange rind, too.

The following are not classic soufflés, as they do not start with a cream sauce, and they omit the egg yolks altogether—a boon for cholesterol watchers. These can be assembled at jet speed!

Here's a great way to use up overripe bananas:

BANANA SOUFFLE

4 ripe bananas	1 tsp. almond extract
½ C. cream	7 egg whites
7 oz. almond paste (marzipan)	½ C. sugar
	Salt

Preheat oven to 375°. In blender, puree bananas, cream, and almond paste and extract. Set aside. Beat egg whites till stiff. Gradually beat in sugar and a pinch of salt. Fold whites into 3 C. puree. Fold mixture into a buttered 2-qt. soufflé dish. Bake 30–35 minutes.

Top with whipped cream to which powdered sugar and almond extract have been added. (Serves 6.)

CHESTNUT RUM SOUFFLE

2 C. sweetened chestnut puree	2 Tbsp. dark rum
4–6 Tbsp. rum	2 Tbsp. sugar
½ tsp. vanilla	1 tsp. vanilla
8 egg whites	½ C. preserved, chestnuts in syrup, chopped
1 C. heavy cream	

Preheat oven to 350°. In a bowl thin chestnut puree with rum and vanilla. Gently but thoroughly fold in the egg whites, whipped until they hold a definite point. Pour the mixture into a 1½-qt. soufflé dish and bake for 40 minutes. Whip heavy cream until it begins to hold a shape and flavor it with dark rum, sugar and vanilla. Stir in preserved chestnuts. Serve the soufflé immediately with the whipped cream.

APRICOT SOUFFLE

2–3	cans whole apricots, peeled, drained, and pits removed (enough for 2 cups of puree)	1	C. heavy cream, whipped
5	egg whites		Grated rind of 1 orange
½	C. sugar	3	Tbsp. confectioners' sugar
	Pinch of salt	2	Tbsp. Grand Marnier (optional)

Preheat oven. Puree apricots in blender. Beat egg whites with pinch of salt till stiff; gradually beat in sugar. Fold into 2 C. apricot puree. Bake in a buttered 1½-qt. soufflé dish that has been placed in a pan of hot water: 350° oven for 30–35 minutes, 375° oven for 25–30 minutes, or 300° oven for 45 minutes. Serve with whipped cream flavored with sugar, orange rind, and orange liqueur if desired. (Serves 6).

Not exactly a soufflé but a close relative:

STEAMED APRICOT PUDDING

½	lb. dried apricots	1½	Tbsp. arrowroot
2–3	C. sweet white wine (such as sauterne, muscatel, white port)	¼	lb. butter
		¼	C. sugar
		5	eggs, separated

Soak apricots for 4 hours or longer in enough wine to cover them, then simmer slowly till very soft. Puree in the blender or food processor. Put puree into a saucepan with butter, sugar, egg yolks and arrowroot, and stir over low heat till it becomes a smooth cream. Cool it a bit. Fold in stiffly beaten egg whites. Pour into a buttered mold or 1½-qt. soufflé dish. Cover with buttered foil and steam atop stove (or in 350° oven in pan of water) for 1 hour. Serve with whipped cream flavored with sugar, apricot brandy, or orange flower water.

You may also cool the pudding, unmold, chill, and frost with the sweeted whipped cream.

To steam this pudding on top of the stove, fill a deep pot with enough boiling water so that the dish placed on a stand is above the water level. Cover the pot and reduce heat to a simmer. Check water level occasionally so that it doesn't evaporate away completely.

A cold soufflé is not a soufflé at all. It is technically a Bavarian cream that has been poured into a dish too small for the amount of dessert mixture. A foil collar supports the excess mixture, so that when the dessert is chilled, the gelatin sets, and the foil is peeled away, you have an illusion, something that resembles a soufflé in appearance but tastes like a Bavarian cream. If you remain unimpressed by such dramatic presentations, you may serve the cold soufflé mixture in custard cups or dessert dishes, or chill in a simple mold and dip in hot water before serving to unmold easily. Just remember that if you should decide the attempt the "trompe l'oeil" of a cold soufflé, you must have a dish that is the right size. A ¾-quart soufflé dish will be just about right for a mixture that measures over a quart or a quart and a half. If you pour the mixture into a 2-quart dish you will be waiting *quite* a long time for it to rise.

Incidentally, Bavarian creams freeze very well and can be brought to proper temperature in a few hours or overnight in the refrigerator.

COLD LIME SOUFFLE

1 envelope or 1 Tbsp. of gelatin	¼ tsp. salt
¼ C. cold water	Rind of 1 lime, grated
4 eggs, separated	Green food coloring (optional)
½ C. fresh lime juice	1 C. heavy cream
1 C. sugar	

Soften gelatin in water.

In stainless steel or enamel pot combine egg yolks, lime juice, ½ C. sugar, salt. Mix well with beater or whisk. Cook over *very low* flame, stirring *constantly* till thickened. Add gelatin and stir till dissolved. Stir in lime rind (and 2 drops green food coloring, if desired). Pour into large bowl.

Beat egg whites at room temperature till they hold their shape. Gradually beat in ½ C. sugar and beat till stiff peaks form. Whip cream till stiff. Combine the cream and the egg whites. Add ⅓ of the cream-egg whites mixture to lime mixture and stir well. Carefully fold in the rest. Pour into a ¾-qt. soufflé dish to which a buttered foil collar has been attached on the outside and secured with a rubber band or string. Chill well, 4–6 hours. Or you may serve as a Bavarian cream in a mold. May be made the day before. Also may be frozen. (Serves 6.)

Cold Lemon Soufflé

Use lemon juice and rind instead of lime, and eliminate food coloring.

Cold Grand Marnier Soufflé

Reduce total sugar to ½ C., add juice and rind of 2 oranges and ¼ C. Grand Marnier. Gelatin may be dissolved in half of the orange juice. Garnish with orange slices if desired.

COLD PUMPKIN SOUFFLE

2	envelopes gelatin	1	tsp. orange peel
½	C. cold water	1	tsp. cinnamon
1½	C. pumpkin puree	½	tsp. ginger
1	C. sour cream	¾	C. brown sugar
3	egg yolks	5	egg whites
¼	tsp. each cloves, nutmeg, salt	¼	C. white sugar
		1	C. heavy cream

Soften gelatin in water, and dissolve over low heat. Heat pumpkin, sour cream, egg yolks, spices, and brown sugar. Add gelatin to pumpkin mix.

Beat egg whites, adding white sugar when almost stiff. Beat cream till stiff. Combine with egg whites. Stir ¼ of cream and whites into pumpkin mixture. Fold in the rest. Pour into 1-qt. soufflé dish with buttered foil collar. Chill. Garnish with pecan halves. (Serves 6.)

This can fill 2 baked 9" pie shells. Top with whipped cream if desired.

Instead of a cold soufflé that could fill a pie shell, here is a pie filling that could be a cold soufflé if you changed its presentation:

RUM CREAM PIE

6 egg yolks (or 3 eggs, separated)
1 C. sugar
1 envelope gelatin dissolved in ¼ C. cold water
1 pt. heavy cream (1 C. if using egg whites)

½ C. dark rum
Shaved chocolate
Chopped candied ginger (optional)
1 cookie crumb crust (gingersnaps are best, but graham or chocolate will do)

Beat egg yolks with sugar till very thick and pale. Add cooled, dissolved gelatin. Beat optional egg whites until stiff; beat the cream till stiff, flavor with rum, and add egg whites. Fold into yolks. Cool mixture till it begins to set, and pour into pie shell. Sprinkle with shaved chocolate. (You may add chopped candied ginger to cream mixture, too.) Top with more whipped cream if feeling sinful. (Serves 8.)

You may use other liqueurs in place of rum. Consider crème de cacao and Kahlúa, crème de menthe, Irish whisky, Amaretto, brandy, and all the fruit liqueurs.

Crumb Crust

1½ C. crumbs—graham cracker, ginger snaps, chocolate, or vanilla

wafers—crushed in the blender
6 Tbsp. butter, melted

Combine with hands and press into pie pan. Bake in 375° oven for 10 minutes.

PART FOUR:

What Am I Cooking?

Introduction: Asking "What Am I Cooking?"

Once you have asked WHY, FOR WHOM and HOW am I cooking, WHAT am I cooking is a question that will almost answer itself. In fact, WHAT am I cooking is the last of questions I ask because its answer, for me, is totally dependent upon the first three. If you know the person FOR WHOM you are cooking, you will cook WHAT he or she might like to eat: favorite foods or something new you suspect he or she might enjoy. If you are cooking for yourself, you will cook WHAT you like or try a new dish you think may become part of your repertoire. You will cook WHAT is available at your market and WHAT is in stock in your pantry. The WHATs of cooking are the raw materials, your available equipment, and the recipes at your disposal. They reflect your budget, your technical abilities, your knowledge. But they are colored by HOW you are feeling when you deal with them.

This last section of *Feedback* deals with some of the WHATs of cooking: recipes, menu planning, et cetera.

Remember that in subjective matters like individual growth and pleasure, an amateur gets as much out of the cooking process as the pro; a bumbling first effort can yield as much satisfaction as a chef's masterful tour de force. Technique and experience are just means to the end, the expression of a food idea in a joyful and personal manner.

297

Chapter 31

WHAT IS A RECIPE?

Attribution, Evolution, and Interpretation

To be a good cook you must enjoy food. Reluctant eaters usually make mechanical and uninspired cooks. Your basic ingredients need not be expensive or unusual—merely as fresh as possible and of good quality. It helps to be somewhat organized if the process is to go smoothly. Spontaneity is wonderful, but chaos can really impede your energies no matter how well-intentioned you are. You can be organized without being constipated.

Some people are intuitive cooks. They have a natural feel for the medium. Others learn by eating, tasting the foods prepared in restaurants and cooked by friends; through travel, trying new dishes, and memorizing the flavors. Some learn by reading cookbooks, others by doing, in cooking classes or teaching themselves. It doesn't matter how you develop and refine your art. Just practice. Cook. Experiment. Take a few chances and, from time to time, deviate from the tried and true. You may surprise yourself. The difference between a good cook and a great one lies in the amount of imagination, creativity, and sense of personal interpretation imparted to the food. The great cook understands the "dance of cooking," when the process takes over and the recipes go along.

When I first began writing, I toyed with the idea of doing a book without recipes. After all, as by now you know, I believe that from the point of view of personal growth and enjoyment, WHY you cook and HOW you feel about it are more important than WHAT you cook. But the process does not exist in a vacuum: There is ultimately a product.

These recipes have been selected not because they are "mine"—in fact, many are not—but because they represent different kinds of cooking energy and allow for the development of personal style.

These recipes are not rigid formulas to be followed like laws of the land. They are ideas, suggestions, auras, impressions. Feel free to make changes according to your personal tastes and preferences. My own food prejudices are so well known that my students jokingly designed my "crest" as mushrooms rampant on a field of garlic butter.

The recipes in *Feedback* are eclectic in origin and have been collected through travel and reading and, above all, from friends who have been willing to share their discoveries and old treasures with me. Good recipes, like good meals, ought to be shared. That is how they get recorded, passed on, kept alive! Too many recipes have gone to the grave with a jealous, insecure aunt who wouldn't reveal her formula for chocolate cake or a grandmother who was too old to remember all the ingredients and details of how she used to make her special cannelloni.

How petty and misguided are those who will not share a recipe for fear that you will steal their thunder. Feel sorry for people who give you a recipe with one ingredient missing or changed just to make you feel like a fool for failing to reproduce their triumph. You'll probably find a similar recipe while reading a new cookbook, or you may be able to invent one that you will like even better, and have a great time doing it, too. It's fun to be a cooking detective.

When I was first married, my former husband used to talk about his grandmother's stuffed cabbage. Rae Goldstein had been preparing this specialty for over fifty years. When I entered the family she was quite old, her eyesight failing. Only once was

I fortunate enough to taste the famous stuffed cabbage. I talked with her about the recipe. She had never written it down but "knew" what went into it and how much.

Unfortunately, she died before anyone in the family could transcribe the recipe while she cooked. So I embarked on a detective's mission: the Cabbage Caper. I think that I made stuffed cabbage once a week for months, trying all the recipes suggested by well-meaning aunts and cousins until I arrived at one combination that seemed to be "it." At least my husband said that it was as good as, if not better than, Grandma's Rae's. It may not be better, but it is greatly enjoyed by our family, especially by her great-granddaughter and namesake, Rachel, who can now make stuffed cabbage any time the craving strikes.

STUFFED CABBAGE (Jewish "Dolmas")

2	medium or 1 very large cabbage, 2–2½ lbs., cored*	2	eggs
		1½	lb. ground chuck
			Salt and pepper
1	onion	2	C. rice, uncooked

Bring a large quantity of salted water to a boil in a deep pot. Parboil the cabbage for about 5–10 minutes, drain, and remove the *largest* leaves. Grate the onion or puree it with the eggs in blender. In a bowl mix the ground chuck, eggs with onions, salt, pepper, and rice. Place a heaping Tbsp. on each leaf, roll up, and spear closed with toothpicks.

In a deep kettle bring to a simmer:

2	10-oz. cans tomato soup, undiluted	1	small chopped onion
		½	tsp. salt
1	can water	1	C. brown sugar
8	Tbsp. lemon juice		

You may add a bit more soup, or use tomato juice, if needed. Drop cabbage rolls in the simmering liquids, cover the kettle,

*Remove as much as possible of the hard center of the cabbage by cutting it out with a sharp knife.

and simmer for about 2½ hours. Baste occasionally. Taste sauce and adjust seasoning.

You may also bake this in a 350° oven for the same amount of time. The proper balance of sweet and sour is up to you. If your budget is tight, use less meat, more rice. The sauce thickens upon reheating. If it is too thin you may reduce it over low heat till the proper consistency is achieved. Keeps in refrigerator a week. This is one of those dishes that tastes better on the second day, or upon successive reheating. (Serves 6–8.)

I was luckier in tracking down another recipe. My friend Helen Nicholas always raved about an Albanian leek pie that her mother made, but as her cooking experience was limited, she couldn't provide many clues as to how to make it. All she offered were glowing descriptions: aromatic, golden brown and puffy, flaky, cheesy, sublime. One day Helen told me that her mother was coming to California for a visit. I asked Helen to write her mother to please make the leek pie while she was here so that I might transcribe the recipe and then we would be able to make it whenever we wanted. Mrs. Nicholas arrived from Auburn, Massachusetts. In her suitcase was a bag of King Arthur flour (unbleached white flour of excellent quality, made in Massachusetts) and something that looked like a broomstick. It was her trusty rolling pin. Helen bought the leeks and cheese, and I provided the pizza pan and the kitchen. Mrs. Nicholas got to work, carefully explaining what she was doing, step by step, suggesting variations as she went along: Some days she used zucchini, some days spinach. Her pan was a little deeper but mine would do. She was incredibly adept at rolling the dough. Perfect circles formed under her hands. She had obviously been rolling dough like this since she was a little girl (just like the women in Italy, who begin rolling pasta once a day when they are eight years old). We watched, mesmerized. The leek pie went into the oven and we waited. We sipped tea and sniffed the air for the telltale aroma that would let us know that it was almost ready. When it finally emerged from the oven, it was just as Helen had described it: golden brown, flaky, puffed in the center. We cut into it and oohed and aahed. It was delicious, as wonderful as she had remembered. We ate and ate till we could hardly move.

Later on, in a more rational moment when I was copying the recipe over (my notes were a bit disorganized because of all the drawings, the notes, the variations suggested, etc.), I realized that this pie was not too far removed from the Greek and Turkish borek I prepare with fillo dough, or spanokopita if we had used spinach. A week later I decided to attempt the leek pie while it was still fresh in my mind. (I believe that you don't really "know" a recipe until you cook it. You may read about it, watch it in class or on a TV cooking program, but until its physical actions are imprinted on your brain by direct action, you don't understand the recipe, nor will you even remember how to do it if you allow too much time to elapse between the watching and the doing.)

I prepared the dough and crossed my fingers, for I had never rolled a perfect circle in my life and especially one that was 18" in diameter. I held my breath and started to roll, using my longest rolling pin and hoping not to stretch the dough too much and make unwanted holes in the crust. It came out! Not only that, the second crust came out as well. I had rolled two perfect (well, almost perfect) circles, and the pie was placed in the oven. I was so excited that I tried to call Helen to tell her of my triumph, but she was not home. I peeked at the pie and sure enough it was puffing up! The smells were incredible, and when everyone came home from school and work we feasted on Mrs. Nicholas' leek pie.

LAKROR ME PRESH—Mrs. Nicholas' Albanian Leek Pie

Dough

3 cups unbleached white flour, sifted with
1 tsp. baking powder
1 tsp. salt
1 Tbsp. Crisco (or any solid shortening)

1¼–1½ C. lukewarm water
½ lb. butter melted with 2 Tbsp. Crisco

Place flour, baking powder, salt, and Crisco in large bowl. Make a well and add the water gradually till the dough holds together. Knead till smooth and lump free. Set aside in cool place—not the refrigerator, if possible. Allow to rest for 2–24 hours, covered with foil or plastic wrap.

Divide the *pete*, as dough is called in Albanian, into two parts. Roll the first half out into a circle about 20" in diameter. Brush well with melted butter with Crisco. Fold in half toward you, and pull the dough into an elongated rectangle the long side facing you. Butter again and fold left to right, a quarter at a time, buttering as you go till you have a packet of dough that is *about* 4" × 4". (Measurements are approximate; dough is malleable and can be pulled to almost any size.) Place in a lightly floured plate and cover with foil. Roll out the other half and repeat the buttering and folding. Allow the dough to rest covered for a half hour while you make the filling. Try to use the least amount of flour possible while rolling out the dough. Wondra is very good for this procedure and is easy to clean up.

Filling

7–8 leeks, white part mostly (about 2 C.)	1 lb. cottage cheese
2 Tbsp. butter	4–6 eggs
3 Tbsp. water	Salt and pepper to taste
3–4 oz. cream cheese (or Alouette, herbed Boursin, etc.) (optional)	Nutmeg, garlic powder, etc. (optional)

Wash leeks well and chop fine. Cook in a saucepan, covered with the butter and water. Steam till tender, about 10 minutes. Add the cheeses, the eggs, the salt and pepper, and any spices you like. Mrs. Nicholas' pie contains only salt, but I find that I want pepper and occasionally nutmeg or garlic.

Butter a 15" pizza pan. Roll out one packet of dough and place it in the pan with about a 1" overlap at sides. Pour in the filling. Roll out the other piece of dough and top the pie. Roll up the edges of the pie, underside overlapping the top piece till the edge is curled up. Brush liberally with butter. Push down on the edge of the rim with the tines of a fork. Bake in a 350° oven for 1 hour. Let rest 15 minutes before slicing. Cut in squares. (Serves 6 for supper.)

The pie may be baked ahead of time and reheated. It is good when it is warm. You may also prepare it ahead of time and refrigerate it, then bring it to room temperature before baking; but it may lose some of its flakiness this way.

If you are nervous about making the crust, cannot roll a perfect circle or even a square or trapezoid, then you can prepare this with fillo dough. The texture will be different, but it will still be grand.

Variation: You may use spinach, Swiss chard, zucchini, or summer squash instead of leeks.

It is the ultimate conceit in cooking to think that there is anything completely new. One night you "invent" a dish and a few months later, while browsing through a cookbook, you see a similar recipe; it seems that "your" dish is fairly common in Rumania! I will call a recipe "original" or "mine" if I stumble upon the combination or idea without having read about it before, but I believe that there are very few "original" creations in the kitchen.

Attribution is a tricky issue. For example, in 1969 I clipped a dessert recipe from the Sunday *New York Times*. It was called "Evelyn Sharpe's French Chocolate Cake." I filed it away, planning at some later date to prepare the cake when the chocolate munchies were upon me. Five years later I was invited to a friend's restaurant for a birthday celebration. The owner, Narsai David, and I had decided to celebrate our birthdays together over a festive meal. Since he had to work that evening, dinner was at his restaurant. His pastry chef, a young woman named Janice Feuer, prepared a cake for the birthday extravaganza. After members of the restaurant staff tasted it, it was given the name "Chocolate Decadence." It was sumptuous, rich, and delicious. The next day I called her to thank her for her efforts and to ask for the recipe. Later on, as I was filing it with the chocolate cake recipes, I noticed Evelyn Sharpe's recipe and remarked to myself that the two were practically identical. There was a tablespoon of butter, a tablespoon of sugar off here and there, but essentially it was the same cake. Now far be it from me to say who invented the cake. Did Janice see the *New York Times* recipe? Did she play with it, make a few changes, and then consider it hers? Or did she spontaneously create this cake out of her head? In fact, it really doesn't matter. What does matter is that we have the recipe, the cake is delicious, and I can pass the recipe on to you. So here is "Chocolate Decadence à la Janice and Evelyn":

CHOCOLATE DECADENCE CAKE

1 lb. sweet chocolate, melted in double boiler	4 eggs, separated Whipped cream
3 Tbsp. sugar	Vanilla
1 Tbsp. flour	2 Tbsp. confectioners' sugar
8 oz. sweet butter, softened	

Combine melted chocolate with sugar, flour, and butter. Beat the yolks lightly and combine with the chocolate mixture. Beat the whites till they hold their shape but are not stiff. Fold them into the chocolate. Pour into an 8" springform pan lined with buttered waxed paper.

Bake in a 425° oven for 15 (yes, *fifteen*) minutes. Cool in the oven with the door left ajar.

If you overcook this cake it gets too dry. Although it may look soft after 15 minutes, it will firm up to the right consistency.

Keep the cake at room temperature. If you are making this days ahead of serving, you may refrigerate it. The cake can be safely frozen. However, it is IMPERATIVE that the cake be brought back to room temperature for a few hours before serving to develop the maximum flavor and texture. Serve with sweetened whipped cream flavored with vanilla. You may garnish with raspberries, whole or pureed, crystallized rose petals, or candied violets. This is *quite rich*, so servings should be small.

Occasionally I have been cooking something for such a long

time that I've forgotten how the recipe has evolved. I have been making Sacher torte and mocha torte for many years. The recipes are conglomerates. I think that originally they were printed in the Sunday *New York Times* as "Ann Seranne's Mocha Torte" and "Paula Peck's Sacher Torte," or maybe it was the other way around. I do know that I preferred the cake from the mocha torte with the Sacher torte frosting, and that I have come to use the mocha torte frosting with a chestnut torte recipe that I changed because the original was too heavy and the baking time was too short. So I thank Ann Seranne, Paula Peck, and the unknown chestnut torte personae for their inspiration, but as the song goes, "I did it my way."

BASIC CHOCOLATE CAKE FOR MOCHA TORTE AND SACHER TORTE

10	egg whites	1	tsp. vanilla
⅛	tsp. salt	8	egg yolks
¾	C. sugar	1	C. flour
½	C. (1 stick) sweet butter		
7	squares semisweet chocolate (7 oz.)		

Preheat oven to 350°. Grease bottoms of three 9″ cake pans (foil pans are good). Line bottoms with waxed paper and grease the paper.

Add salt to the egg whites, and beat till peaks just form. Add the sugar a bit at a time, beating constantly. Beat a few more minutes till stiff and glossy.

Meanwhile melt the butter and chocolate over hot water. Cool a little and add vanilla. Then add the chocolate and butter to the egg yolks, stirring with a wire whisk. It will be thick. Add ⅓ of the whites to the chocolate mixture and stir well. Then pour on top of remaining whites and sprinkle with flour. Fold all together with whisk, being careful not to overmix, but not leaving any white lumps showing.

Pour into pans and bake 25–30 minutes. Turn onto rack and peel off the paper. When cool, frost with mocha butter cream. This cake freezes well. (Serves 12–16.)

Mocha Butter Cream

1 C. sugar	¼ C. strong coffee
⅓ C. water	1½ C. (3 sticks) sweet
¼ tsp. cream of tartar	butter
4 egg yolks	2 Tbsp. dark rum
5 oz. semisweet chocolate	

Beat egg yolks till light and fluffy. Melt the chocolate in the coffee over hot water. Combine the sugar, water, and cream of tartar in a small pan and bring to a boil, stirring only till sugar dissolves. Boil rapidly till syrup spins a thread (236° on a candy thermometer). Gradually beat the syrup into the beaten egg yolks and continue to beat till the mixture thickens. Add melted chocolate. Beat in the butter a little at a time. Add rum. Chill till thick enough to spread. (Makes 4 cups.)

SACHER TORTE

When cake is cool, spread apricot preserves liberally between layers and pour frosting over the cake, smoothing sides with spatula. Chill well. Serve cake almost at room temperature.

Frosting for Sacher Torte

3 oz. unsweetened	1 C. sugar
chocolate	2 egg yolks or 1 whole egg
1 C. heavy cream	1 tsp. vanilla
1 Tbsp. light corn syrup	

Heat chocolate, cream, corn syrup, and sugar in a small heavy pan, stirring till sugar is dissolved and chocolate is melted. Raise heat to medium and cook till 224°–226° on candy thermometer (soft ball). Using a small wire whisk, beat the hot mixture gradually into the egg or yolks. Stir in vanilla. Pour hot frosting over top and sides of cake. It will firm up when it chills.

CHESTNUT TORTE

6	eggs, separated, and one or two extra whites		chestnut puree (or 1 15½–oz. can)
1¼	C. sugar	1	C. blanched almonds, ground in blender with
1	Tbsp. vanilla		¼ C. sugar
2	C. unsweetened		

Have all the ingredients at room temperature. Preheat oven to 325°. Beat yolks with sugar till very thick and pale.* Beat in vanilla. Fold in chestnuts and almonds. Beat whites till stiff. Fold into chestnut mixture. Pour into 2 well-buttered 8" springform pans. Bake 60 minutes in 325° oven.

Cool in pans, after loosening edges with a knife. Fill between layers and frost top and sides with mocha butter cream (see mocha torte recipe). You may decorate cake with marrons glacés, or chocolate sprinkles, or almonds. This cake may be frozen.

Some recipes in my files were copied over onto index cards so long ago that I have forgotten whose they were or where I found them. I've been making the following pâtés for years. I remember that the recipes were part of a long magazine article on pâtes, but recently when I was rereading Paula Peck's *The Art of Fine Cooking,* some of the pâté recipes looked strangely familiar. Obviously these were hers that I found reprinted in the magazine, possibly with no credit given. Over the years I have added a pound of pork sausage to the baked pâté because I find that it gives more body to the loaf and extends its lifetime in the refrigerator by about 5 days. I've dropped the cognac and cut down a bit on the livers and flour, picked up a clove or two of garlic, reduced the salt, cut down on the chicken fat, and omitted the MSG altogether. In the country pâté I have increased the chicken livers, cut down on the fat, and increased the spices. So are the recipes mine or Paula Peck's? She was certainly the inspiration. What matters, of course, is that the pâtés are wonderful, the recipes well tested, and that we can share them.

* Eggs and sugar will thicken more quickly if beaten in a slightly warmed bowl or in a bowl that is placed in another bowl of warm water.

BAKED PATE

1½ lb. chicken livers	½ C. chicken fat
2 cloves garlic, minced	1 tsp. each salt, white
½ C. heavy cream	pepper, ginger, allspice
3 eggs	1 lb. pork sausage
4–6 Tbsp. flour	
1 large onion, minced	

Heat oven to 325°.

Puree everything but sausage, a bit at a time, in the blender. Pour the liver puree into a bowl. With your fingers, mix pork sausage into puree. Pour into greased loaf pans* or mold. Cover pans with double thickness of foil. Place in pan of hot water and bake for 2 hours.

Chill well. Keeps in refrigerator 6–10 days. Do not freeze. Serve with buttered toast or French bread and butter as a first course. As an hors d'oeuvre, you may use French bread rounds, melba rounds, rye or pumpernickle breads.

Makes 2 2–lb. loaves and 1 1–lb. load. (Serves 12–16.)

COUNTRY PATE

1 lb. boneless veal	3 eggs
1 lb. pork shoulder	½ C. cognac
½ lb. pork fat	8 large cloves garlic
all finely ground	½–1 tsp. each nutmeg,
1 lb. ham	allspice, cinnamon
½ lb. pork fat, roughly	4 tsp. salt
ground	2 tsp. white pepper
2 lbs. chicken livers	Bay leaves
¼ C. heavy cream	8–10 sheets pork fat (enough
½ C. flour	to cover each loaf)

Heat oven to 400°. Put ground meats in large bowl and break up with a fork.

In blender puree livers with cream, flour, eggs, cognac, garlic, and spices, a bit at a time. Mix well with the ground meats. Your

*Tinfoil pans are fine.

fingers are your best tools! Pour into loaf pans and cover each loaf with 1–2 bay leaves and a sheet of pork fat. Cover with a double thickness of foil. Place loaves in pan of hot water and bake 2 hours.

Remove foil and bake 20 minutes more. Remove from oven. Cover the pâtés with foil again and weight* till cool. Chill. Keeps for 2 weeks. Serve with French bread, buttered toast, gherkin pickles. (Makes 3 2-lb. loaves of pâté and 1 1-lb. loaf.)

Even something as common as Jewish chopped chicken liver has as many recipes as there are families. I know a woman whose mother used to make chopped liver with the ratio of one dozen hard-boiled eggs to one pound of chicken livers!

Some like it creamy, some like it chunky, some like the onions browned, some like the onions almost raw. Some call it pâté, but to me it's

CHOPPED LIVER

1	lb. chicken livers	¾ C. finely minced onions
8	Tbsp. rendered chicken fat ("schmaltz")**	3–4 hard-boiled eggs
		Salt

Sauté the chicken livers in 4 Tbsp. chicken fat till done, turning often. Mince the onion and sauté it in 4 Tbsp. chicken fat till soft and pale gold. Chop the eggs by hand or in blender, briefly, one at a time. Put into a bowl. Add onions. Then chop livers and pan juices a bit at a time in blender and add to the eggs and onions. Season with salt and chill.

*To weight the pâtés place full tin cans or wooden blocks over the loaves, then heavy books or other objects on top. This process forces the melted fat around the baked pâté to act as a preservative when the loaves are chilled.

**To render chicken fat, cut it into small pieces with a kitchen scissors. (It's too slippery to slice easily with a knife.) Put it in a pan over low heat. Pour off the melted fat into clean jars as it accumulates.

Add some chopped onion to the pan and cook the cracklings and onions till golden brown. Drain on paper towels. Sprinkle with salt and you have gribines, a delicacy which I call Jewish soul food. The fat will keep in the refrigerator for months. It can be frozen. The gribines are devoured so fast, I've never had to store them. If you have any left over, keep them at room temperature for a day.

Note: Keeps 2–3 days in refrigerator. Great with rye bread and melba rounds. Don't chop the livers too finely. The texture should not be pasty—you may add up to 2 more hard-boiled eggs. Just keep the chunky texture. (Makes 3½ C. , approx.)

Here is another example of recipe evolution. My friend Mark Strand had been in Brazil for a year on a Fulbright scholarship. He was coming to California for a visit and I wanted to make a special dinner that would remind him of his good times in Rio. So I decided to prepare feijoada, the Brazilian national dish. I knew that it was a combination of meats, black beans, and rice, served with greens, and accompanied by orange slices, sort of an Afro-Latino soul food. My recipe was a combination of three, part Paula Peck, part Time-Life, and part Rosa VanLengen, a Brazilian neighbor who graciously offered her time and expertise. I notice that Miriam Ungerer has a version of this dish in her book *Good Cheap Food,* only she calls it Black Beans and Rice. I'm sure you may have seen similar recipes in "soul food," Southern, and Caribbean cookbooks. The French have their variation. It is called cassoulet. Before the authenticity experts get up in arms, let me say that I know that the recipes are not "the same thing." I realize that they come from different origins and are not connected historically. But they are related on the tongue. Since both feijoada and cassoulet represent a good deal of time and effort, I suggest making enough for two meals or serving them for a large party. They always produce a very festive feeling around the dinner table.

BRAZILIAN FEIJOADA

⅓	C. olive oil		Bacon fat (optional)
5	cloves garlic, minced	1½	lb. chorizo, sliced
2	large onions, chopped	1	lb. Polish sausage, cut
2	small green peppers, diced		into 1" pieces
2	C. dried black beans, washed and soaked overnight, drained	1	small jar dried beef (optional)
	Water	2	tsp. salt
2–3	lb. pork shoulder, or leg in 1" cubes	½	tsp. pepper
		⅔	C. orange juice
		½	C. red wine

Heat oil in deep pot. Add garlic, onions, and peppers, and sauté till tender. Add beans and fresh water to cover. Cover the pot and simmer 1 hour or more until the beans are tender. Drain excess liquid. In the blender, puree 2 C. beans with some of the cooking liquid. Return the puree to the pot.

Sauté the pork in a large skillet in a bit of bacon fat or oil till golden. Also sauté the chorizo. Add both to the beans. Add the Polish sausage and dried beef if desired. Adjust seasoning, adding salt and pepper to taste.

Pour juice and red wine into the pork skillet and reduce by about half. Add liquid to beans. Bake in a 350° oven for 30 minutes. Serve with rice, sliced oranges, greens with hot sauce, and fried bananas if you like.

BRAZILIAN HOT SAUCE

Combine:

½	C. fresh lemon juice	4	bottled Tabasco peppers, drained and minced
1	tsp. finely minced garlic		
½	C. finely minced onions		

Serve with greens.

BRAZILIAN GREENS

½ lb. lean bacon, diced
2 lb. kale, collard, or
   dandelion

greens—about 4 large
bunches.
Water

Heat bacon in deep kettle and cook till almost done. Add the washed, sliced greens and ½ C. or so of water. Steam till tender. Salt and pepper to taste.

FRIED BANANAS

6 Tbsp. butter
4 Tbsp. brown sugar
6–8 peeled and halved ripe
   bananas—not plantain
   (not too soft, however)

Grated rind of 2 oranges
½ C. fresh orange juice
   Grated coconut
   (optional)
2 Tbsp. Myers rum

Melt butter in a large sauté pan. Add sugar and cook a few minutes, till it caramelizes. Add bananas, orange rind, juice, coconut if desired. Cook till mixture is bubbly and bananas are slightly browned and tender. Add rum. Serve with whipped cream or ice cream.

Note: If you do not feel like assembling this at the last minute, you may put the bananas in a buttered baking dish, cover with the juice, butter, sugar, and rind, and bake in a 400° oven for about 25 minutes. Then sprinkle with rum.

Obviously, you don't have to serve these just with feijoada. They are a delicious dessert with whipped cream or ice cream, or as they are.

CASSOULET

Beans

2	qt. water	4	onions, diced
2	lb. or 4 C. Great Northern or small white beans (variation: 1 lb. kidney beans, 1 lb. dried peas)	4	cloves garlic, crushed
		½	lb. salt pork, blanched and diced
		½	tsp. ground cloves
		2	Tbsp. salt

Bring water to a boil in large kettle. Add beans and bring back to boil. Boil 2 minutes, then let sit 1 hour (or soak overnight). Drain. Cover with fresh water and add onions, garlic, salt pork, and seasoning. Simmer, covered, 1 to 1½ hours. Drain.

Meat

2	lb. lean pork, cut into 1" cubes	1	large can plum tomatoes, chopped, or 2 C. tomato puree
2	lb. lean lamb, cut into 1" cubes	2	Tbsp. salt
	Bacon drippings or rendered salt pork	1	Tbsp. oregano or marjoram
	Cooked duck or goose, in sections (optional)	1	bay leaf
4	onions, chopped	1	lb. Polish or garlic sausage in ½" slices
4	cloves garlic, crushed	1	lb. pepperoni cooked for 30 minutes in boiling water, then sliced ¼ thick
2	green peppers, chopped (optional)		
1	C. wine		Bread crumbs (optional)
2	C. or more beef bouillon		

Brown pork and lamb in bacon drippings or in rendered salt pork. Set aside. Sauté onions, garlic and peppers in drippings till soft. Combine meats and onion mixture in deep kettle. Add wine, bouillon, tomatoes, spices, and herbs. Bring to a boil. Reduce heat and simmer, covered, 1 hour. Discard bay leaf. Combine all meats, beans, sausages. You may cover top with bread crumb layer. Bake at 350° for 30–45 minutes. (Serves 10–12.).

It is important to give credit where credit is due. If someone gives me a recipe I want to tell others whose idea it was. My good friend Paul Jacobs was a sensational cook. Every winter he made persimmon pudding to serve at Thanksgiving and Christmas feasts, or over a cup of tea for those of us who were lucky enough to have been at his house when there were glorious leftovers. The original recipe was given to him by a friend in Boston. He made a few changes; I have made a few changes of my own; I hope that you will try the recipe and feel free to put a bit of yourself in it as well.

PAUL JACOBS' PERSIMMON PUDDING

2½ C. sugar
1¼ C. butter, melted
2½ C. sifted flour
¾ tsp. salt
2½ tsp. cinnamon or Chinese Five Spice powder
4 C. persimmon puree (about 8–10 very ripe persimmons pureed in blender)

5 tsp. baking soda dissolved in 5 Tbsp. hot water
5 Tbsp. brandy
1 Tbsp. vanilla
1 C. raisins and/or currants
1 Tbsp. lemon juice
¾ C. chopped walnuts
5 eggs, lightly beaten

Add sugar to butter. Stir in the flour, sifted with salt and Five Spices or cinnamon. Add persimmon puree, soda, brandy, vanilla. Add raisins, currants, lemon juice, nuts, and eggs. Put in greased pudding molds and steam for 2½ hours either in a 325° oven in a pan of water or on top of the stove on a rack above water in a covered kettle. Watch to see that the water does not evaporate. Serve warm with hard sauce. This makes about 3 2-lb. loaves.

Hard Sauce

Cream 1 C. sweet butter with 2½ C. confectioners' sugar, sifted. Add 4 Tbsp. or more of brandy.

Note: To ripen persimmons rapidly, keep them at room temperature in a brown paper bag with a few apples. The puree freezes very well, as does the baked pudding after thawing.

If you are eating at a restaurant and one of the dishes is especially good, it can't hurt to ask for the recipe. Many chefs are proud to share. In fact, some books are just compilations of recipes from famous restaurants. Some may be too complex for the home cook or require odd ingredients or unusual equipment, but most are easily adapted to the average domestic kitchen. I was pleased to be given this recipe by Alice Waters of Chez Panisse Restaurant in Berkeley.

CHEZ PANISSE ALMOND TART

1 C. toasted sliced almonds	1 Tbsp. kirsch or Amaretto
¾ C. sugar	1 Tbsp. Grand Marnier
¾ C. cream	¼ tsp. almond extract

Crust

¾ C. flour	Pinch of salt
4 Tbsp. butter	Vanilla or grated lemon rind (optional)
2 egg yolks	
2 Tbsp. sugar	

Combine crust ingredients one hour ahead of time and chill. Roll out between sheets of waxed paper and lift carefully into a 9" tart pan. Preheat oven to 375°. Mix filling ingredients. Let sit a few minutes and mix again. Pour into tart shell. Bake 20–30 minutes, till caramelized. May be glazed under the broiler. (Serves 6.)

The first time I made the almond tart I had trouble with the crust. It was so rich it was tricky to handle, even chilled. It crumbled and cracked when I tried to lift it off the pastry marble and into the pan. The next time I rolled it out between sheets of waxed paper, chilled it in the freezer for a few minutes, and then pushed it into the tart tin. The wax paper peeled off easily because the crust was quite cold. Another time, I made two of these tarts in class. There were no holes in either crust but one tart was perfect and one leaked all over the oven. I was glad that this was not the first time I had tried the recipe or I might have been discouraged. Instead we took it philosophically, ate the perfect tart, decided that it was definitely worth the effort, and cleaned the oven later. Better luck next time.

If someone gives you a recipe and you try it but it doesn't "come out right," don't be paranoid and suspect sabotage. Don't feel that you were inadequate to the task. Try to enjoy the adventure of playing with a new recipe. Think of what you can do the next time to make it better, to make it represent your style of cooking. The person to please is yourself; if you are satisfied, generally others will be too.

If you try a recipe and it is not "just right" for you, add a touch of your own. Don't be apologetic because a traditionalist scoffs at your use of lemon in pea soup or cloves and tomatoes in onion soup. You can reject formulas and traditions if they don't take into account your particular tastes and desires. What may excite you may not be loved by all. You are not, I hope, cooking to win popularity contests, so keep experimenting with a free conscience until you develop your personal cooking signature.

Ordinarily I find split-pea soup too heavy and dull in flavor. But this soup is filled with surprises. The lemon makes it seem lighter, the whipped cream and bacon provide interesting texture contrasts. The champagne may seem extravagant, but it adds a light sparkle and you can always finish the rest of the bottle with the soup. You may not want any more dinner!

SPLIT PEA SOUP WITH CHAMPAGNE AND LEMON

1	lb. green split peas	½ C. or a bit more dry champagne
2	qt. chicken broth	
1	onion, cut in half	1 C. unsweetened whipped cream
1	Tbsp. grated lemon rind	
	Juice of 1 lemon	About 10 slices bacon, fried crisp, crumbled
4	Tbsp. dry sherry	

Bring the peas, the broth and the onion to a boil and simmer about 1 hour, stirring occasionally. You may remove the onion or mash it into the pea puree. Add the lemon rind and juice and simmer about 15 minutes more. Add sherry and adjust seasoning. The champagne goes in at the very last minute. Top with whipped cream and crumbled bacon. (Serves 6–8.)

An unconventional onion soup:

ONION AND TOMATO SOUP

½	C. butter		
4–6	onions, sliced thin	4–6	C. beef bouillon (3 cans
1	clove garlic, minced		undiluted and 2 cans
½	bay leaf		water)
¼	tsp. thyme	2	C. tomato puree
½	tsp. cloves		Salt and pepper

In a large, heavy saucepan melt butter and stir in onions, the slices cut in half and the rings separated. Add garlic, bay leaf, thyme, and cloves, and cook over lowest possible heat till the onions are pale gold in color, about 20 minutes. Stir in beef bouillon and cook over low heat for 20 minutes. Add tomato puree. Cover the pan and cook 10 minutes more. Season with salt and pepper.

Serve in individual bowls either garnished with croutons and grated cheese or topped with a poached egg and chopped chives, with a side dish of grated cheese. (Serves 6.)

Note: For more traditional onion soup, add 2 more onions, omit tomato puree and cloves. Put into individual ovenproof bowls. Top each with fried or toasted bread and grated Swiss cheese, and place under the broiler until the cheese is melted.

Cooking should not be a competitive sport. (You may compete against yourself to improve, but that is a self-imposed game of discipline. It is not competition in the public arena.) Pleasure should not come from defeating others but from playing for the enjoyment of the game itself. No two persons will prepare things in exactly the same way. We are not machines yet, thank goodness. I can teach a class of fifteen students how to make crème caramel and everyone's interpretation will be slightly different. One caramel will be thinner, one darker; one custard will be firmer, another creamier. It may be served as part of a rich French dinner, or after steak and salad.

EASY CREME CARAMEL OR FLAN

¾ C. dark brown sugar*
2–3 Tbsp. hot water
2 C. half and half (light cream)

½ C. white sugar
2 eggs plus 2 extra yolks, or 3 eggs
1 tsp. vanilla

Preheat oven to 325–350°. Melt brown sugar in a heavy saucepan with hot water. *Stir* well till sugar is dissolved. Don't let it burn. When the caramel is bubbly, pour into individual custard cups or a mold. Set aside to cool.

Scald but *do not boil* half-and-half with white sugar. In a bowl mix eggs lightly. Pour the hot cream gradually into the eggs, *stirring constantly*. Add vanilla. Pour into cups on top of caramel. Place cups in a pan of hot water and bake 45–60 minutes.

Chill well. (When cool, cover with plastic wrap.) Just at serving time run a knife around the edge of the custard and unmold in serving dishes. You may garnish with berries. May be made 2–6 days ahead. *Do not freeze.* (Serves 6.)

For an interesting variation inspired by the Alice B. Toklas cookbook's "Custard Josephine Baker," add grated lemon peel, 3 sliced bananas, and a few tablespoons of Amaretto.

---

*You may use white sugar, but be careful not to burn it. White is more traditional, brown is easier to handle. You don't have to wait for it to turn brown!

Even if we have ingredients of the same quality, identical equipment, and cooking skills, and plan to reproduce the same menu, our interpretation of a recipe will be different because of our individual body language, mood, energy level and personal palate. "Sauté over high heat for five minutes" tends to mean just that. But how high is high to you if you have a gas range, not an electric one? "Add cream gradually." O.K. Gradually means a little at a time. How much is a little? A teaspoon at a time? A few tablespoons, a quarter cup? "Cook till the juices run out," or "Reduce the sauce." How much? How long? Is it thick enough? "Season to taste." What a copout! Well, not really. Whose tastebuds must you please, yours or the writers'? It's your dish and their recipe. Who is eating it? I tend to season with a heavier hand than some cooks. I like clear, direct flavors, nothing obscure or subtle. I don't want to have to hire a detective to find out if that is a bit of cinnamon in the lamb—I want to know. Others may prefer nuances and so may you. We don't all taste things the same. Some who smoke a good deal may not taste at all. And after three powerful cocktails many people don't know cinnamon from oregano! When a recipe says one to three teaspoons of chopped garlic the writer may be hedging, but you will have to make a decision. In some families one teaspoon of minced garlic passes by unnoticed.

Some like the idea that there is endless freedom of interpretation in recipes. You can add the nutmeg or leave it out. Two or four tablespoons of tomato paste are O.K. and you can add as much liquid as you like to attain the "desired consistency." However, if nonspecific instruction makes you tense and indecisive, then stick with the more restrictive recipes till you feel confident enough to improvise.

Cooking is like chemistry and physics: Laws exist, yet freedom within the laws is possible. But cooking is also like art: Laws exist to be broken and freedom is essential.

Here are two recipes for filet of sole. One is a relatively classic version of sole Normande, the other an offbeat variation of sole Florentine. Which is closer to your personal cooking style and your palate?

FILET OF SOLE NORMANDE

1	C. vermouth or dry white wine, approximately	¾	C. sautéed sliced mushrooms
¼	C. minced green onions	1	can cream of shrimp soup (optional)
4	Tbsp. butter	1	C. cream
1½	lb. filet of sole, in 12 small pieces, if possible (or cut 6 big pieces in half lengthwise)	4	Tbsp. Wondra flour
			Salt and pepper
		¾	C. grated Swiss cheese
		¼	C. grated parmesan (optional)
½	lb. crab meat		
¼	lb. tiny cooked shrimp		Butter

Into a heavy saucepan with a well-fitting lid, pour about ½" wine. Add the green onions and butter and bring to a boil. Reduce heat to a simmer and add the pieces of sole that have been rolled up into spiral "turban" shapes and held together with a toothpick. They are to be poached standing up, the top of the spiral easily visible. Cover the pan and steam the fish for about 5 minutes, or until the fish turn white but remain slightly pink in the center of the spiral. Transfer the fish to a buttered baking dish and remove the toothpicks carefully. Surround and sprinkle with crab meat, shrimp, and mushrooms.

To the poaching liquid in the pan add the cream of shrimp soup and bring to a boil. Mix cream and flour, and add to soup; heat till the sauce is thickened. Season with salt and pepper and add about ½ C. Swiss cheese. Pour this sauce over the fish spirals. Top with more grated Swiss cheese, and parmesan if desired. Dot with butter.

At this point you may refrigerate the dish and bake it later at 350° for 25 minutes, till bubbly, glazing under the broiler for the last 5 minutes. Bring it to room temperature before baking. If you have prepared this just before serving time, then the fish should still be warm and all you need do is glaze it under the broiler to brown and melt the cheese.

If you are opposed to Wondra, or instantized flour is not part of your Basic Pantry, then melt butter and add 4 Tbsp. flour in a saucepan, then add the poaching liquid and cream and cook till thick. If you cannot find cream of shrimp soup omit altogether or add a Tbsp. of tomato paste for color. And finally, if you cannot afford crab and shrimp, omit and simply call this sole with mushrooms. (Serves 6.)

FILET OF SOLE WITH RAISINS AND SPINACH

2 lb. spinach or 2 pkgs. frozen chopped spinach, thawed
12 Tbsp. butter
1 bunch green onions, chopped
Parsley
Grated rind of half a lemon
1 clove garlic, minced (optional)
Salt, pepper, nutmeg
6 large filets of sole or 12 small pieces

1 C. dry white wine or vermouth
4 Tbsp. flour
1½ C. cream
½ C. raisins, soaked in Marsala or sherry
Cinnamon (optional)
½ C. grated parmesan cheese
Pine nuts or almonds (optional)

Wash the spinach well and steam till wilted; rinse and drain. Chop finely. (Or squeeze the excess moisture out of the thawed frozen spinach.)

Melt 8 Tbsp. butter in a saucepan and add the green onions, parsley, lemon rind, and garlic if desired. Stir fry a few minutes. Add the spinach and sauté a few minutes more. Season to taste with salt, pepper, and nutmeg. Place the spinach mixture in a buttered baking dish.

Roll the filets of sole into spiral "turban" shapes and fasten with toothpicks. Pour the white wine into a saucepan and bring it to a boil. Place the sole spirals in the wine. Lower the heat, cover the pan, and simmer about 5 minutes till the sole is almost done—white on the outside and a little pink in the center. Remove the sole from the poaching liquid and place atop the spinach bed, carefully removing the toothpicks.

Melt 4 Tbsp. butter in a saucepan and add the flour. Stir till combined, then add the cream and the poaching liquids. Cook till thickened. Add the drained raisins and season to taste with salt, pepper, and some cinnamon, if you like. Pour over the sole and spinach. Top with parmesan cheese and pan-toasted pine nuts or almonds, if desired. Bake in 350° oven for 25–30 minutes, till bubbly. (Serves 6.)

Here are two recipes for risotto, the classic and the baroque. Which represents you today?

CLASSIC RISOTTO ALLA MILANESE

6	C. chicken broth	¼	tsp. saffron filaments*
8	Tbsp. butter	¼	C. white wine
2	C. rice	½	C. parmesan cheese
½	C. chopped onions		

Simmer broth and keep simmering. In a different pan melt 4 Tbsp. butter and stir in rice with the onions till well coated and golden. Add 1–2 cups of broth at a time and cook uncovered, stirring occasionally, adding additional broth up to 4 C., till liquid is absorbed. Dissolve the saffron in wine and steep in the last 2 C. of broth. Add to rice and let most of it absorb. Add 4 Tbsp. butter and all the cheese. Mix quickly with a fork. This is creamy, a bit soupy, but the rice should be al dente.

To the cooked risotto you may add 1 C. peas or mushrooms cooked in butter, sautéed shrimp and garlic, or 1 C. sautéed chicken livers.

*Saffron is the dried stigma of the crocus flower. You can buy it in strands, dried in its natural form, or powdered. I think the latter is a bit medicinal in taste.

PAELLA—The Baroque Risotto

12	pieces chicken, or more	4–6	C. chicken broth
	Olive oil	1	tsp. saffron steeped in ¼
2	large onions, chopped		C. vermouth
2	green peppers, chopped	1½	lb. shrimp, shelled and
1	Tbsp. garlic, minced		deveined
1	lb. ham, diced	36	clams, scrubbed well,
1	can diced tomatoes		steamed open, with
	(about 2 C.)		juice reserved
1	tsp. coriander, ground	1	box frozen peas, thawed
2	Polish sausages, sliced	½	C. sliced black olives
2	chorizos, sliced	¼	C. pimento strips
4	C. long grain rice		

Dredge chicken in a paste made of:

2	Tbsp. oregano	3	Tbsp. red wine vinegar
3	tsp. salt	4–5	Tbsp. oil
1	Tbsp. cracked black		Minced garlic (optional)
	pepper		

Sauté seasoned chicken in oil till lightly browned. Add onions and peppers to the pots (this will fill two large oven or stove-top casseroles with lids, or one jumbo kettle). Add garlic and ham. Stir. Add tomatoes, coriander, sausages, and chorizos. Add rice, then broth and saffron in wine. Place shrimp on top to steam. Bring to boil, then lower the heat, cover the pot, and simmer for 30 minutes. Stir well. Add clam broth if the rice is not done and all the liquids have been absorbed. Stir in peas, olives. Heat a few minutes. Top with the pimento strips and the clams.

You may prepare paella ahead of time and heat in 350° oven for 20 minutes, adding additional broth if needed. (Serves 10–12.)

Personal style is expressed not only in the kind of recipes we select, what we add or omit, but also how we present the dish after we've prepared it. When I first found the following recipe it was suggested that I serve the orange filling stuffed back into hollowed orange shells. I tried it that way a few times but decided that it was a little cute and just not me. So I've decided on ramekins. To others the orange shells may be prettier and an artistic touch. Choose your own sytle of visual presentation, but do try the recipe:

ORANGES GLACEES

3	large juice oranges, or	¾–1 C. heavy cream
	1¼ C. juice	Grand Marnier
1	C. sugar	(optional)
6	egg yolks	

Halve oranges, squeeze out the juice. (Optional: save the shells.) Measure the juice and add water if needed to get 1½ C. juice. Put juice in a deep heavy saucepan with sugar. Bring to a boil over high heat, stirring till the sugar is dissolved, and cook till syrup spins a thread (232° on candy thermometer), about 5–10 minutes. Don't let it burn.

While syrup is heating, beat egg yolks till they are thick and light. Gradually beat in the hot orange syrup till very thick and cool. Fold in cream, stiffly whipped and flavored with Grand Marnier if desired. Freeze the mixture in a tray or bowl for a few hours till it is firm enough to hold its shape. Remove the pulp from the orange shells and spoon the orange mousse into the shells. Or pour directly into ramekins, and omit the orange shell routine. Sprinkle with chopped pistachio nuts or shaved chocolate, if desired. Cover with heavy foil and freeze till ready to serve. Keeps about 2 months in freezer. (Serves 6.)

Chapter 32

.MENU PLANNING:

What Is a Perfect Meal?

One of the things that has annoyed me over the years has been students calling to say, "Joyce, I'm serving your lasagna on Saturday. *What* should I serve with it?" I try to explain to them that *my* menu is not necessarily *theirs*. How I combine tastes, textures, and colors may not be the way they would do it. My menus change according to my mood (HOW I AM COOKING) and the people FOR WHOM I am cooking. One day I might serve lasagna at the start of the meal, followed by a light meat course, Italian style. Another day lasagna would be the center of the meal, preceded by an antipasto.

A meal is like a piece of music or a painting. The foods are the notes or pigments, the menu is the chosen format or composition and the signature of the artist or chef is visible. I cannot sign my name to your creation and you oughtn't to use mine. Styles in art and cooking vary wildly; they are what make a menu unique, not the specific foods or recipes. Some of us are logical and controlled, others loose and random. One cook can prepare a series of five beautiful dishes, all totally "unbalanced" (in the traditional sense of the word) and seemingly unrelated to each other, and serve them as a meal. Another can set forth a dinner that is composed like a musical score, with quiet periods and a few crescendos, where all parts relate to the total theme. Neither is more correct.

For example, here are two similar menus for a summer meal:

Fresh tomato bisque

Whole stuffed salmon en croûte

Lettuce and watercress salad vinaigrette

Lemon Bavarian cream with raspberry sauce

or

Pâté with buttered toast

Whole stuffed salmon en croûte

Broccoli hollandaise

Stuffed grilled tomatoes

Green salad with cheese and apples

Cold chocolate almond soufflé

Madeleines

Both menus have as their "pièce de resistance" the whole fish en croûte. But one chooses a simple soup for openers, a salad after, and concludes with a light and refreshing dessert. The second menu has a rich opening course, a vegetable with a rich and flashy sauce, an embellished salad, and a rich and creamy dessert with a rich and buttery cookie. Obviously a more baroque hand is at work here. (Or someone who has taken one cooking class too many and wants to show you how much he or she has learned, alas, all in one meal!!)

In this country of how-to-do-it books, books with neat solutions to simple or complex problems, people assume that "perfect" menus exist which produce ideally balanced meals. In the history of classic French cuisine, such formulas have, in fact, evolved. Boiled potatoes are suggested as the ideal accompaniment for fish; nutmeg is proposed as a good accent for spinach while basil is for tomatoes. Traditionally, braised cabbage is the companion for roast goose and turnips for duck. While it is possible to learn the accepted combinations by purchasing a food encyclopedia such as the *Larousse Gastronomique,* you'll soon discover that ritualized meal planning is not always the sign of a good meal or a good cook. A menu can be a classic and still be badly executed or dry and uninteresting because nothing of the cook's personality is expressed. While I could give you a list of prescriptions for creating a "balanced" menu, I won't. Formula menus are usually routine, uninspired, and impersonal.

For example here are two Thanksgiving menus, one the conventional menu cookbook type, one far more personal:

Cream of pumpkin soup

Roast turkey with chestnut stuffing

Creamed onions

Brussels sprouts with brown butter

Mince pie

or

Clam chowder

Roast turkey with cornbread stuffing

Chinese stir-fried celery with almonds

Yams with apricots and orange rind

Chocolate butterscotch pie

The first menu is certainly recognizable as one you've seen and eaten many times before. The second, while it is conventional in sticking to the turkey, does add a few odd turns to the standard vegetables and goes its own way with the soup and the dessert. I know a food historian who, by hearing what you made for Thanksgiving dinner, can analyse your social and ethnic background. And he is about ninety-five percent accurate, so much do our foods tell about us. (Remember, you cook who you are.) This is especially interesting because Thanksgiving is an "American" holiday, as opposed to Christmas, when people usually prepare foods that reflect their ethnic origins.

What if it were Christmas and you didn't feel like eating roast goose, or mince-and-apple pie, or turkey or ham or roast beef for that matter? What if you wanted lettuce soup instead of salad—or a cold soup in the dead of winter—or shish kebab or even a bowl of chili? Would you feel free to say to hell with tradition, I'll cook what I'm in the mood for, or would you proceed robotlike into the kitchen to do the same old thing? Why not takes chances? After all, you might discover that your family was bored to death with the old repertoire and ready and willing to try a new Christmas menu.

If you go to the market and the spinach you had scheduled for supper looks tired and wilted, but the artichokes and green beans look fresh and inviting, be flexible. If the butcher has run out of pork loin that you had planned to serve for dinner, don't panic. And don't go running frantically to six more markets in search of the missing pork loin or spinach or comice pears that your market no longer has in stock. Conserve your energy for the cooking! Leave room in your life for chance and improvisation. Let what you find at the market direct you, not a written menu or the list in your hand.

Cooking in the head can be as exciting as cooking in the kitchen. Instead of entering the market with recipes revolving in your mind, what if you set out with this point of view: Here is the stuff. What does it say to me? What happens when you see an artichoke or cabbage? Is it the greenness that calls to you, the leafiness, the mysterious core concealed within the many layers? Perhaps some of the vegetables lying side by side in the bins suggest new combinations and other possibilities for approaching them. The crisp green pepper plays up the soft fleshiness of the round tomato. Red and green, soft and crisp, juicy and dry. What about the shiny purple eggplant? What a surprise to discover its creamy pulp when you cut into the thin smooth skin. Flashy outside and subtle interior. How does that mix with the peppers, where you discard the interior and use just the outside? Ratatouille came together, I suspect, because of the visual beauty of the combined ingredients. The diverse colors, shapes, and textures cried out for fusion in the pan. That is why I refuse to follow the recipes that tell me to cook it for hours. I don't want to lose my initial response. I want the individual colors and textures to remain distinct, not dissolve into a gray mass.

RATATOUILLE

Olive oil
2 onions, sliced thin
3–4 cloves garlic, minced
1 eggplant, peeled and cubed
2 green peppers, in strips

About 6 zucchini, sliced
3 tomatoes, sliced
½ lb. mushrooms
Salt and pepper
Pesto (see p. 331) or fresh sweet basil

Film two large saucepans with oil. Add the onions and garlic to one, the eggplant to another. (If you don't own *two* large pans, cook each vegetable separately and combine later on.) Sauté the onions for a minute or two, then add the green peppers. Cook till crisp but done. Set aside. Sauté the eggplant till tender but not brown. You may need to add a bit more oil to keep it moving in the pan. Set it aside.

Film the pans again with oil. In one sauté the zucchini till tender crisp. Add the sliced tomatoes and steam, covered, for a minute or two. In the other pan, stir fry the mushrooms briefly. Combine all the vegetables and season to taste with salt, pepper, and fresh basil or 2–4 Tbsp. pesto. Heat just momentarily. You may put the ratatouille in a casserole, top with breadcrumbs and grated cheese, and bake 20 minutes in a 350° oven, or serve directly from the sauté pan. (Serves 6-8.)

Don't overcook the vegetables. They will give off too much water and get soggy, and the whole thing will look like a monochromatic mush.

If you make this without the eggplant and mushrooms and add 2–3 more peppers, you will have an Italian variation of ratatouille called peperonata.

Leftover ratatouille is excellent inside omelets.

Formula menus do not provide the answers to these questions of personal taste. Keep in mind that WHAT you feel like *eating* may not be WHAT you feel like *cooking*. HOW are you feeling? Meditative or full of High Energy? Are you cooking for yourself or for somone special? Do you want a crunchy vegetable such as celery or green beans to set off the creamy mashed potatoes? Do you want the chicken sweet or tart or spicy hot?

Do you want the chicken sweet?

MONTMORENCY SAUCE FOR HENS OR DUCKS OR HAM

2 C. ruby or tawny port	Juice of 1 orange
2 cloves	2 Tbsp. butter
½ tsp. each nutmeg, allspice, thyme	1 can pitted black Bing cherries, drained
1 tsp. grated orange rind	1–2 Tbsp. cornstarch, dissolved in some of the
½ C. chicken stock	cherry juice
½ C. red currant jelly	

Combine port, spices, and orange rind, and simmer till reduced by half. Add stock and currant jelly, and stir till dissolved. Add orange juice and butter. Bring to a boil. Add cornstarch, stirring constantly till thickened. Add cherries.

Roast 6–8 Cornish hens in 400° oven for about 1 hour, basting with melted butter. When done, arrange on platter with watercress garnish. Pour some sauce over birds and serve remainder in sauceboat. Sauce may be made ahead of time (or frozen) and reheated. It may be used for 2 roast ducks, or 6–8 chicken breasts, or ham steaks, or whole ham.

Or sweet and creamy?

APPLE SAUCE FOR CHICKEN AND GAME BIRDS

6	Cornish hens, split, or 2 chickens, disjointed, or 12 boned chicken breasts	¼	C. chicken stock
		⅔–¾	C. calvados
		⅓	C. yellow or dark raisins
		4–5	apples (try Pippins or Granny Smiths), peeled and sliced
	Salt and pepper		
1	C. butter		
¼	C. diced celery	¼	C. sugar
¼	C. onion, chopped	2	egg yolks (optional)
1	apple, diced	¾	C. cream

Sprinkle birds with salt and pepper. Melt ½ C. butter and sauté the birds on all sides till lightly browned. Add celery, onion, diced apple, chicken stock, and ¼ C. calvados, and cook, covered, 20–30 minutes, until the birds are tender. Meanwhile, in a small saucepan, heat the raisins in the rest of the calvados till they plump up. Set aside. Sauté apples in the rest of the butter and the sugar until they are browned and tender, coated by the sugar-butter caramel. Add the raisins in calvados and heat through. Combine the egg yolks and cream (or use just the cream) and stir into the cooked apples. Pour the apple-raisin-and-cream mixture over the birds, and heat all the pan juices and apple sauce together for just a minute. (You may assemble the entire dish ahead of time and warm it in a 350° oven, covered, for 20 minutes, then glaze under the broiler.)

Or sweet and tart?

BIGARADE (ORANGE) SAUCE FOR DUCKS OR HENS OR PORK

⅓ C. fine julienne* of orange rind	3 Tbsp. lemon juice
White wine	¼ C. Cointreau, Triple Sec, or Grand Marnier
⅛ tsp. each ground ginger, allspice, nutmeg,	¼ C. white wine
2 Tbsp. brown sugar	Grated rind of 1 orange
⅓ C. white sugar	2–4 Tbsp. red currant jelly
1 Tbsp. wine vinegar	2–3 tsp. cornstarch
¾ C. orange juice	¼ C. wine, broth, or orange juice

Simmer julienned orange rind in white wine to cover for about 5–10 minutes and season with ginger, allspice, nutmeg, and brown sugar. In a heavy saucepan combine white sugar and wine vinegar, and cook over medium flame till sugar melts and caramelizes. Add orange juice, lemon juice, liqueur, ¼ C. white wine, and grated orange rind. Stir well and cook for about 5 minutes. Add jelly. Stir till melted. Dissolve cornstarch in wine, broth, or orange juice. Add to boiling sauce, stirring constantly till thickened. Add julienned rind to sauce.

May be made ahead of time and reheated. (Also may be frozen.) Good with two ducks, four Cornish hens, sautéed or baked chicken breasts, or roast pork.

Or tart and creamy?

---

*Remove orange rind with potato peeler. Slice into thin strips (you may stack a few at a time, shiny side down, for better traction). Just remember to use a *sharp* knife.

ORANGE LEMON CHICKEN

4	thighs, 4 breasts, and 4 drumsticks, or 12 small pieces of chicken	¼	C. dry white wine or vermouth
½	C. butter	1	C. heavy cream
	Oil		Salt and pepper
	Juice of 2 oranges and 1 lemon	1½	Tbsp. cornstarch dissolved in 4 Tbsp. wine, orange juice, or water
	Grated rind of 1 orange or 1 lemon or 1 tsp. dry rind of each	¼	C. grated parmesan cheese
1	tsp. tarragon		Paprika
¼	C. madeira		

Sauté chicken in butter with a bit of oil till golden and almost cooked through. Remove the chicken from the pan and place in a baking dish. To the butter in the pan add the citrus juices and rinds, and the tarragon. Add wines. Stir the mixture over low heat and gradually add cream, stirring with a whisk to keep it from curdling. Add salt and pepper to taste. Thicken the sauce with cornstarch solution, added while sauce is bubbling, stirring constantly. Pour sauce over chicken. Sprinkle with parmesan and a dash of paprika.

Bake in 350° oven for 25 minutes. You may glaze under the broiler to brown. (You can refrigerate after sauce is added, and heat later.) (Serves 6.)

Or tart and spicy?

MOROCCAN TAJINE OF CHICKEN WITH LEMONS AND OLIVES

3½	lb. chicken, cut in 8 pieces	1	tsp. salt
4	Tbsp. olive oil, or butter and olive oil mixed		Ground black pepper
		2	fresh lemons, seeded and quartered
1	C. onions, diced	1	C. water
2	tsp. paprika	24	small, ripe green olives, pitted
1½	tsp. ground ginger		
1	tsp. turmeric		

Brown chicken in oil and set aside. Sauté onions in the same oil till soft and golden. Add spices and fresh lemons, chicken, and water. Bring to a boil and simmer, covered, for 25–30 minutes. Add olives and heat well. (Serves 6.)

Or sweet, creamy, and spicy?

POR AJAM—Indonesian Chicken and Pineapple

3	Tbsp. oil	2	Tbsp. lime juice
2	lb. boned chicken meat, cubed	1	Tbsp. Indonesian soy sauce (or soy mixed with a little molasses)
1½	C. diced fresh or canned unsweetened pineapple	1	tsp. chili pepper flakes
½	C. minced onions	1½	tsp. salt
3–5	cloves garlic, minced	2–3	tsp. grated lime rind
2	C. coconut cream (see below)	1	onion, thin sliced and fried till crisp

Heat oil; sauté chicken and pineapple till pale brown. Add onions and garlic, coconut cream, lime juice, soy, chili flakes, salt, and lime rind. Cook 15 minutes, till tender; garnish with fried onion. You may remove chicken and reduce sauce if not thick enough.

Coconut Cream

1	C. grated unsweetened coconut	2¾	C. *hot* heavy cream

Combine and let stand 30 minutes; squeeze through cheese-cloth or strainer, for 2 C. coconut cream.

Or spicy hot?

POLLO AL DIAVOLO—Broiled Chicken

Basting sauce

1	stick butter or margarine, melted	1	tsp. crushed red chili pepper flakes, or more to taste
½	C. olive oil		Salt and lots of black pepper
	Juice of 1 lemon		
2–3	cloves garlic, finely minced	½	C. onions, finely minced
2–3	Tbsp. vinegar		

Combine all ingredients except onions. Broil the chicken for 15 minutes on the back side and 10 on the skin side. Baste often with the marinade. During the last 5 minutes mix the onion with the remaining marinade and spread on the chicken. Grill till browned. Serve with lemon wedges.

This is enough sauce for 10–12 pieces of chicken, or 3 small broilers, split.

Naturally, a little knowledge of the history of foods—how they have been served— and some experience in eating can help you in structuring your meals. If you were planning a very spicy curry dinner and wanted to use cucumbers in a cooling salad, you might mix them with yoghurt and mint. If you wanted a cucumber salad that was a bit heartier to accompany a robust pot roast, you might try a rich and spicy sour cream dressing.

CUCUMBER SALAD

Peel 2 large, 3–4 small cucumbers and slice them very thinly. Sprinkle with salt and let sit for about an hour. Drain the liquid that accumulates in the bottom of the bowl. Serve with a dressing made of:

1 C. thick sour cream	1 tsp. salt
1 Tbsp. sugar	1 tsp. dry mustard
2–3 Tbsp. white vinegar	

You may add thinly sliced green onions or radishes to the cucumbers.

Perhaps you will change your mind while cooking and turn the salad into a soup!

CACIK—Yoghurt and Cucumber Salad

2 large cucumbers, peeled, seeded, and diced finely	Salt, white pepper
1 clove of garlic	1 Tbsp. dried mint, or 3 Tbsp. fresh mint, chopped
1½ C. yoghurt	2 tsp. white vinegar
1 tsp. oil	

Sprinkle cucumbers with salt and drain in colander for a half hour. Crush garlic to a fine pulp. Add a few Tbsp. of yoghurt to the garlic, then add the mixture to the rest of the yoghurt, add oil, vinegar, and stir well. Season to taste and add cucumbers and mint.

TURKISH CACIK—Cold Yoghurt and Cucumber Soup

4	cucumbers, peeled, seeded, and diced finely	1–2	C. water
	Salt		Olive oil to taste
2	cloves of garlic, crushed	1	pt. yoghurt
	Pepper		Chopped dill or mint to taste
2	Tbsp. white vinegar		

Salt cucumbers and let stand 20 minutes. Rinse well. Mix well all the ingredients except dill or mint, and let macerate 2–4 hours in refrigerator. Serve very cold. Add dill or mint just before serving. (Serves 6-8.)

The Bulgarians add ⅓ C. chopped pan-toasted walnuts to this soup.

The Persians add 1 chopped hard-boiled egg, ½ C. plumped raisins, 1 Tbsp. dill, and ¼ C. minced green onion, and serve with an ice cube in each bowl.

You may develop a preference for certain taste combinations which you'll use over and over again. You'll find yourself on binges, adding thyme to everything one week, cinnamon the next. But your palate and taste preferences will evolve and change as you do lots of eating and lots of cooking. You may discover that your taste buds *are* unusual or you may find out that you truly do enjoy the traditional boiled potatoes with fish, nutmeg with spinach. Then you can be a traditionalist by choice, not necessity, and enjoy your meal without being hung up on the need to be considered "outrageous."

There should be no "right" and "wrong" in menu planning. Formulas can be changed when you feel the desire to change them. If you want three vegetables and no salad, O.K. If you'd like fruit twice in one meal, go ahead. Even though the "experts" say that you shouldn't serve two fruits or two cream sauces in one dinner, you may *want* to. If you feel free to think for yourself and allow the dishes to happen naturally, they will taste "related." One night you might want to cook a classic

French or Italian dinner with all the courses in traditional sequence, the appropriate wines; the next night you might serve an international hodgepodge: Chinese soup, Indonesian beef, Moroccan carrots, and a French dessert. You can walk the path between tradition and innovation at will.

CANTONESE CREAM OF CORN AND CRAB SOUP

6	C. chicken broth	⅓	C. diced cooked ham or
1	17-oz. can of creamed corn.		canadian bacon (optional)
1	Tbsp. cornstarch dissolved in ¼ C. water	2	eggs, beaten Salt and pepper
¾	lb. shredded crab meat		
½	C. chopped green onions, green part only		

Bring broth to a boil. Add the corn gradually. Thicken with cornstarch solution. Add crab meat, diced ham if desired, minced green onions. Stir in the beaten eggs at the last minute and season to taste. If you don't like or can't afford crab, add 1½ C. diced cooked chicken. (Serves 6).

INDONESIAN BEEF SATE AND PEANUT SAUCE—A Steak Kebab

1	tsp. crushed chili peppers	1	tsp. lemon rind Juice of half a lime
1½	tsp. dark brown sugar	1½–2	lb. lean, tender
6	Tbsp. crunchy peanut butter		beefsteak cut into 1" cubes
2	C. hot water		

Simmer all ingredients except lime and beef for 15–20 minutes. Remove from heat and add lime juice. Thread beef on small skewers. Pan broil, turning till brown on all sides. You may grill these over charcoal. If so, cut the meat in larger cubes to prevent overcooking. Dip in sauce and serve extra sauce on side.

RICE PILAFF

⅓ C. chopped onion
4–6 Tbsp. butter
2 C. long grain rice

4 C. boiling chicken broth
Salt and pepper

Optional

almonds
raisins
pine nuts
peas
sautéed mushrooms
walnuts and garlic sautéed in butter
grated cheese

Sauté onion in butter till soft and transparent. Add rice and stir in butter till grains are opaque. Add broth, salt, and pepper. Cook covered, over low heat, on top of stove for 20 minutes or bake in 350° oven, covered, for 30 minutes or until liquid is absorbed. Stir in desired optional ingredients when done.

You may substitute brown rice, whole rye, or whole or cracked wheat for the white rice. Or you may combine different grains—but cook them separately to assure perfect texture to each grain. Brown rice takes anywhere from 45–60 minutes to cook; whole rye takes 45 minutes; wheat berries take 60–90 minutes. The ratio is generally 2 C. water to 1 C. grain, but look to see if the whole wheat berries need more water after 1 hour.

MOROCCAN CARROTS

6 Tbsp. butter, or a bit
more
2 bunches of carrots,
sliced
1 small onion, thin sliced
¼ C. dry vermouth
½ tsp. nutmeg

3 Tbsp. brown sugar
½ C. currants or yellow
raisins
Grated orange or lemon
rind (optional)
Cinnamon (optional)

Melt butter and add the carrots, onion, vermouth, nutmeg, sugar, and currants or raisins. Cover and cook till tender. You may add grated orange or lemon rind, and cinnamon.

MOCHA POT DE CREME

2 C. heavy cream	1 tsp. vanilla
½ C. sugar	6 egg yolks
3 Tbsp. instant coffee	
2 Tbsp. cocoa or grated chocolate	

Heat oven to 325°. Scald the cream, but don't let it boil. Mix it with sugar and add the instant coffee and cocoa, stirring till dissolved. Add the vanilla. Beat the egg yolks till pale in color. Add to the cream, stirring constantly. Strain into baking cups and place the cups in a pan of hot water. Bake 35 minutes, chill. Can be made the day before.

For coffee pot de crème, omit cocoa.

For vanilla pot de crème omit cocoa and coffee, and increase vanilla to one tablespoon.

You may add almond, lemon, or orange flavorings as well. (Serves 6.)

By being independent and personal, you won't have to pay attention to fads and fashion in foods and menu planning. I read recently in a magazine that moussaka was "out" this year and gazpacho was "in," that coq au vin and duck à l'orange had been pushed aside by duck with green peppercorns. Yoghurt may replace crème fraîche. Cocktail parties are making a comeback. And so is the midnight supper. Really, who cares? Who calls the shots, your mouth or your social insecurity? Menu and food fads are usually followed by people I call "The Cooking Groupies." Groupies in the kitchen? That homey place which puts us in touch with our families and ourselves? Yes.

Like the teenybopper camp followers of rock and roll, cooking groupies live from lesson to lesson of visiting famous chefs and cookbook authors, and for them a lunch with Paul Bocuse,

Michel Guérard, James Beard, or Jacques Pépin is almost the equivalent to making it with Mick Jagger.

Learning how to cook is not always the groupies' primary concern. Many are competent cooks who have been taking lessons and collecting cookbooks for years. In fact, the celebrity chef's "coq au vin" recipe may not be as good as one they already know. It's social insecurity, not ignorance, that fills the seats at these demonstrations. What is important is the "event," being there to *see* the experts whip the egg whites, being able to tell a friend, when she asks why you are chopping the onions in a certain way, that that's how Simca or Jim does it.

What an expenditure of time, money, and energy is involved in the meal-as-social-status game. A while ago the Sunday *New York Times* ran an article about the "Jet-Set Chefs" on their kitchen-storming tours of the country. These tours are often sponsored or put together by entrepreneurs of cookbooks and equipment. In the promo brochure of "The Good Cooking School" in New York, not a school but a multimedia big-business enterprise, they refer to this as "talent management." (And here I had thought that this term only applied to the likes of Sammy Davis, Jr.!) These organized demonstrations are, in fact, Big Business. It *costs* to break bread (whole wheat buttermilk at that) with Simca Beck, Paul Bocuse, or Jean Troisgros.

It's hard not to smile when you see people on the subway or bus reading in a gourmet magazine about "The Hunt Breakfast" and planning to serve it next Sunday for brunch. About as close to "The Hunt" as most of us will ever get is "The Job Hunt" or "The Bargain Hunt." Don't you find something slightly ludicrous in those cookbook menus entitled "The Midnight Supper for Eight After the Theater ," or "Supper for Six by the Pool"? With theater prices as high as they are, few have money left over for dinner for eight, and energy after driving the baby-sitter home. And the pool? How about "Dinner on the Fire Escape" or "Picnic on the Porch"? I guess these titles won't sell too many cookbooks to people who aspire to greater things. Why not cook a meal that is so good, and shared with friends you like so well, that the backyard becomes a truly wonderful place rather than a reluctant substitute for the country estate with pool that you haven't got? A good reality can be so much more satisfying than a self-deceiving fantasy.

Not all fantasies have social pretense as their *raison d'être*. Fantasy has a place in cooking. You can create a meal that is travel or theater. You can set the mood, provide the atmosphere, the music, the aura of being somewhere else in space or time. A Persian feast, an Indian banquet, a romantic candlelight supper for two: These are not only within the realm of possibility, they are enjoyable to prepare. Your friends will really appreciate the energy you put out, the research, the food and the mood you created. They will be only too happy to come along on your trip! Not every meal you cook has to be earthy, spontaneous, unpretentious. For an Indian Fantasy Meal, you may choose to have a paisley spread on the table, and lots of yellow, orange, and white flowers. Arrange all the condiments in a series of bowls in the center of the table, their diverse colors and shapes playing against each other. A little ethnic music could help set the scene. The following recipes are suggestions (not a fixed menu), examples of the variety of color, texture, and aroma of Indian food. Curry is not just something in a yellow cream sauce!

TANDOORI CHICKEN

Combine in blender:

2	C. yoghurt	1	onion, grated
¼	C. or more lime or lemon juice	½	tsp. salt
			Black pepper
1	Tbsp. ground coriander	1	tsp. ground ginger
½	tsp. cayenne	¼	tsp. cloves
2	cloves garlic, minced	¼	tsp. cardamom
1	tsp. or more paprika	½	tsp. turmeric

Pour over 12 small pieces of chicken. Marinate 12–24 hours, turning occasionally. Bake in 375° oven for 40 minutes, basting with marinade, and crisp under the broiler for 10 minutes. Sprinkle with additional paprika for a bright orange color. (Serves 6.)

You may do this with a butterflied* leg of lamb. Marinate for 24 hours. Broil for 30 minutes, fat side down first for 15 minutes, then turn onto the other side. Baste with remaining marinade. Season with more salt and pepper to taste, and serve with rice pilaff and lemon wedges.

SORPAATEL—Nani Rao's Pork Curry

3 lb. pork cut in 1" cubes
4 Tbsp. butter
1 C. onions, chopped
5 cloves garlic, minced
1 tsp. ginger
½ tsp. ground cloves
1 tsp. cinnamon
½ tsp. black pepper
½ Tbsp. turmeric
2 Tbsp. chili powder (not chili pepper!!!)
3 C. water

Sauté pork in 2 Tbsp. butter. In another pan sauté the onions and garlic till soft in the rest of the butter. Add these to the pork, along with the ginger, cloves, cinnamon, pepper, turmeric, and chili powder. Stir well, add water, and simmer for about an hour, till tender. Check to keep water from evaporating. Serve with rice and assorted condiments. (Serves 6.)

LAMB CURRY

6 Tbsp. butter
3 onions, chopped fine
2 tsp. coriander
1 tsp. cumin
½ tsp. ginger
¼ tsp. garlic powder
3–5 tsp. curry powder
¼ tsp. or more cayenne
½ tsp. cardamon
½ tsp. turmeric
½ tsp. cloves
½ tsp. cinnamon
Salt and pepper
1 small leg of lamb (about 2½–3 lb.), cut in 1" cubes
1 C. beef broth or onion soup
1 C. yoghurt or coconut milk
Diced apple, lemon rind (optional)

*Boned and opened up in a flat shape that resembles a butterfly.

Melt butter. Add onions and spices and diced apple and lemon rind if desired. Cook for 5 minutes. Add meat and broth. Cook 25 minutes. Add coconut milk or yoghurt. Simmer 20 minutes. Serve with rice and assorted condiments. (Serves 6–8.)

EAST INDIAN SHRIMP CURRY

¼	lb. butter	½	tsp. salt
1–2	cloves garlic, minced	½	tsp. pepper
1	large onion, minced	¼	tsp. cayenne
3	stalks celery, chopped	½	tsp. nutmeg
1	Tbsp. chopped parsley	¼	tsp. ginger
1	bay leaf, crushed	1½	C. chicken broth
	Pinch each thyme,	1	C. dry white wine
	marjoram	2	lb. shrimp, shelled and
½	tsp. dried mint,		deveined
	crumbled	1	green pepper, diced
2	cloves	1	can water chestnuts,
¼	tsp. basil		sliced
2	Tbsp. curry powder		

Melt butter in large saucepan and add garlic, onion, celery, parsley, bay leaf, thyme, marjoram, mint, cloves, basil. Cook till soft. Then add curry, salt, pepper, cayenne, nutmeg, ginger. Mix well and stir. Cook 5 minutes. Slowly add broth, and when mixture thickens add wine. Cook over low heat for 30 minutes. Add shrimp, green pepper, water chestnuts. Heat through till shrimp are pink. Serve with rice, chutney, and condiments. (Serves 4–6.) You may want to try this recipe with crab meat or boneless fish filets cut into bite-size pieces.

CURRIED CAULIFLOWER

½ C. oil or butter
½ tsp. mustard seeds
½ tsp. cumin seeds
1 Tbsp. grated ginger root
½ C. minced onions
1 tsp. salt
½ tsp. turmeric
2 lb. cauliflower, cut into flowerets

1 small tomato, chopped
½ tsp. sugar
½ tsp. diced chili pepper
½ tsp. ground cumin
1 C. peas (optional)
2 Tbsp. fresh coriander, minced (cilantro or Chinese parsley)

Heat oil. Add seeds, ginger, and onions. Stir 1 minute. Add the salt, turmeric. Cook 2 minutes. Add cauliflower, tomato, sugar, chili pepper, and cumin. Lower heat and cook covered till cauliflower is tender. Add peas the last few minutes. Stir in coriander just before serving. (Serves 4–6.)

DHALL—Lentil Curry

½ lb. lentils
2 C. water
2 oz. melted butter
1 onion
1 clove garlic
1 Tbsp. coriander
1 tsp. turmeric

½ tsp. cumin
½ tsp. chili
1–2 Tbsp. vinegar
Grated lemon rind (optional)
Salt

Boil lentils in water till soft. Fry onion and garlic in butter for a few minutes, then add the spices, which have been made into a stiff paste by mixing with weak vinegar. Fry a few minutes. Add the lentils with all the liquid and add salt. Add lemon rind if desired. Simmer about 10 minutes.

SAFFRON RICE

8 Tbsp. butter
2 2" cinnamon sticks
4 whole cloves
Seeds of 4 cardamom pods
1 C. minced onions (optional)
2 C. Basmatti rice or long-grain white

4 C. water
1 Tbsp. brown sugar
2 tsp. salt
1 tsp. saffron threads steeped in hot water for 10 minutes

Heat butter. Add spices, and onions if desired, and sauté 5 minutes. Add the rice. Heat and stir 5 minutes. Add water and sugar and salt and the saffron. Bring to a boil, then reduce the heat and simmer 24 minutes. Incidentally, the leftover rice, prepared without onions, makes for a great rice pudding.

YOGURT WITH FRESH VEGETABLES—Indian Salad

1 cucumber
1 Tbsp. chopped onion
1 Tbsp. salt
1 C. yoghurt

1 ripe tomato
1 tsp. toasted cumin seeds
1 Tbsp fresh coriander, minced

Peel cucumber and remove seeds. Chop. Mix with the onion and salt and let stand a few minutes, then squeeze out excess moisture. Mix with yoghurt, chopped tomato, cumin seeds, coriander. Cover and chill at least one hour.

See eggplant garam masala (pp. 37, 37n.) for another Indian dish that might be part of this meal.

CURRY CONDIMENTS

Chutney, sweet and hot

Fried bananas

Plumped raisins

Deep-fried onion rings

Chopped macadamia nuts or peanuts

Dried banana chips

Coconut flakes or chips

Raw fruits and cucumber slices

Papaya, watermelon rind pickles

Pappadums, deep fried

Grated lemon or lime rind

Chopped hard-boiled egg

For a Persian Fantasy Meal you might throw a rich red or turquoise-blue spread on a low table or on the floor. Have lots of roses floating in bowls of water. Serve some of the following dishes:

BORANI ESFANAJ—Persian Spinach Salad

1 lb. fresh spinach	Salt and pepper
1 small onion, minced	1 tsp. dried mint leaves, crumbled very fine, or 1 Tbsp. fresh mint, finely chopped
1 Tbsp. oil (or 2–3 Tbsp. butter)	
3 cloves garlic, finely minced	
1½ C. yoghurt	2 Tbsp. chopped, pan-toasted walnuts

Wash spinach and chop coarsely. Mix with minced onion. Cook in its own moisture in frying pan, tossing frequently, over low heat, till all the water is evaporated. Add oil and garlic and sauté 3 minutes. Turn spinach into a bowl, let it cool completely, then mix with yoghurt. Season to taste with salt and pepper. Sprinkle with mint and pan-toasted walnuts. Serve cold. This is excellent as a sandwich filling with pita or Arab bread.

ASHE MASTE—Persian Hot Yoghurt Soup

Form into walnut-sized meatballs:

½	lb. ground beef	1½	tsp. salt
1	small onion, grated	½	tsp. pepper
½	tsp. salt	5	C. water
½	tsp. pepper	⅓	C. lentils
1	egg (optional)	¼	C. parsley, chopped
¼	tsp. cinnamon	½	C. green onions, chopped
4	C. yoghurt		
¼	C. rice	1	C. canned chick-peas, drained
1	egg		
1	Tbsp. flour	1–2	garlic cloves
½	tsp. turmeric		Butter
¼	tsp. cinnamon	1	Tbsp. dried mint, powdered

Put yoghurt in 3-qt. pot. Add rice, egg, flour, and seasoning, and beat well. Add 4 C. water and mix. Add lentils and cook over low heat for 20 minutes, until thickened. Add 1 C. more water. Add meatballs and simmer 10 minutes. Add vegetables and chickpeas and simmer 15 minutes.* Stir often to avoid curdling. Chop garlic fine and sauté in butter. Add garlic and mint to the soup. (Serves 8.)

*1 C. noodles added at this time makes this ashe reshte.

GEISI POLO, or MISMISHAYA—Persian Lamb with Apricots

3–4	Tbsp. butter		¼	tsp. ginger
2½–3	lbs. lean lamb, cubed			Water
1–2	onions, chopped fine		½–¾	lb. dried apricots,
	Salt and black pepper			soaked and chopped fine
1	tsp. ground coriander		½	C. raisins, soaked
1	tsp. ground cumin			(optional)
½	tsp. cinnamon		2	oz. ground almonds
½	tsp. saffron		1	tsp. rose water

Sauté meat in butter. Add onions, spices, and water to cover. Simmer 30 minutes. Add apricots (and raisins) and almonds and simmer 30 minutes more. Add rose water. May be served over chelo rice (pp. 352–53) or combined with half-cooked rice in layers in a pot (rice layer, meat, rice, then rice on top) and steamed 20 minutes.

CHELO KEBAB or Shish Kebab

1	onion		2	tomatoes, quartered
2	Tbsp. olive oil		2	green peppers, quartered
4	tbsp. lemon juice			Square chunks of raw
2	tsp. salt			onion (optional)
½	tsp. black pepper			
2–2½	lb. lean lamb, cut into 2" cubes			

Cut onion into thin rings, or grate. Add oil, lemon juice, salt, and pepper. Marinate meat in this mixture for at least 2–3 hours at room temperature or overnight in refrigerator, turning occasionally. String the lamb on 3 or 4 long skewers. Thread the tomato, pepper, and onions on separate skewers. Broil to taste on charcoal or under broiler (pink, 10 minutes; well done, 15 minutes). serve with pilaff or chelo rice (see pp. 341, 352–53).

The Persians dip the grilled meat in raw egg yolk and sprinkle with powdered sumac. However, if this is a bit too exotic for you, serve the shish kebab with yoghurt mixed with finely chopped fresh mint leaves or finely pulverized dried mint. Or with yoghurt mixed with garlic, finely minced and lightly sautéed in butter.

KEBAB VARIATIONS

Armenian Style

Combine 4 cloves crushed garlic, 1½ tsp. salt, ½ tsp. each of ginger, allspice, cloves, and pepper, and a bay leaf. Mix well with cubed meat and add 1 C. sour cream. Mix thoroughly and refrigerate, covered, for 3 days.

Afghan Style

Coat cubed meat with salt and pepper. Combine 1 C. yoghurt, 2 cloves crushed garlic, 2 Tbsp. lemon juice, and fresh (or dried) thyme, and marinate the meat; keep in refrigerator overnight. Skewer quartered lemons with lamb.

Moroccan Style: Qodban

Marinate 2 lbs. lean lamb in 1" cubes for 2–4 hours at room temperature in:

¼	C. lemon juice	1	tsp. turmeric
½	C. olive oil	½	tsp. ground cumin
2	Tbsp. chopped fresh coriander (optional)	1	tsp. salt
		¼–½	tsp. cayenne
1	Tbsp. minced garlic	1	tsp. ginger

CHELO—Persian rice

1	lb. long-grained rice (2 C.)	3	Tbsp. hot water
		1	egg yolk
5	Tbsp. butter		

Cook the rice till just done (7–10 minutes) in 4 qt. water with 3 Tbsp. salt. Drain and rinse in warm water. Heat a heavy-bottomed saucepan or oven-proof casserole over low heat and add 2 Tbsp. butter and 1 Tbsp. hot water and coat the bottom evenly. Mix ½ C. cooked rice with egg yolk; spread it evenly over the bottom of the pan. Fill the pan with remaining rice, making a mound in the center. Make deep hole in center of mound, cover, and bake in 350° oven for 15 minutes.

Remove cover and sprinkle with 3 Tbsp. melted butter and 2 Tbsp. hot water. Cover and bake for 30 minutes. Remove from oven and let it sit on cool surface for 10 minutes for easier removal of crust. Stir rice gently to make it fluffy, and place on platter. Remove the crust and serve heaped on the rice or separately.

IRANIAN BAKLAVA

4 C. blanched almonds, finely chopped	1 lb. melted sweet butter (or a bit less)
4 C. sugar	1 C. water
1 tsp. ground cardamom	2 Tbsp. rose water
1 lb. fillo pastry	

Chop almonds. Mix with 2 C. sugar and cardamom. Butter a 9"x13"x2" baking dish. Put three layers of fillo in pan, brushing each with melted butter. Spread some almond mixture on top. Add more fillo, more butter, more almonds. Put a bit more pastry on top and brush with butter. Cut into diamonds. Pour melted butter over it evenly. Bake in a 350° oven for 35–40 minutes.

Boil remaining 2 C. sugar and water for 20 minutes on medium heat. Add rose water and pour over baklava.

Usually I find baklava too sticky and sweet with honey. Unlike the Greek and Turkish variations, which use walnuts, cinnamon, and honey, this baklava is sweet and aromatic, but not sticky.

The intimate candlelight dinner for two can take place in the dining room, on the living-room floor, even in the bedroom. The setting and music, the flowers, will be determined by how well you know the taste of your guest.

A SENSUAL DINNER FOR A SYBARITIC TWOSOME

COLD AVOCADO SOUP

2 small or 1 large ripe
  avocado, peeled and
  diced
2 Tbsp. grated onion
½ C. heavy cream

1½ C. hot chicken broth
½ tsp. salt
¼ tsp. pepper
2 Tbsp. dry sherry

Puree the avocados and onion with the cream in the blender. Add the puree to the simmering broth in a saucepan (*not* aluminum). Simmer 2 minutes and add seasoning and sherry. Taste. You may serve hot or chilled. Garnish with sour cream sprinkled with chili powder.

STEAK AU POIVRE

2 Tbsp. cracked black
  pepper
2 filet steaks, 1–1½" thick
¼ C. dry white wine or
  vermouth
1 Tbsp. lemon juice

1 tsp. Worcestershire
  sauce
4 Tbsp. brandy
  Salt
2 Tbsp. butter
1 tsp. oil

Press cracked black pepper into steaks. Pound in with flat side of cleaver and let sit at room temperature for a few hours. In a cup assemble wine, lemon juice, Worcestershire, and brandy. Heat a large skillet sprinkled with salt. Put in butter and oil, and sear meat on both sides. Cook till rare, about 3–5 minutes on a side. Place meat on warm platter. Add the wine mixture to the butter in the pan, heat to bubbling and just slightly reduced. Pour over the meat and serve at once.

Another variation:

STEAK AU POIVRE VERT

Sauté 2 filet steaks to taste, preferably rare. Keep warm on heated plater.

Sauce: Combine with mortar and pestle

2 Tbsp. drained green peppercorns, crushed	2 Tbsp. Dijon mustard
4 Tbsp. brandy	2 Tbsp. vermouth

Add to pan juices. Then add ½ C. heavy cream. Pour over steaks. You may use this sauce with pork chops.

ASPARAGI CON PROSCIUTTO E PARMIGIANO

Steam asparagus standing up till crisp but cooked. Take about six stalks, wrap with a slice of prosciutto, and place in a buttered baking dish. Continue to do this till the asparagus are used up. Sprinkle with parmesan cheese and dribble melted butter with freshly ground black pepper over the top. Bake in a 400° oven about 5–7 minutes, or glaze under the broiler if they are still hot when you assemble them.

STRAWBERRIES WITH RASPBERRY SAUCE

1	pkg. frozen raspberries, thawed	Marnier, or framboise liqueur
2	tsp. lemon juice (optional)	2 Tbsp. honey
3	Tbsp. Cointreau, Grand	2 baskets strawberries hulled, halved if large

Drain most of the raspberry juice and save it. Puree the raspberries in the blender. Add lemon juice if desired, liqueur, and honey. (You may push through a strainer to remove the seeds if you like, but you'll have less sauce.) You may want to thin the sauce with some of the reserved raspberry juice. Cover prepared strawberries with sauce.

This sauce is good over pineapple wedges, poached peaches or pears, sliced bananas, or custard, rice pudding, cold lemon soufflé, etc. This recipe makes enough for four—save the extra for breakfast.

Chapter 33

WHAT IS A COOKBOOK?

It seems only natural that while writing this book I've had to clarify for myself what I expect from a cookbook. To the publisher a cookbook is 7 inches × 9 inches and 325 pages long, has a gimmick, and makes money. To the cooking student it provides the answers to a million questions. To the social aspirant it offers novelty and panache. And to me, an inveterate cookbook reader and cooking teacher, it presents the opportunity to meet a new person and hear another point of view.

A cookbook is a statement about its author's palate. That is why, when asked to name my favorite cookbook or which ones I recommend, I find it difficult to answer. Enjoying someone's recipes is like wanting to dine at their table. There are some at whose table I would like to sit nightly, others I would like to visit but only occasionally.

It is part of my job as a cooking teacher to be informed as to what's in print. I try to read most of the new books as they bounce off the presses, and I am often amazed by the amount of poor advice and misinformation. One book, for example, advises you to form a Linzertorte and place it directly, without a pan, on a baking sheet. What it neglects to tell you is that you may be cleaning melted Linzertorte and burnt raspberry jam out of the oven for days!

Books by reputable authors tell you to soak mushrooms in acidulated water for a half hour to get them clean. So what if the mushrooms get so waterlogged that all of their juices and flavor evaporate as soon as they hit the sauté pan? Some books tell you to brown garlic, which gives it a woody texture and a bitter taste, and gives you a case of indigestion to boot! Others say to parboil shrimp for twenty minutes when two will do, or to baste goose with a fat-soaked cloth when there is enough fat *in* the goose to keep you draining the pan every half hour. You are advised to cook asparagus in a flat pan for twenty minutes, but nobody tells you that the tips will fall off when you try to remove the asparagus from the water! I could go on for hours; in fact a book could be written just on the errors and misinformation in cookbooks. Even when recipes have been well tested and the writer's advice is sensible, there will still be mistakes in cookbooks. Maybe even this one. What's sad about this is not that there are errors but that the people who buy the books and cook the erroneous recipes blame themselves! They feel incompetent and get discouraged.

A cookbook should not intimidate you or make you feel unprepared and inept. Some cookbooks act as instruments of terror! The instructions have been made so unnecessarily complicated that the reader is discouraged from ever trying. Can anything so difficult, involved, and time-consuming be worth the effort? (Only if you are attracted perversely to the inherent challenge.) Cooking, like eating, is for everyone, not just the anointed few. If a cookbook is so obscure and esoteric, if the ingredients are hard to track down, who needs it, except the food snob?

There are some cookbooks I find myself using over and over again, while others sit on the kitchen shelf collecting dust. Initially they looked "interesting" and I thought that eventually I'd get around to trying some of the recipes. What seemed provocative in a quick glance at the bookstore proved disappointing when I had some time to really read it. The recipes just didn't give me the urge to rush into the kitchen, or they were too familiar.

What then are the signs of a good cookbook? First and foremost, a *good cookbook makes you want to cook*. It stimulates your imagination as well as your palate. It makes you want to get your hands in. Its presentation of an old recipe just might inspire you to cook a dish you'd grown tired of. A cookbook can be a *shopping source*, tell you where to find ingredients and what to look for after you have found them. It can be a *problem solver*. If you have been having difficulty with a certain recipe or technique, a book may describe it in a manner that makes it easy for you to understand. And it can be *read for pleasure:* Some books I have enjoyed immensely, for their attitude or ambiance, even though I never cooked a recipe in the text.

Eventually you'll find a few cookbooks whose authors will become your friends, whose moods will reflect yours, whose tastes you share. This will come about through trial and error, personal experimentation, recommendations from friends. Some books will be so close to your tastebuds you will hardly alter a recipe. Others won't jibe with your personal taste, even though you may like the basic premise of the book.

Experience *is* the best teacher. After you've been cooking and eating for a while you'll be able to skim through a cookbook, read the recipes, and get a feeling for what the food will be like. Just as a conductor can read a musical score and "hear" the music, you'll "taste" the recipes and know if they are for you.

What follows is a list of cookbooks that I have used and enjoyed for years. Some you may be familiar with, and others may be just the ones you are looking for.

Some Basic All-Purpose Cookbooks

The Joy of Cooking, Irma S. Rombauer and Marion Rombauer Becker. Indianapolis: The Bobbs-Merrill Company. This book has been around since 1931, and a recent updated version is now available in paperback (New York: New American Library/Signet, 1973). It is endlessly informative and thorough, also enthusiastic and encouraging.

The New York Times Cookbook. New York: Harper and Row, Publishers, 1961.

The New York Times Menu Cookbook. New York: Harper and Row, Publishers, 1966.

The New York Times International Cookbook, New York: Harper and Row, Publishers, 1971.

Edited by Craig Claiborne, who collected the recipes from professional chefs and good cooks. They are outlined simply so you can follow without too much trouble.

The Complete Kitchen Guide, by Lillian Langseth-Christensen and Carol Sturm Smith. New York: Grosset & Dunlap, 1965. A paperback primer which defines cooking terms, measurements, and equipment. It is a valuable cooking dictionary.

Feasts for All Seasons, by Roy Andries de Groot. New York: Alfred A. Knopf, Inc. 1966; paper, McGraw-Hill Book Company, 1976. This man is a perfectionist, a fanatic for details, knowledgeable. We share similar food preferences. I love his recipes and trust his tastebuds implicitly. This book has inspired me upon numerous occasions. Although de Groot is blind, he "sees" everything with his nose and exquisite palate.

Art of Good Cooking, by Paula Peck. New York: Simon and Schuster, Inc., 1966; paper, 1970.

Art of Fine Baking, by Paula Peck. New York: Simon and Schuster, Inc., 1961; paper, 1970.

These are classics and well worth tracking down. The baking book is still the best in the business. I use the cooking book often because I enjoy the seasoning and the homey vitality of the food.

Cooking with Helen McCully Beside You. New York: Random House, Inc., 1970. A simple, direct, practical book; some good recipes, easy to follow.

Good Cheap Food, by Miriam Ungerer. A William Cole Book. New York: The Viking Press, 1973; paper, New American Library/Signet, 1975. Not only a practical book that makes you want to get out into the kitchen, but one that is a pleasure to read. While giving us excellent recipes, Ms. Ungerer is articulate, funny, and able to convey the enjoyment of the cooking process.

Economy Gastronomy, by Sylvia Vaughn Thompson. New York: Atheneum, 1963. Another no-nonsense, homey book with good advice, good recipes, and "style."

Michael Field's Culinary Classics and Improvisations. New York; Alfred A. Knopf, Inc., 1965; paper, Vintage Books, 1973. What to do with leftovers in the grand but traditional manner.

Special thanks to Julia Child for her television programs, which showed the American public that cooking could be fun. While her first books are verbose and formal, the recipes often overly complex, her latest book, *From Julia Child's Kitchen* (New York: Alfred A. Knopf, Inc., 1975), is just as informative and more personal·in tone. Ironically, I find her book based on the television series, *The French Chef Cookbook* (New York: Alfred A. Knopf, Inc., 1968), by far the easiest to use.

SPECIALIZED COOKBOOKS

The Greengrocer, by Joe Carcione. New York: Pyramid Books, 1971.

Cutting Up in the Kitchen, by Merle Ellis. San Francisco: Chronicle Books, 1975. All you need to know about vegetables and meat.

Diet for a Small Planet, by Frances Moore Lappé. New York: Friends of the Earth, for Ballantine Books, 1969. The argument for eating less meat; how to combine carbohydrates to increase protein content.

Leaves From Our Tuscan Kitchen, by Janet Ross and Michael Waterfield. New York: Vintage Books, 1973. The original was written in 1899! How to enjoy vegetables as the center of the meal.

The Vegetarian Epicure, by Anna Thomas. New York: Vintage Books, 1972. Excellent recipes to increase one's appreciation of the nonmeat way of life. (Except that the too-runny crepes may cause fear and trembling with neophyte chefs.)

The Time-Life *Foods of the World.* New York: Time-Life Books.
An interesting series that was published from 1968 to 1970. There are lots of recipes from everywhere, and glorious photographs which are an inspiration to get you cooking. Not all the books are equally good, but the general cultural information is excellent and the pictures are great.

All the Penguin paperback books by Elisabeth David:
Mediterranean Food, 1950.
French Country Food, 1951.
Italian Food, 1954.
Summer Cooking, 1955.
French Provincial Cooking, 1960.
These are for experienced cooks. The recipes are loosely written and the ingredients are not always measured. But there are more recipe ideas per paragraph than there are per chapter in many other books on the same subjects.

The Fine Art of Italian Cooking, by Giuliano Bugialli. New York: Quadrangle—The New York Times Book Co., 1977.

The Classic Italian Cookbook, by Marcella Hazan. New York: Harper's Magazine Press, 1973.
Italian Family Cooking, by Ed Giobbi. New York: Random House, Inc., 1971.
These are basic, easy-to-follow, authentic Italian recipes. The pasta and vegetable sections are especially informative and interesting. And the food is delicious!!

Italian Regional Cooking, by Ada Boni. New York: E. P. Dutton and Co., Inc., 1969. This is a more detailed book on Italian cooking, with the dishes arranged by provinces. Hard to read, alas—the recipes are printed on gray paper. Remaindered, it can be picked up at a fraction of its original cost.

Good Things, by Jane Grigson. New York: Alfred A. Knopf, Inc., 1971. A very personal book with some excellent recipes by an English food writer who has an international palate.

Food for the Emperor, by John D. Keys. Los Angeles: Ward Ritchie Press, 1972.
The Pleasures of Chinese Cooking, by Grace Zia Chu. New York: Simon & Schuster, Inc., 1962; paper, Cornerstone Paperback, 1974.
Both books have tantalizing recipes and are easy to follow, no mean feat in Chinese cooking. Although there are hundreds of Chinese cookbooks, these are my favorites.

The Taste of Country Cooking, by Edna Lewis. New York: Alfred A. Knopf, Inc., 1976. American Southern cooking at its finest. Enjoyable to read.

A Book of Middle Eastern Food, by Claudia Roden. New York: Alfred A. Knopf, Inc., 1972; paper, Vintage Books, 1974. When I was in London I picked up a Penguin paperback of this book and brought about ten copies back for friends. It was published here a few years later. By then I had cooked my way from one end of the book to the other. The most complete and interesting book on Middle Eastern cooking I've found anywhere.

Couscous and Other Good Food from Morocco, by Paula Wolfert. New York: Harper and Row, Publishers, 1973. For those who are hooked on Moroccan cooking with its regional nuances.

The Art of Greek Cookery, by the women of St. Paul's Greek Orthodox

Church, Hempstead, Long Island. Garden City, N.Y.: Doubleday & Co., Inc., 1961. What a collection of family recipes! Many variations on a theme. You will really see personal interpretations of classic recipes at work.

SOME BOOKS ABOUT COOKING TO READ FOR PLEASURE

The Passionate Epicure, by Marcel Rouff. New York: E. P. Dutton & Co., Inc., 1962.

The Art of Eating, by M.F.K. Fisher. New York: The Macmillan Company, 1937, 1954.

With Bold Knife and Fork, by M.F.K. Fisher. New York: G. P. Putnam's Sons, 1968.

The Alice B. Toklas Cookbook, Garden City, N.Y.: Doubleday Anchor (paperback), 1954. There's more to this book than just hashish cookies. What wonderful stories about Alice, Gertrude, and their friends! Great recipes, too.

The Food of France, by Waverley Root. New York: Atheneum, 1958; paper, Vintage Books, 1966.
The Food of Italy, by Waverley Root. New York: Atheneum, 1971.
All you could ever hope to know about the food of these countries.

The Auberge of the Flowering Hearth, by Roy Andries de Groot. Indianapolis: The Bobbs-Merrill Company, 1973. Great reading, good recipes even if they are complicated and a bit rich for the average palate and pocketbook.

The Foodbook, by James Trager. New York: Grossman Publishers, 1970; paper, Avon, 1972. Whenever people ask me when tomatoes were first eaten, who invented pasta, etc., I send them to this book.

The Psychiatrist's Eat Anything Diet, by Leonard Pearson, Ph.D., and Lillian R. Pearson, M.S.W., with Karola Saekel. New York: Peter Wyden Books, 1973; paper, Popular Library, 1976. This book was designed to help overweight persons tune in on what they really want to eat, foods that "beckon" or "hum." It is the author's thesis that if we ate just the food we crave we would eat less and would ignore foods that are merely substitutes for our real food desires. There are some very interesting exercises for the general reader, thin or fat, to increase awareness of emotional conditioning in eating habits and the sensual properties of food.

34

WHAT COOKING EQUIPMENT DO YOU NEED?

People Power vs. Machine Power

Lately as I stroll through the department-store housewares sections and cooking specialty shops I notice that the atmosphere has changed. I no longer smell food. What I smell is money. Cooking has become Big Business. Two-hundred-dollar machines are selling like forty-nine-cent pancake turners. *Forbes* business magazine in March of 1976 ran a lengthy article on the multimillion dollar food industry in America. They report that 90% of our households have mixers, 45% have blenders, 38% have dishwashers, 17% have slow cookers (Crock Pots), and 44% have full-size freezers. Money seems to be no object. People are willing to spend $25–$50 for imported knives, $30–60 for pots and pans, not to mention $140 for "kitchen centers," $230 for mixers with dough hooks, etc., and $225 for food processors.

To capitalize on the country's cooking mania, manufacturers are saturating the market with food-preparation appliances. There are machines that roll and cut pasta, churn ice cream, make yoghurt, grind peanut butter, sift flour, and form cookies and pâté à choux electrically. The consumer is bombarded with advertising and special mailings. Houseware festivals feature famous guest chefs and cookbook authors demonstrating the latest equipment. The accent is on the "show business" of cooking rather than on the process of cooking. (One of the most sobering experiences of my life came after I had given a lesson in one of our leading department stores. Some of the people who avidly devoured the food I'd prepared confessed that they had been at the store all week, for most of the demonstrations. Many were unemployed or had limited incomes, and it was a golden opportunity to get a meal. Not exactly the audience the store or I had expected.)

Commercialism is often tinged with morality, the "right" way to cook a fish, the "correct" pans for omelets and crepes, the most "efficient" Crock Pot for stewing. The cooking business thrives on the insecurity of the novice and the snob appeal for the accomplished cook to have the newest and most fashionable equipment. Only the person with a strong sense of self can resist the come-ons of buying more and more to keep up with the trends.

With so much equipment on the market the average buyer goes into a catatonic trance when entering the housewares department. To help the bewildered shopper there are books that describe and define the different types of pots, pans, gadgets, and machines, since the sales help says, "I don't know . . . I just work here."

Even sadder is how the money continues to flow long after the first wave of expenditures. To justify buying a new $200 time-saving device, more money is spent for books with recipes designed especially for the machine and cooking classes to show how to use it properly. Invent a better mousetrap and someone will find a way to invent more mice.

It may seem obvious to say that a pot is only as good as you are, but this fact remains largely concealed from the aspiring cooks who cross my path in class or those I overhear in department stores nervously asking the sales clerks what to buy.

Think of innocent people, cooking magnificently for years with dime-store custard cups, unaware that their crème caramel might not be perfect because they didn't have imported French porcelain ramekins! Can you recall memorable meals eaten in tiny local restaurants or in friends' homes where the old cast-iron pans, the inexpensive aluminum roasters, the chipped plates and unmatched silver, affected the quality of the meal not one iota? Great food is the product of good ingredients, skill, and loving inspiration. The pots and pans are merely vessels for the food idea and its physical presence. The cook creates and affects the dish, its tastes and textures. It really doesn't matter whether it's been prepared with imported cutlery and casseroles, supermachines, or cheapo pots and pans from Goodwill.

One weekend I went to visit friends who lived in an isolated village in Northern California. I had called to ask if there was anything they wanted me to bring from San Francisco. They expressed an immense craving for Japanese food. So before I left I stopped at the Japanese market and bought some raw tuna for sashimi and some meat and vegetables to make sukiyaki. When I arrived they were happy to see me and my parcels, and were looking forward to the prospect of the dinner we were to prepare together. I was caught off balance when I stepped into their tiny kitchen to find a small piece of warped wood which served as their "cutting board" and a penknife with which to prepare the meal! Of course it would have been easier and more "professional" to have had a sharp knife for the intricate slicing required by the nature of the dishes we were preparing, but putting the meal together was challenging and fun. When we finally and triumphantly brought dinner to the table, it was delicious!

So if your kitchen is short on storage space and you don't have unlimited funds to buy equipment, here's some advice.

When buying cooking equipment, it is best to acquire things *as you need them*. I know that it's tempting to take advantage of those alluring special sales on sets of pots and pans. However, their sizes will not always be suitable for your particular needs; there will always be two or three out of the six pots that you will hardly ever use. Financially you will have saved nothing and these useless but "matching" pans will take up precious storage space in your pantry. Better to buy a few good pots of the capacity that you usually need, for four or six or two, and maybe one for those rare moments when you feel like cooking for a crowd and can afford to.

Buy *heavy-duty* pots and pans that will last a long time. Don't skimp on quality to save a few dollars. Your initial investment may seem high compared with the usual bargain assortment presented in department-store sales, but replacing cheap equipment every few years adds up.

To find out what equipment is best and durable, ask friends who cook about their favorite pots and pans and how long they have had them. May I suggest visiting a restaurant supply store first, then a reputable department or hardware store. Some specialized "gourmet" equipment stores are overpriced and push lots of extraneous stuff you really don't need. Shop around. Very often discount houses will carry the exact item you want for less money than the sale price in specialty shops.

Just recently I was asked if I believed in the "macho" kitchen. It was the first time I'd heard the expression, and I asked my friend what it meant. He said, "You know, Joyce. A kitchen filled with machines. My machine is bigger and faster than your machine." Well, I knew the kind of kitchen he was talking about, and I realize that it is impossible to have a chapter on equipment without getting into the topic of machines. It is a subject about which I have strong yet ambivalent feelings. I know that the average person does not have endless hours to spend in the kitchen and that for many the drudgery of cooking far outweighs the joys. Not everyone may enter into the meditative space or enjoy the physical tasks involved in preparing a meal. We are a nation that loves to push buttons and speed things up. I shudder to think what would happen if there were a massive power failure that lasted for days or weeks. Would people have forgotten how to cook altogether after all these years of machine technology in the kitchen?

But meanwhile, the machines are everpresent and in fact seem to be multiplying as fast as the population. So we had best discuss what you need and might *really* use as opposed to what you will have fun with but don't really need.

What about electric knives and knife sharpeners? One is an extraneous gadget for people too lazy to learn how to slice. The other is a voracious knife eater that keeps you running to the store for replacements to your knife collection. About electric can openers, the less said, the better! You'll spend more time unjamming the works than it takes to open the can manually. Microwave ovens are for people who want to heat and eat, not cook. They are great for quickly thawing frozen foods and are the mainstay of most of the fast-food restaurants all over the country. Even "gourmet" restaurants are into the thaw-and-heat microwave method. Microwaves are here to stay, alas, but have little to do with the joy of cooking.

Electric peanut butter machines, crepe pans, and Crock Pots are hardly essential, though they are fun to use. You can buy freshly ground peanut butter at many stores, you can make crepes with plain old frying pans, and with some organization of your time you can simmer stews and the like in casseroles and dutch ovens.

However, there are a few pieces of electric equipment you will want to buy and should. If you like to bake, a good mixer with extra bowls is a fine investment. If not, a hand mixer will suffice.

The latest star on the cooking equipment horizon is a very expensive one indeed, the food processor at a mere $225. Due to the amount of money spent on its promotion and its amazing press coverage in such diverse publications as *Gourmet, Vogue, Esquire,* and *The New York Times,* there has been a virtual stampede of consumers racing to buy this machine ever since it was made available to the American public. How *did* we survive all these years without it? And if we have a blender, do we really need it?

For those who have not seen "The Machine" in operation, let me describe it. It is a high powered chopper-blender-mixer which saves incredible time and effort in the kitchen. It chops onions in minutes, makes a pint of pesto in seconds, minces mint leaves and parsley to perfection in moments. It mixes piecrusts, shreds vegetables, grates cheese, makes mayonnaise, minces meat for hamburger, and supposedly does everything except eat the food for you.

Now a good blender can also chop nuts, puree fruits, vegetables, and soup, and make sauces like hollandaise and mayonnaise. It can grate cheese and make bread crumbs, pâté, and pesto. However, it cannot slice vegetables, chop onions, mince parsley, grind meats, or blend pastry as the food processor can. The blender requires more time and patience. You have to stop occasionally to scrape the sides of the jar and dislodge the food which may have become clogged around the blades. So while you can grate the cheese and bread crumbs, and puree the pâté and pesto, you can only do one half cup at a time for maximum efficacy.

I find it rather ironic that the cooking establishment has jumped on the processor bandwagon with such force. For years the cultists of "haute cuisine" pushed doing everything in the kitchen by hand. The only "right" and virtuous way was the long way, from scratch. No electric mixers were allowed, just the whisk and the copper bowl; no blenders, just the grater, the mortar and pestle, and the ubiquitous food mill. If Escoffier didn't have it in his "batterie de cuisine" it was outlawed for use by the cooking elite. But now that the three-star Michelin chefs are using "The Machine," it is permissible to sing, rather belatedly, the praises of the Industrial Revolution.

It is important to remember that while machines can be a help in the kitchen, they can also remove you further from the cooking process.

I am willing to concede that a processor chops mint and garlic faster than I can with my cleaver. It blends a piecrust more quickly than I can with my fingertips. It certainly chops eight onions faster than I can (although it still cannot eliminate the tears that come from having to peel and chunk them by hand before I get to use the machine). But all this talk of speed and efficiency is missing a major point: that cooking can be a pleasurable means of spending time, not something to be gotten over with as quickly as possible.

There are still some people who actually enjoy feeling the mushrooms and onions under their fingertips. They like the tactile process of slicing, the way it feels when the objects and the blades alternately resist and surrender. They delight in the smell of mint and garlic on their hands. And above all they like the *energy* they feel after a good workout in the kitchen.

As your moods and needs change from day to day, so can your cooking methods. Don't be bound by rigid rules and set procedures for doing everything. Occasionally you may need the kitchen as a place to unwind after a day that has been frantic and too speedy; you may want to do things the long way around, not for any moral reasons, but to get your hands in and relax. Onion-chopping time can become clear-the-head time.

Let's keep the new technology in perspective. Machines are convenient, efficient, and fast. Gadgets are fun. However, there is joy in work you do with your hands. Just because you have machines you don't always have to use them! Cooking can be creative, tactile, sensual, relaxing, liberating—not just an exercise in pushing buttons. People have been cooking for centuries in a variety of successful ways. "New Waves" will come and go. What really matters is the *now* of you in the kitchen.

GENERAL INDEX

INDEX OF RECIPES

388

392